Can You Hear Me Whisper

IRINA REICHES

ISBN 978-1-956010-27-5 (paperback)
ISBN 978-1-956010-28-2 (digital)

Copyright © 2021 by Irina Reiches

All rights reserved. No part of this publication may be reproduced, distributed, or transmitted in any form or by any means, including photocopying, recording, or other electronic or mechanical methods without the prior written permission of the publisher. For permission requests, solicit the publisher via the address below.

Rev. date: 09/14/2021

Rushmore Press LLC
1 800 460 9188
www.rushmorepress.com

Printed in the United States of America

To my amazing granddaughter, Israela, who stepped unexpectedly into my life with her charming perfect smile, sunshine, and love. Izzy is a rare gift from the Almighty.

Foreword

We have no control over the circumstances of our birth, neither the time, place nor parents. I was born during the horrors of the Holocaust to two Jewish newlyweds in Vilna, Lithuania, then part of the Soviet Union quickly occupied by the Nazis. Statistically speaking, I had little chance of surviving. Over 95% of Lithuania's Jews were exterminated - a more complete destruction than befell any country affected by the Holocaust.

My father was among those murdered. I never knew him, but I intend this book to honour those very few who insisted on preserving a flicker of humanity among the consuming flames of war and annihilation; and who often paid the price of their courage with their lives.

I will never know precisely why I defied the odds. But I know for certain that it was largely attributable to one remarkable woman whose decency overcame her fear and who enabled an infant girl whose nearly entire family was executed to share her story.

The evils of war are often so incomprehensible that they tend to be forgotten in the years to come. As one of the few who were saved, I believe it would be a crime to keep silent.

Prologue

I was twenty-seven years old when I died.

On April 4, 1943, we were playing Schubert's *Death and the Maiden* with my string quartet at the Officer's Club at the old city hall in Volozin. I was engrossed in my memories. In this same place, ten years earlier, I had participated in a violin competition. My mother, Bella, had sat crying in the audience for most of the time I played.

Heavy, burgundy drapes graced both sides of the large, oval ballroom. There were four high Imperial-styled columns in each corner. The gold leaf was worn out, but its presence created an indisputable majesty. Two enormous crystal chandeliers from the Napoleonic era were dimly lit, illuminating the parquet floor with intricate designs created by local masters more than a hundred years ago. Divine sounds of my favourite composer floated through the air, trying to escape reality.

Two couples were dancing in the middle of the ballroom. One of the pretty women reminded me of my beloved Raisa. She had the same petite body, the shining cascade of curly, blond hair, and the same dreamy romantic quality about her movements.

Suddenly, I felt someone staring at me. I turned my head to the right. Orlovich!

She was sitting in the back booth next to the head of the local police who was wearing a German uniform. There was no escape. I felt a sharp pain of unexpected fear in my chest and in my head. What should I do now? I never imagined someone from Vilna would arrive in this remote town in Byelorussia.

There was clear recognition in her eyes. Pani Orlovich leaned closer to her neighbour and whispered into his ear.

I waited for two minutes, then got up to leave discreetly. Two German officers were by the door waiting for me. This was the moment I died—not two days later when they actually shot me in the yard just for fun.

1

"How old is Raisa?" Israel asked his friend Jasha.

Israel was aware that she was looking at him all through the evening. He pretended not to notice.

"Maybe seventeen. She is stunning. Don't dream, Izia. Raisa is not exactly our class."

Raisa was a little princess known for her beauty, charm, and her warm and ready smile. She was admired by her family and everyone who met her. Despite her family's wealth, Raisa had a reputation for being very compassionate, gentle, and kind.

She was petite—5 feet, 2 inches—with sky-blue eyes, blond curls touching her shoulders, and full, inviting lips that were half open in a smile. She was so young; so innocent.

Class or no class, Israel believed that should he dare ask Raisa for a dance, he would not be rejected.

When he did invite Raisa, she blushed. Her hand trembled. She danced gracefully following his every move.

The next morning, Israel woke up with a headache and a fever. He had no strength to get up or to have a cup of tea. He stayed home all day.

In a week's time was his birthday; he would be twenty-four. Israel wished his mother was in town. His mother, Bella Israelit, was stuck in some distant village in a part of Belorussia, which after the division of Poland by Hitler and Stalin, was under Soviet rule. Bella Israelit was having difficulty getting a permit to return to Vilna.

Israel kept his mother's photo next to his bed, Actually, it was a photo of his mother, his older brother, Osik, and him. It was taken just before Osik left for France.

Osik was an ambitious, hard-working young man, who could not tolerate the recent ghetto bench policy which prevented Jewish students at the university to sit together with other students. He found it too humiliating. He chose to stand at the back of the auditorium in protest during classes.

Osik was a real intellectual who wished to make the world a better place. He dreamed of going to Palestine to build a Jewish State. But first he wanted to become an engineer. Osik left to study in Paris and was doing pretty well on his own. He wrote long letters home and didn't seem to miss Vilna.

Israel, on the other hand, loved his hometown. Vilna was a centre of Jewish culture in Eastern Europe. There were more than one hundred synagogues, educational institutions, professional guilds, a Jewish public school, a Jewish theatre, choirs, and a Gymnasium that taught in Yiddish and Hebrew. There were two Jewish choirs that sang in Yiddish—one was the choir of the Jewish Educational Society, and the other was the Gerstein choir which was named after its conductor. There were also two daily Jewish newspapers and many political groups.

In Vilna there were many Jewish craftsmen including hat makers, tailors, bronze workers, and leather men; Jewish life was blossoming. Of the 220,000-person population, 60,000 were Jews. Israel was apolitical. He was surrounded by good friends, enjoyed life, and loved classical music. He had played violin and piano since he was seven years old and had won many competitions all over Poland.

In the late afternoon his friend Jasha dropped by and was surprised to find him in bed.

"My God, Izia, I came by to take you out. You look sick!"

"I will be fine. Don't worry."

Israel did not feel better for quite a few days. On Friday afternoon he had dozed off and did not hear the front door open. The delicious smell of homemade chicken soup woke him up. It was a familiar smell, very much like that of his mother's soup. Suddenly, he was ready to eat.

"Please, try a little. It is good for your health." Gentle, beautiful Raisa was holding a pretty bowl on a lovely cobalt-coloured plate with a Chinese design. "I brought it from home. Please try it."

"Raisa, how did you know that I was sick? How did you find me? I cannot believe it."

"Are you really surprised that I found you? Happy to see me?"

"Happy? Am I happy? I am in heaven. I think that I am dreaming." Israel managed get up from his bed. "I already feel better. I don't think I am sick anymore."

"Izia, just have some chicken soup. I will not stay long. It is getting late for the Sabbath."

Raisa tiptoed into her spacious family home from the back entrance. She could see the light in her father's room. Her mother, Masha Kaplan, was still in the kitchen. Raisa hugged her, holding her tightly.

"Mama, I want to marry him. I want to be his wife."

"My sweet baby, you are too young; too young to think about a husband."

"There is nobody else for me. I was born to be his wife. Israel is my *bashert*!"

Masha Kaplan put her arms around her youngest, prettiest daughter and kissed her forehead. She held her curly head on her large, loving chest.

"My dear maidale, these are very strong words for such a young, innocent child like you." She stroked her daughter's cheeks and hair while rocking her gently. It seemed like only yesterday that her little baby (who she liked to call Shirley Temple) was sitting on her lap in the movie theatre watching *Bright Eyes* or *Curly Top*. Raisa looked like the precious, little, American star. Now her Raisala was talking about marriage.

"I want to marry before *Pesach*," whispered Raisa, hugging her mother's neck.

"Go. Get ready for Sabbath," Masha said as if she didn't hear her daughter.

Masha looked at the angelic face of her favourite daughter and became aware that Cupid had smiled; it had happened. Girl and boy had met! Raisa was a seventeen-year-old princess who loved her family, adored her mother and her brother, and loved to dance. Her life was bursting with joy. Israel was dashing and oozing with charm. His sweet violin pierced Raisa's heart. Sparks flew. Their budding love was full of promise in the beautiful spring.

That same spring Raisa graduated from Sofia Gurevich Gymnasium. The teachers were excellent. Many of them taught at the University level.

Raisa had many friends. She was known for her generosity. Everyone talked about how during *Purim* she had brought a lot of *shlachmones* from home. She filled two or three huge baskets so everyone could have a treat.

Her best friend, Gita, couldn't afford to go to Sofia Gurevich Gymnasium because her parents had to support a family of seven children. Instead, Gita went to Ikh Duh Arbet to learn how to sew, knit, and embroider. The school, established in 1920, was where Jewish girls went to be trained in crafts. Gita gave Raisa an embroidery item as a present for each of her birthdays.

Gita's father was a talented artist who painted. Gita had an older brother, a brilliant Zionist poet, who had died during an awful typhoid epidemic. Her brother's death was a tragedy for her, and she mourned for him for seven days while sitting on the floor wearing torn clothes as she sat Shiva. After graduation from school, Gita left for Palestine.

Israel came to the house to introduce himself and to ask Raisa out. They went for a walk along the river, and talked for hours while sitting on various benches. Raisa asked Israel many questions. She wanted to know everything about him.

"Raisala, it is almost ten o'clock. I better bring you home." Israel got up.

As they were approaching the elaborate iron gate of a large, stone mansion, they could see Raisa's father on the second-floor balcony. He saw them and came down.

"I apologize if we are late. Thank you for allowing me to take Raisa out. I would like to do it again," Israel said politely.

"It is not up to me. It is up to her if she wants to go out with you again," her father replied in Yiddish. Raisa blushed, ran upstairs, and watched through the window as Israel shook her father's hand and slowly disappeared from view as he walked away.

The two days that Raisa didn't hear from him seemed to be the longest and most boring in all her happy and cheerful life. She couldn't talk or think about anything but Israel.

The next time they met, Israel invited Raisa for a walk to the Castle Mountain in the middle of the city, behind the Cathedral. She had never been there before. She was touched that he brought them lunch and remembered to bring her favourite pastry, Stephania. As Israel unwrapped the seven-layered piece of cake and gave it to her, his long, elegant fingers touched her hand. Raisa felt electricity flow through her entire body. She thought herself to be the luckiest person on the entire planet.

On their next date, they went to see the show *Hansel and Gretel*. Raisa loved it. After the show, Israel took her to a charming, little coffee shop called Sztralla on Mizkevicho Street, just two blocks away from her home.

"Raisa, will you marry me?" Israel asked, gently touching the curls around her chin.

Their honeymoon was spent in Palanga, on the Baltic Sea. Raisa's parents bought them a car as a wedding present.

Raisa idolized everything about her husband: his voice, his eyes, the way he looked at her, the way he talked to her family and their friends, the way he walked, the way he treated her, and the way he played the violin. Israel called her his "angel."

In her prayers, Raisa promised G-d that she would live up to being his wife. She believed that she was born to make him happy. Whenever she looked into his eyes, a warm, loving wave rushed through her heart, touched her dimples, and stopped at her knees.

Every morning Raisa ran to the bakery for fresh pastries, Swiss cheese, and butter so that Israel and she would enjoy a breakfast in their garden.

Their Polish maid, Zoysia, cooked delicious and traditional Jewish meals such as boiled buckwheat with fried onions. Raisa made sure to ask Zoysia to prepare Israel's favourites: *zimus* with carrots, chicken liver, *lockshen kugel* with raisins, *borsch* with marinated beetroots, even *cholent*. For Sabbath, Raisa's mother made Napoleon cake especially for Israel. She also made sure to get him the sour pickles, that he liked so much, which were actually produced in Trokai.

After a late lunch in the afternoons, Israel would usually stay home, play violin, sing romantic songs, and encourage Raisa to sing along. He claimed she had a very pleasant voice. Nobody had ever said that to her before. Her sister Leah had a terrific ear for music. Leah sang in the Yiddish theatre, but not Raisa.

"I love to hear your voice," Izia said as he kissed her and swung her around the mahogany coffee table.

On August 23, 1939, just before Hitler occupied Poland, the Soviets signed the Molotov-Ribbentrop Pact dividing Poland.

The Soviets were feeding the Nazi war with petroleum, copper, nickel, platinum, lumber, and rubber from India, 500,000 tons of phosphates, 900,000 tons of milk products, 1,500,000 tons of grain, and zinc purchased from the British Empire. On June 15, 1939, the Soviet Red Army invaded the eastern part of Poland and Lithuania.

In November the Soviets allowed the Lithuanians to claim Vilna as their capital and to rename it "Vilnius." Then things changed fast. It was difficult to absorb what was happening or to figure out what to do next. Nobody expected Soviet tanks to roll into the city streets, yet there were hundreds of uniformed Russians arriving every day. Kids were excited to watch tanks rolling on the main street and to chat with the friendly soldiers. Adults were more cautious and were afraid of Communists.

In June 1940, Moscow issued an ultimatum demanding a change of governments. The three Baltic states were incorporated into the Soviet Union as the Estonian, Latvian, and Lithuanian Soviet Socialist Republics.

The Soviets took complete charge of Vilnius. The Russians were fairly generous to the poor and forbade people to refer to Jews using derogatory names. The Soviet authorities wasted no time, however. They promptly confiscated private property, arrested priests, high government officials, the intelligentsia, and business people. They began with the deportation of Lithuanian Zionists. In total, close to forty thousand people were put in trucks traveling deep inside Russia. Most died later in camps from hard labour and starvation.

Late one afternoon, Russian officers arrived at Raisa and Israel's apartment and ordered Israel to follow them.

"Please don't take him. Take me. He never did anything wrong. He is not a Capitalist. We are not a bourgeois family," Raisa begged a young, red-headed Russian in uniform.

"Raisa, don't worry. Please calm down. Everything will be fine." Israel hugged her, ready to go.

"No, no, nothing will be fine! Please, please take me instead of him. We just got married. Don't take him away!" she begged again.

The two young men seemed frustrated with her. Surprisingly, they said nothing and left.

The Soviets established their own government and put their own people in charge claiming that the Lithuanians asked for their help. Many Jewish people, Socialist in their inclination, trusted the Russians and worked closely with them.

Before the Russian occupation, Israel had been a musician in a local club, but the Soviet authorities closed it. Everyone was out of work. Because Israel spoke beautiful Russian, he made friends with some young officers and started working in the town's department of education. He had plenty of free time to spend with his young wife.

They read books and newspapers together, discussed politics, took long walks in the evenings, and shared chocolate ice cream cones in the little café across the street from their bright and spacious apartment.

"I find pregnant women very seductive," Israel teased Raisa when she first began showing signs of their baby growing inside her. Israel chose different names every day.

Once their baby girl was born, the grandparents, sisters, and friends showered the young couple with the most exquisite gifts. Raisa's sister Leah bought a baby carriage from Belgium. Their housekeeper, Zoysia, made lacy, pink curtains to hang in the sunny room designated for the new baby. Zoysia's husband painted the walls of the nursery with funny fantasy scenes from different fairy tales. Theirs seemed to be the nicest nursery in the entire world. Maybe the British queen had a nursery like theirs for her children.

"What a magnificent daughter we have, Raisala. Do you realize how blessed we are, how good God is to us?" Israel asked again and again while rocking their little angel with big, blue eyes that looked straight at him. She was bundled in lace and soft pink blankets.

Does she recognize me already? he wondered. "Sonia, Sonechka, ku-ku-ku! Look at me! Look here! I love you. I adore you. I am your Papa. I will always be there for you. I will take good care of you. You are my lucky, little girl. You already brought us so much *nachas*. One day you will be ready to marry, and guess what? Your papa and mama will walk you to the *chupa*."

"Izenka, the way you talk to her, it melts my heart." Raisa had tears in her eyes.

"Why tears?" Israel kissed her cheeks while holding the baby in his arms. "Why, my silly angel?"

"These are good tears. From joy, from our happiness. I must have done something terrific to deserve you."

Israel had plenty of time to spend with Raisa and their baby, Sonia. By the time she turned one year old, they were planning another child.

"How many children would you like us to have?" asked Raisa.

"We will stop at five. I want us to build a big, happy family."

Israel's mother was still far away in Byelorussia. Bella Israelit had graduated from a Russian Gymnasium. She was born in 1895 at a time when the majority of the population in Vilna was Russian. Jews had lived in Vilna since the fourteenth century when the Grand Duke of the Polish-Lithuanian Commonwealth had invited merchants, artisans, and traders to develop his nation. In 1795, the Russian Empire annexed Vilna after the partition between the Russian Empire and Germany.

Vilna became the home of great modernist Yiddish poetry, important Jewish publishing houses, theatre, the final resting place of the Vilna Gaon and was the birthplace of the YIVO Institute.

The city known today by its Lithuanian name, Vilnius, was once part of the Polish-Lithuanian Commonwealth. Until the end of World War II, Vilna/Wilno (Yiddish/Polish) was a majority Polish- and Yiddish-speaking City. Lithuanian speakers were always a small fraction of its population. The Jews of Vilna were comfortable with both Russian and Polish culture.

After 1922, the new Polish government immediately started to eradicate Russian, hiring Polish teachers, opening Polish schools and a New Polish University. Successful Jews were quite cooperative and blended easily with the new changes. The new president at the time, Pilsutzky, was good to the Jews in that he didn't allow physical violence against them.

Israel's mother, Bella, spoke perfect Russian and Yiddish at home. Her children went to the Polish Gymnasium and read books in all three languages.

But still Yiddish was the language of choice for most families.

The year before Israel danced with Raisa for the first time, Bella Israelit, who had been a widow for five years, met a Jewish businessman from Glubokoje, married him, and went to live in his home town.

When life began to look dangerous in Byelorussia, Israel's resourceful, intelligent mother miraculously managed to come back to Vilna. Knowing how elegant Israel's mother was, Raisa got a new haircut before Bella's arrival to make a good impression. She chose a style she had seen in a Hollywood movie.

"Izia, how do you like her hair better, with her natural curls or this new look?" Israel's mother asked her son.

"I like her anyway she chooses to be: in pyjamas, a fancy dress, with long curls or short hair. Raisa is always the most beautiful woman to me."

His answer was a music to Raisa's ears.

Bella Israelit arrived two weeks before *Pesach*. She was clearly thrilled with Israel's marriage to Raisa, and to see him so much in love.

"Mama, you can stay with us as long as you wish. We have a big apartment." The young couple welcomed her with open arms.

"My dear *kindalech*, I will not stay long; only until things settle down a bit. It cannot be such chaos for much longer."

"In difficult times, it is wise to be together. My parents are leaving soon to Valakumpija, to our dacha. Everybody. My sisters, Leah and Sara, are coming with their families. Mama, you should stay with us. Please. Izia missed you. He has spoken a lot about you. We will always take good care of you." Raisa was sincere.

They spent *Pesach* together at Raisa's parents' home. On April 12, there were thirty-two people sitting at the table for Seder.

Masha Kaplan made sweet and sour stew, cookies from dough boiled in honey, and traditional Vilna *tsimes* with carrots, beans, potatoes, onions, and prunes. Her specialty were latkes and pies made from matzah flour and stuffed with fried onions and jam.

Raisa's father reclined on cushions at the head of the table. The kids searched for *afikomen* (as they did every other year) and received generous presents. *Pesach* was the most beautiful holiday to spend with family, as usual.

By the end of April 1941, Raisa and Israel had left for their dacha with the rest of the family. Bella Israelit decided to stay in their apartment in the city.

The smell of the pine in the country was supposed to be good for their health. The kids were busy playing outside, swimming in the lake, and gathering wild mushrooms and blueberries.

Delicious stillness soothed the soul. The sky was an innocent shade of light blue dotted with the tiny, yellow spots of young spring trees. Scrawny, naked branches awoke from a prolonged cold winter. The trunk of a huge, old tree in an open field was cut to form an inviting and comfy resting spot pretending to be a chair. Every tree had its own time for budding. The middle of May was a sheer symphony absorbing such harmony.

Lying on the soft, fresh grass and looking up, Raisa and Israel were mesmerized by the variety of shades of greens, light yellows, and deep, dark avocados that intercepted the dazzling array of new leaves. It was almost magical to witness nature in such virginal splendour crossing the boundaries in baby steps, from bush to bush and tree to tree. Here at this moment, they were relieved from their anxiety by the blossoming spring, listening to the sounds of the water gently lapping against the shore of the river.

There were no new words to say anymore. Raisa was holding Israel's hands afraid to move, afraid to change her position.

"I cannot live without you, Izia."

"Why should you? I will always be next to you."

"I am afraid."

"What are you afraid of? What is the worst that can happen?"

"I don't know, but I am afraid."

The grey and black clouds stretched across the sky. The sun's rays occasionally pierced through openings, illuminating the ripples and brown ducks floating in unison along with melancholic seagulls. A few of the ducks dipped into the water and stuck out their behinds which looked like split wet stones, occasionally betrayed by the skinny, red legs which protruded from their bellies. Some waddled out of the water to shake out their feathers; others gracefully circled in the air, lazily flapping their wings.

After the children went to bed, the grownups sat down to play cards. Nobody said a word for a while.

"You are young; you have energy. But for me, it is too hot. I am tired. I am going to bed," Raisa's father said, breaking the silence as he got up from his chair. Raisa's mother, Masha, followed him.

"I don't feel like playing." Raisa went to the kitchen to have a cold lemonade.

2

In May 1941, the Russians were departing fast. Over three days, some three thousand Jews left with them.

Raisa's older brother, Sema, seemed restless. He planned to leave with the three thousand other Jews who were leaving Vilna. Raisa went to the train station to say goodbye. She loved Semka. He was a bit different and thus difficult to handle for her parents.

Sema wanted to improve the world; to do some good. In 1937, their father had sent him to Palestine to buy orange groves. But Sema found Palestine to be harsh and boring, so he came back home, to Vilna.

Hiding in a corner behind a tree, Raisa watched his straight, tall figure on the stairs of the train wagon. Sema was not alone. Next to him was standing a young woman whom Raisa had never met. They were looking at each other and laughing. There was obviously something special between them.

Raisa moved forward closer to them. The train started to whistle and was ready to leave.

"This is my beautiful sister, Raisa," Sema said, surprised she had come to the station.

"My name is Fania." She had beautiful, straight teeth and a big smile. "I'm very pleased to meet you. Semka has told me a lot about you and your husband, Izia."

She called him Semka, thought Raisa. *They must be intimate.*

A few hours later the Soviets would not allow anyone to cross the border. People were stranded at the train station with no place to escape.

The bombings started in June. People mistakenly thought the bombings were another emergency training session that had become common at the time. The retreating Red Army trucks zoomed by. There were many dead people on the country roads. A mass exodus had begun.

On June 24, 1941, German forces bombed the city. The next day, German soldiers marched through the streets of Vilna and were greeted with flowers by local Lithuanians. Lithuanians had always held Germany and German culture in great esteem. They placed their aspirations for restored independence from the Soviet Regime on the expectation of a Nazi victory.

Without further delay, the provisional government, encouraged by the Germans, subjected Jews to the restrictions Germans had already imposed in Poland. The Jews who had lived under Soviet occupation since 1940 had no access to information trickling through the territories occupied by Nazis. Additionally, they were ill-prepared for the German attitude toward them. Most didn't expect equal rights with non-Jews, but they had hoped the Germans would leave them alone.

Almost immediately, the Germans, with the support of the local police, established different lines in bakeries for Jews and non-Jewish people. When the doors opened early morning, they let in ten gentiles for every one Jew. Soon, Jews were forbidden to walk on the sidewalk. If they did, they could be arrested.

Jews were forbidden to sit on benches in public parks and gardens. They were barred from public transport. Every public vehicle was required to post a sign saying NON-JEWS ONLY. Jews were also prohibited to own radios or to sell their property. They were restricted to purchasing food with ration cards at two small food stores. The curfew started two hours earlier for Jews than for other citizens.

Fascists took away valuables from Jewish homes and made an inventory of the furniture, often taking the more expensive pieces. Local reporters gave them information about wealthier homes. Some Jews tried to hide their valuables with their Lithuanian friends.

Jews were arrested for minor infractions or for no reason at all. Jewish men were often grabbed at random on the streets by Lithuanian police dressed in civilian clothes. Numerous trucks overcrowded with Jews lined the streets, and one often witnessed groups of fifty to one hundred Jews marching on the streets with a German convoy.

Some locals were actually called *hapunes* because they snatched men between fifteen and fifty years old off the street and pretended to take them to work. In reality, according to the German's carefully prepared plans, they took them to Ponary Forest to a rather small clearing not far from the rail station.

On July 11, 1941, shootings began at Ponary Forest, a village twelve kilometres from Vilnius. It became a death factory. The Soviet authorities had built huge concrete pits to store fuel but failed to ever use them for that purpose. When those pits were full of dead bodies, the victims were forced to dig their own graves before they were shot by Gestapo and local cooperators.

Over the course of summer 1941, more than 21,000 Jews were killed. Jews in the city had no idea where others were being taken. Nobody wanted to believe that people were actually being murdered. Those who weren't taken were ridiculed and tormented. Fascists made religious Jews shave their beards and forced them to dance in the middle of the main square to Hasidic music.

The Jewish population was to pay the Germans a contribution of five million marks; they had to give away all their money and valuables. Germans, Poles, and Lithuanians, all in Nazi uniforms, distributed ration cards for food. Work permits were issued for the purpose of serving Germans. Jews had to wash floors and windows, unload supplies, chop wood, and do anything else they were ordered to complete.

Jews were forced to do odd jobs including cleaning the streets and public toilets. All Jews had to wear a white square of fabric on their chests and backs with a yellow circle and the letter "J" in it. Later, these were replaced with white armbands with a yellow star, and soon after that, just a yellow star. Germans shot people if they caught them without the bands.

Jewish men were taken away every day. At first, they were told that they were being taken to work. Men were ordered to take towels and soap with them. Some whispered that they were taken to shooting grounds.

On the 1st of September, Fascists staged an incident to cause a provocation. They left two dead Germans on the corner of Dijoy Street and accused the Jews of killing them. All residents of the neighbourhood were taken that night to Ponary or the Lukishki prison, the oldest prison built in the centre of Vilnius during the Tsarist regime in the 1860s. Its prisoners had been those disloyal to the regime.

On the 4th and 5th of September, the situation in the town grew more tense. Jewish residents were forced to leave their homes on Strashuno, Rudninku, Mesino, and other streets in the centre of Vilnius. They were given thirty minutes to pack and move to the ghetto. They could take only as much luggage as they could carry.

On September 6th, the remaining Jewish people were told to take whatever they could carry and to leave their homes. No transportation was allowed.

The Jewish population assembled in the old historical ghetto. They waited in the courtyards for whatever was to come next. The old, dilapidated neighbourhood had been sealed off, pushing everyone inside. People ended up sleeping five and six in one bed, and occasionally with strangers they had never met before.

There were two ghettos created on the 6th of September: a large one with a central point on Rudninku Street, and a smaller one on Stikle and Jidu Streets.

Many Jews from other streets were taken directly to Ponary. Sick and elderly people were taken to the smaller ghetto; people who specialized in a craft were kept in the bigger ghetto.

It was unusually cold for the end of September out in the country. Days became shorter; kids went to bed earlier. Baby Sonia was the centre of attention. Leah had twins, ten-year-old girls, and Sara had two children, nine and six years old.

One chilly afternoon, a young, poorly dressed, tired-looking woman with a baby in her arms walked into their garden. There was something familiar about her.

"Raisa, you don't remember me? I am Fania, Sema's wife. We got married in Belorussia."

Raisa's parents were stunned.

"Is this Sema's child?" asked her father.

"Yes. She is. We named her Esther, after my grandmother. Sema was arrested a few days after she was born. I had no place to stay. Everybody was running east."

"Don't worry. We will take care of you. Masha, bring something to eat."

She must have been pregnant when I met them at the train station, Raisa thought but said nothing. There was a cute innocent baby, Sema's child.

Baby Sonia was like a living doll with clear blue eyes and a contagious smile. Everyone wanted to play with her.

"Our little angel seems to be the happiest when she is with you, Izia," said Raisa's father as he watched Israel throw Sonia up in the air like a light ball. "You can do whatever you want with her. She has no fear. Just pure joy."

Leaves stressed by the weather were turning brown and yellow and were shedding fast.

On this particular afternoon, the rain started and continued until dark. Everyone seemed tired and too scared to talk about what was going on in the city, in the ghetto. The exhausted adults were ready to retire by nine o'clock.

Bang! Bang! Bang! For a few weeks now they had been afraid of hearing that knock on their door. Jews were being grabbed by the local police wherever they could find them.

"Izia!" Raisa quickly took Israel's hand to escape through the back door.

They had discussed this moment many times before. If the Germans came to take them, Raisa and Israel would go to their neighbour, Orlovich, who promised to obtain Aryan papers for them.

With their blond hair and blue eyes, they could easily pass for Poles. They could then figure out how to help their family. The Orlovich family had worked for Raisa's father for forty years. The Orlovich were invited to all the weddings, bar mitzvahs, and family *simchas*. They could be trusted one hundred percent. Rather, if anyone could be trusted, it was them.

The narrow trail snaked through the garden into the fields and disappeared. Raisa and Israel knew the way to the modest, little house hidden between the pines away from the road.

The door was not locked. Mrs. Orlovich and her husband sat at the kitchen table.

"Sorry, we know it's late, but they came tonight," Raisa whispered.

"Good, you found your way in the dark. We were waiting for you. Thank God you were out here in the country. In Vilna, I don't think one Jew is left in their home. Everyone is in the ghetto."

"What will happen now to my family?" A pale and frightened Raisa felt like fainting.

Pani Orlovich gently picked Raisa up before she could fall on the low, green couch near the wall of the large kitchen oven.

"Tomorrow morning the first thing we will get you the right papers for everybody in your family."

Israel put his hands gently around Raisa's face and looked into her big, teary eyes.

"Raisa, darling, try to calm down. Please. There are a lot of good people in this world."

Pani Orlovich offered them something to drink and to eat.

"Thank you. We all had dinner tonight. We are really not hungry." Israel seemed calm.

"I want to know where they took my mother and father, my baby, everybody...." Raisa couldn't stop crying and leaned on Izia's shoulder.

"We will know tomorrow. Now it is time to go to bed. Like the old Russian proverb says, 'Morning is wiser than evening,'" said Mr. Orlovich.

"Where did you put all your valuables? Your ware? Jewelry?" asked Pani Orlovich in her sweet, soft voice while looking straight at Israel. "I can keep them for you till the war ends."

"Most of the valuables my father-in-law buried in the garden."

Raisa tried to pinch Israel under the table.

"It is cold outside. Like winter. You are shivering," said Mr. Orlovich, a bit distraught.

"It's safer for you to sleep in the barn. What do you think?"- asked his wife.

"Whatever you say. We are grateful for your kindness. You are risking your life and your safety by helping us." Israel was calm but visibly tired.

"Who wouldn't? You are so young; so innocent. You don't deserve to suffer. Nobody does."

The barn wasn't very close to the house. Orlovich prepared lots of warm, cozy blankets on the top of the hay for them. They fell asleep, frazzled, in each other arms.

Raisa opened her eyes to the sound of a rooster. It was pitch black in the barn. Izia was sleeping as deeply as a baby. She curled closer to his warm body and dozed off again.

"Shnell, shnell!" someone shouted outside.

Izia was still asleep when the door of the barn swung wide open. A man in a German uniform barged in.

"Come out, fast! Move!" he ordered.

He was a very young soldier, obviously Polish.

"Let us go. Take me, don't take my husband," pleaded Raisa.

"Move! Last night Pani Orlovich came to tell us you were hiding in the barn. Move! Hurry up!"

It was still raining, and it was a cold, windy morning. Israel and Raisa followed the soldier on a narrow, muddy road before being pushed into a row of about forty people surrounded by guards with rifles.

It was difficult to walk on unpaved dirty road. One elderly woman slipped on the wet leaves.

"Don't stop. Move!" the guard yelled at the people who had stopped to help her. He prodded her with his rifle. A few minutes later, the woman fell again. This time the guard shot her.

Hungry, shrieking crows and chirping birds responded. Another deadly shot. One was afraid to breathe; they just looked ahead without so much as backward glance.

Overhead, twisted branches wickedly pierced the sky. The small leaves of birch trees shivered, shaking in the wind. High bushes of black currants grew abundantly on both sides of the road.

"Raisa, run!" Israel whispered to Raisa while holding her trembling hand.

"I am not going anywhere without you!"

"I am tall; I cannot hide. But you are tiny. Don't worry about me. I will be okay. Run!" Israel pushed her into the ditch.

Raisa tripped, then heard the shots. There were probably others who jumped out of the convoy. Paralyzed by fear and too scared to open her eyes, Raisa didn't move.

The rain stopped. The sky was dark with black clouds. Most of the trees were brown or bare, and a lonely mountain ash with heavy clusters of red berries on empty, skinny branches stood in front of Raisa. A few trees retained their bright yellow leaves; it was as if they were letting some sunshine in.

Raisa had nowhere to go but back to the city to look for her family and to find her Izia.

In late October 1941, the smaller ghetto was eliminated. The larger ghetto was fenced. In narrower streets, wooden and brick walls were installed. The *Judendrat* settled in the building of the former Realschule on 6 Rudninka Street. There were police offices established in the ghetto. Jewish policemen watched to make sure all Fascist directions were followed.

The Fascists enjoyed changing the selection protocol for killing Jews. On one day young Jewish boys who were taken to work were told to go to the sauna. They were locked inside a shed where they were burned. There were a few synagogues in the ghetto. On October 1, 1941, Yom Kippur, all Jews who were praying in them were taken to Ponary. Many Jews hid in *melinas* shelters when atrocities such as these took place.

There were quite a few *Judendrat* offices responsible for various aspects of life in the ghetto: a work office, a social service office, a maintenance office, an office of culture, a medical office, and a funeral office. There was a hospital that primarily kept patients with infectious diseases, a children's home in the hospital, and a drugstore in the ghetto. There was also a sports field, though nobody seemed to go there, and a library. The children in the ghetto were taught in schools organized by schoolteachers.

Meanwhile, the local police continued to grab Jews wherever they could find them. They were immediately taken to the open pits in Ponary Forest to be killed.

A young woman arrived in the ghetto one day with the story of how she had been taken to Ponary with her husband and her two young children. They were all told to undress, and then they were shot. She woke up on a pile of naked bodies and managed to walk to the village. An elderly Polish peasant let her in, dressed her in *shmattes*, housed her for two days, but was afraid to keep her longer. This young woman wept as she talked, but nobody believed her story. A well-known, well-liked Jewish paediatrician named Dr. Steinberg felt sorry for her. He said that she must be crazy to make up such a story and was probably in shock after being taken from her house with her children. Later, other people arrived with similar horror stories, asking to be believed. People didn't believe them; couldn't believe them. The stories were unreal and too scary, particularly for those families whose men had been taken away.

Within a few months, life in the ghetto became organized from inside. Jews had schools and a theatre. Nobody was dying from hunger, but they all went to bed at night not knowing if the Germans would come to take them away.

Raisa found all her family together with her little baby, Sonia. She waited, but Israel never showed up in the ghetto. Raisa had no clue what happened to people who had walked on that country road.

Leah's husband, Abrasha, had a brother named Misha Zagin in Byelorussia near Volozin. He was a family doctor. It seemed that Jews had a better chance there. Their father was planning to escape to Volozin.

Every day in the ghetto could be the last. The biggest danger was for young children. Older ones could go to work but young ones were taken away without any warning during the day and night.

"Raisa, you cannot keep the baby here. We have to do something," her sister Leah whispered at night.

"I cannot part with Sonechka. Whatever happens to me, wherever I will be, at least my baby will be with me."

"That is very selfish talk. Don't think about yourself. Think about Sonia. She has a chance with a *goyshe* family. *Goym* don't take boys. They may take a girl." Leah was adamant. "We still have money. We should look for somebody."

"Who can we trust after… Orlovich?"

"Raisala, we have to. We have to hope that there are some good people with a heart. We have to." Raisa's mother was rocking the pink bundle in her arms.

With her blond curls and blue eyes, Raisa walked bravely outside of the ghetto walls searching for help to place her daughter.

"There is a noble Russian lady who comes here. If you want, I will ask her," a Polish shoemaker told Raisa.

"She said if it is a girl, bring the baby to her house," the shoemaker told Raisa a few days later.

He gave her the exact address.

That same evening, Raisa put on her best dress, wore a peasant handkerchief over her blond curls, wrapped Sonia in a big, woolen shawl, and placed her in the beautiful baby carriage Leah brought for Sonia from Belgium.

As she was leaving their cramped, little room, Fania stopped in front of her.

"Raisa, where are you heading?"

"Fania, I have an address to take my Sonechka."

"What do you mean to take your Sonechka? What about my Esther?"

Feeling ashamed and guilty for not even thinking about her brother's baby, Raisa froze on the spot.

"What do you want me to do?"

"Just take my Esther wherever you take Sonia." Fania was clear it was the only right thing to do.

"Do you want to come with me?"

"What are you talking about? Look at me with my dark, frizzy hair. They will spot me immediately. You have *shiksa* looks. You are safe. Go, I will pray for you and for our innocent girls."

After Fania safely placed sleepy Esther next to Sonia, Raisa rushed out, daringly pushing the baby carriage on the familiar streets of her hometown and walking on the sidewalks where she was no longer permitted to walk.

It was a grey, fall evening. There were no leaves outside, and it was cold. The three-story home was in a very well-kept, non-Jewish neighbourhood on the banks of River Vileika. Raisa saw a spacious entrance with a carved marble staircase leading to the second floor. She rang the bell. Her heart seemed to be jumping out of her chest.

A tall, regal-looking lady of about fifty opened the door. Raisa knew her name was Elena Stepanovna Sokol. She had short, wavy hair, small, grey eyes, and a straight, goyshe nose. She was wearing a green, silk dress with black, low-heeled leather shoes. Elena Stepanovna was expecting Raisa. She understood how dangerous it was to leave the ghetto and to cross town all by herself.

They stood in the middle of the dining room next to a large, oval-shaped, oak table with a cranberry-coloured crystal bowl in the middle. There was an old Russian icon in a delicate gilded frame nesting beside a burgundy-coloured Persian carpet hung carefully on the wall. Next to it was a splendid mahogany cabinet with numerous porcelain figurines similar to the ones Raisa's father brought from Germany before the war.

In the right corner, a tall fireplace covered in white and blue tiles rose from the parquet floor to the high ceiling. A stunning, young woman with huge, deep-blue eyes and long, chestnut curls tucked behind her small ears was leaning against the warm tiles. Raisa noticed an ornate oak door that opened into the next room. She could see a magnificent piano reflecting a delicate old clock like a perfect mirror. It rested on a huge, silk carpet with Chinese designs.

Elena Stepanovna picked up the sleeping Sonia who was wrapped in an embroidered, pink satin blanket trimmed with lace. She cradled the baby in her arms and called her daughters over to look at the lovely child.

"Lucenka, this one is for you. Irina, come closer. This doll with the big eyes is for you," she said as she handed Esther to her youngest daughter, Irina.

"Please take good care of them. Tell them about me. I may not survive this war." Raisa's voice was quivering.

"Trust me. I have two girls of my own. These two, Irina and Lucia. They will help me. Soon the war will be over. It cannot last too long. I am too old to move homes. We are not going anywhere."

"Elena Stepanovna, how will I ever repay you?"

"Don't think about it. It is all in God's hands. I feel bad enough that you cannot stay with us. It would be too risky."

"I know. I have to go back to my family in the ghetto. I am sorry. I hope you don't mind that I brought you two girls. I could not refuse my brother's child."

"Try not to worry about the girls. Take care of yourself; don't do anything foolish."

"We are planning to leave the ghetto in a few days. We have family in Byelorussia. People say it is much safer over there."

"May God bless and protect you."

3

Two days after Raisa brought Sonia and Esther to Elena Stepanovna, their family managed to escape the ghetto. Raisa's father, Joseph Kaplan, found two Polish peasants who drove them through the night over the Lithuanian border to Byelorussia.

For the last ten years, Leah's brother-in-law, Misha Zagin, was the only local doctor there. He was devoted to his patients, and they adored him. The Germans left him alone to work in the hospital. Dr. Zagin had some Polish patients who offered to hide him, his immediate family, and his relatives in case it became unsafe. Dr. Zagin was not ready to hide yet.

"Misha, you are not afraid of what is happening now?" Raisa asked nervously.

"*Hashem* rules this world. I believe He still wants me to take care of more patients."

Their house stood alone, one mile from the village, Gorodki. No neighbours could be seen.

One month passed. Life seemed almost normal. Every Friday night, the family sat in the dining room and had a real Sabbath meal with a chicken soup, *cholent*, and warm, home-baked *chala*.

Outside, an early fresh snow sparkled under the moonlight. Dr. Zagin honoured Raisa's father by making a Sabbath *Kiddish*. Everyone joined in singing *zmiras* before starting the meal.

Raisa felt like *Hashem* was in the room with them. Her heart ached for Israel. She had a slight hope that he was alive and hiding somewhere.

They had had no news about what was happening in Vilna for a long while. Then Misha found out that many people had been taken to Ponary.

"*Hashem* protected us. We escaped at the last split second. It is a *nes*, a real *nes*. We have to pray thanking *Hashem* for saving our entire family," Raisa's father said.

He had aged over last few months. *Iza takes care of us*, was the only thought in Raisa's mind.

One morning, Misha took Raisa with him to the hospital he worked. Sometime around noon, an awkward, skinny peasant walked into reception. On seeing Dr. Zagin in his white coat with a stethoscope around his neck, the man, who was named Vladek, got shy, took off his hat, and sat quietly in the corner on the edge of a small, metal chair in the narrow waiting room. It was prearranged that Raisa would go with Vladek to check some safe places in case they had to hide. Meanwhile, the family could continue to stay together with the Zagins in their large, lovely home. There didn't seem to be danger in this quiet corner. Not yet.

Raisa followed Vladek through the hard-packed, narrow trail in the forest. It was peaceful. They didn't meet a soul all the way to his modest hut. Vladek's wife, Zosia, was very sweet. When Zosia hugged Raisa, she quivered with the memory of Pani Orlovich hugging her.

"You will find good with us. Pan Zagin is a saint. His heart is gold. You can stay with us till the war is over."

Under the table in the kitchen, covered by a straw rug, was a small opening into a square cellar. You could stand upright, and three people could sleep there.

"Nobody knows about this cellar. You will be safe." Zosia tried to catch Raisa's eyes, but Raisa couldn't look straight at her.

"You don't like it? Should we check other places?" asked Vladek. Raisa didn't answer. If they could be trusted, she would stay here, if need be, or wherever they offered for them to stay.

It was late afternoon and Raisa was eager to get back to her family. She would stay in Vladek's cellar with her parents. It would be sufficient for the three of them.

Vladek was hesitant about letting her go back alone, but dressed in a warm, peasant coat with a wool, flowery scarf around her shoulders, Raisa indeed looked like any other pretty girl from the village. It was relatively safe for her to walk alone.

"Don't come with me. I can find my way from here," she insisted.

The days were already short but there was still about an hour of daylight left. It felt chilly. Warm rays of the afternoon sun caressed her face. Raisa listened to her own crisp steps on the snow while thinking about her baby, Sonia, and her beloved Israel. She wondered where he was at that very moment. Maybe, just maybe, Israel was thinking about her and their baby, Sonechka, in this same moment.

Light, gentle snowflakes began to fall. Her two nieces must be outside making a snowman. They had been talking about it the night before. Raisa hoped she might still join them until the sun went down. She was almost there. She could already spot the house behind the bare trees. The quiet was soothing to her tired soul. They must be all inside. Why had she thought otherwise? It was too cold to build a snowman. Getting anxious to be home, Raisa walked faster. And then she froze. Someone was lying in the snow on the front porch. And then someone else and her mother. Raisa ran forward. There was blood, red blood on the snow, piles of pink snow. Then she saw them all… Dead! They were lying in the snow around the house. Raisa collapsed.

Vladek and Zosia found out that local peasants in German uniforms came to the house and ordered everyone, including Misha's wife and children, out to the backyard. The doctor had been at the hospital. The same afternoon, Misha was arrested and tortured. They shot him in his office.

Raisa stayed with Vladek and Zosia for three long years. During the daytime, she was in the cellar. They would let her out for five or ten minutes at a time at night.

Vladek often woke up in the middle of the night to have a drink of vodka. Some nights he got so drunk that he wobbled around the house unable to find the door.

"I may go tell you are staying here in the cellar," Vladek sometimes threatened when he was drunk.

"Don't listen to him. He does not understand what he says," Zosia would say, trying to calm Raisa who was frozen with fear.

There were countless nights and days when Raisa thought she may be the only Jew left on the planet. Raisa wasn't even sure she wanted to survive. To be the only Jew left would be an unbearable punishment. Deep within her soul, Raisa hoped and prayed that *Hashem* would save her Israel. She talked to him constantly. He understood her. Even if Israel was in heaven, Raisa knew he heard her voice; he knew that she was living but that her soul was dead. Her soul had died on that cold afternoon when Raisa returned from Vladek's hut to find the dead bodies of her family.

Raisa had no idea that throughout 1942–1943, the Germans had continued the systematic extermination of Vilna's Jews, including the expulsion of many to camps in Latvia and Estonia.

Despite the exterminations, cultural and social welfare activities in the small ghetto continued.

The United Partisan Organization, made up of various underground political groups, operated in the ghetto.

The second Vilna ghetto was liquidated by the Germans in September 1943. Most of the surviving Jews in work camps were murdered at the beginning of July 1944, shortly before the liberation of the city.

In July 1944, the Russians were actively bombing Belorussia. When the Germans finally left, it looked safe for the Jews to come out of hiding.

There were many Russian tanks on the roads. Some of local residents reconciled with the Nazi occupation. They just wanted the war to end and were afraid of bombings on all sides. Many were uneasy about Communists, but others ran to greet the Russian soldiers to thank them for the liberation.

Many surviving Jews streamed on both sides of the roads, barefoot and emaciated. There was nothing to do but walk. But walk where?

Raisa kept pinching herself that she was alive; she could walk in the daylight like a human being. It was a sunny July day; very warm. She had forgotten about the times she could go outside during the day.

Raisa walked for hours, maybe six or seven. She felt like flying, like she had wings. She felt like singing and surprised herself by singing Polish songs, most probably because she was subconsciously afraid to be recognized as Jewish. She was still crippled by frantic fear.

Every day in Vilnius, Jewish people met at the main square to check for survivors of the nightmare of the war. There were hardly any men or children.

"The Kaplan home has no walls," people used to say before the war. They welcomed guests every Friday night. Now there were no more walls and no more houses. Each one of them was bombed to the ground. None of Raisa's family members were coming back.

There was one place she had to go, however. Raisa found the house easily and rang the bell.

Elena Stepanovna opened the door, hugged her, and held her in her arms for a few moments. Finally, they sat at the oak table in the dining room. Everything looked exactly as Raisa remembered. Every detail was etched in her brain and her memory. Raisa felt cold shivers run down her spine, and her stomach was in knots.

Elena Stepanovna put a vinaigrette salad on the table and brought fresh *borsch* in from the kitchen. The familiar aroma filled Raisa's tired nostrils.

The door into one of the other rooms was open. There stood a little girl in a summery yellow dress with blue flowers. Very well groomed, Sonia had neatly combed braids behind her ears. She looked straight at Raisa, a total stranger, then quickly ran to Elena Stepanovna and held tightly to her arm. Raisa and Elena Stepanovna looked at each other in silence.

"And little Esther?" Raisa asked timidly. She had no idea what had happened to Fania.

"Fania survived. Her sister came to pick up Esther last week." Elena Stepanovna looked away. There was sadness in her soft voice and tears in her eyes. Raisa was fraught with panic and did not know what to say or do. *Was she supposed to take Sonia immediately?* She thought. *Take her where? What could she offer her at this moment? What did she feel? Did she lose all her feelings while hidden alone for three years in the dark, small hole under the ground?*

"Did you go see your family home?" asked Elena Stepanovna.

"I did. It was bombed; there's nothing left. Are your daughters still living here with you?"

"Lucia is not with us anymore. Irina is married. You can stay with me for now."

"Thank you."

"One needs time to forget. We should not tell Sonia anything till you find a place to live and decide for yourself what are you going to do next." Her voice was soft and soothing.

"Elena Stepanovna, you are a saint. You are the nicest person I have ever met in my life."

"I am not a saint. I am a very ordinary woman. We have to think about how to bring you back to normal life. And how not to upset Sonechka. She is too young to understand what happened."

"Thank you. I am going to listen to you. Sonia should know nothing. I have no right to upset her. Staying with me will confuse her. I am a stranger to her. A complete stranger. To tell you the truth, Sonia is a stranger to me as well."

"With time, you will learn to love her again. She is just a little girl who needs love."

"I don't know what love means anymore. I don't think I have feelings left in my empty heart. Like a robot…I feel like a robot. Am I crazy?" Raisa started to cry.

Elena Stepanovna took a white, starched napkin from her pocket to wipe Raisa's tears and moved her chair closer to hold her hands.

"Raisa, you can stay with me as long as you want. Time is the best medicine. You are very young. Your pain is too raw. Sonechka is your child. You are her mother. Believe me, things will work out. These are not normal times, but everything will be back to normal someday."

"I hope you are right."

Elena Stepanovna put Raisa in a big salon with a piano that her oldest daughter, Lucia, used to play. Raisa shivered remembering how she and Izia played Chopin's romantic songs together on a similar piano at her parents' home before this horrid war. That night, Raisa covered the piano with the silk, Persian carpet that was on the parquet floor. She didn't want to look at it…there were too many memories squeezing her chest and giving her sharp stomach pain.

Little Sonia roamed easily from room to room, touching porcelain figurines and the elaborate ivory elephants displayed on the mantelpiece. Something about Sonia walking freely into her room made Raisa exceptionally troubled.

One afternoon, Sonia walked over to piano and pulled down the carpet.

"Don't touch it!" Raisa yelled at her.

Sonia continued pulling on the carpet, wanting to see the black, shiny piano as it was before it was covered. Raisa jumped nervously from her comfortable fauteuil and slapped Sonia's hand hard. Scared, Sonia started to cry and ran out of the room.

"Sonechka, don't go in there. Don't disturb her." Raisa was ashamed of herself for hitting Sonia when she heard Elena Stepanovna's soothing voice.

Raisa knew she should not be so jittery, so strung out. *What to do, what to do? How long will it last?* She thought. She wanted to hide; she was wracked with fear and guilt over her lack of feelings for her own child, for Iza's child. The safest place to hide was in bed. She would close the doors, close the curtains, and go to sleep. Raisa couldn't sleep at night but being tired during the day caused her to doze off in the deep, comfortable chairs of the elegant room.

In May 1945, the war was completely over. Within a few months, one could legally leave Vilna. Raisa desperately needed to escape. Vilna was choking her. She couldn't shake her fear or her memories.

At night she woke up sweating; the same dream kept appearing. Raisa saw Israel. They were floating in the air. In the dream, she was aware that she was dreaming. They were happy. Then there was a shot, and Israel fell down covered in blood.

Most nights, she couldn't sleep, as much as she wished to fall asleep and maybe not wake up. Sometimes Raisa could barely breathe; she cried behind the closed door of her spacious room, crouching like a baby in her mother's womb in her luxurious bed. Raisa felt like a ghost and had a hard time believing that she was alive. She would pinch herself. She felt dirty and dead and walked the streets with constant pain in her back and chest. She was good at hiding her chronic pain, however, and showed her still-beautiful smile to the outside world.

July 17th was Raisa's twenty-third birthday. Elena Stepanovna prepared a nice dinner and set the table with gorgeous Limoges dishes she acquired before the war. There were fresh flowers in the middle like in old times in the Kaplan home.

"Raisa, your priority now is to take care of yourself. You are young, just twenty-three years old. I don't dare ask many questions, but don't blame yourself; don't be hard on yourself."

"Elena Stepanovna, there is something terribly wrong with me. I feel like running; like I'm lost. I'm sleepy and deeply disoriented. Please say something that can help me."

"Have patience. With time, you will find a nice place to live. You will find a new husband. Then you will take Sonia and you will give her your love."

"Elena Stepanovna, I am so miserable. What kind of mother can I be? What can I offer to my little girl? She will grow up hating me."

"For now, go out and meet other people. Your people."

"I don't want to talk to anyone. There are many days that I have difficulty breathing. My heart is empty; my soul is empty. I must be a damaged and broken vessel. I don't feel alive, yet I want to be alive. Most of the time I want to sleep, hoping to see my family in my dreams."

Raisa didn't want to talk about her past, about her family. She lived inside her head. Many nights she went to bed around nine o'clock and hoped not to wake up, not to think, and not to remember. But she always woke up. Maybe God wanted her to live longer, but why? And for what purpose? God? Which God? There cannot be a God in this world. How can people dance and laugh? Don't they remember, don't they know?

Raisa wondered if maybe it was better for Sonia to stay with Elena Stepanovna and to never know that she was born Jewish. Many times, while lying in Vladek's cellar, Raisa believed that if she survived, she would be the only Jew left in the world. Why should Sonia experience this life of fear? She didn't have to be Jewish. She could be Russian. She could have a chance of a normal, peaceful life. What could she offer her? Where would she take her? Where would they go? There were still many anti-Semites around whispering loud and clear that not enough Jews had been killed.

Raisa wished to disappear from this place, from the city of her birth, from these streets soaked in blood. She wanted to forget it ever existed; she couldn't bear the thought of staying in her hometown. She desperately tried to disconnect, to forget the nightmare, the hell of war.

"I am leaving tomorrow morning for Lodz. Most Jewish people go there," Raisa announced one evening to Elena Stepanovna.

"Have a safe journey. Take good care of yourself."

Was that all she had to say? How come Elena Stepanovna didn't ask her about Sonia? How come she didn't reprimand her?

Raisa hid a photo in her bra that she had taken two weeks prior with Sonia. Sonia looked cute with a short haircut, a cute bow in her hair, and a flowery, silk dress. She was standing on the chair behind Raisa looking straight at the photographer with her intelligent eyes. She would not be taking Sonia with her. Raisa did not want Sonia to know she was her mother.

The photo warmed her heart. She talked to Israel each night, asking him to protect Sonia from wherever he was. She wanted Sonia's life to be easy. Sonia should obtain a good education, get married, have maybe four children, and never know she was born Jewish.

The train was arriving in Lodz. Raisa had no idea what to expect. How would she manage? She asked herself again and again why she was alive when everyone else was gone. What had happened to her Izia?

Raisa arrived in Germany and got a position in the United Nations Relief and Rehabilitation Administration since she understood English and German, and fluently spoke beautiful Yiddish, Polish, and Russian. There she helped people organize their papers to go to Palestine, Canada, or the United States. Most people wanted to go places where they had relatives.

On September 6, 1946, an old, gaunt, emaciated-looking woman almost jumped at her, embraced her, and did not let her go.

"Raisa?"

"My God, I don't believe my eyes!" Raisa was embracing Bella Israelit, Izia's mother. She immediately noticed the tattooed number on her arm. Raisa had no idea Bella Israelit had survived. How was it possible?

"Where is our baby?" Bella Israelit asked Raisa.

How could she answer? Unable to control herself, she started to cry.

"Is Sonia alive?"

Raisa nodded, unable to speak.

"Where is she?" insisted Bella Israelit.

4

It was June 1944, and three-year-old Sonia stood on the second-floor balcony gripping the iron rails, mesmerized by the reddish-orange, loud bursts that were covering the sky far beyond the roofs of the houses. She wasn't a bit afraid of the rackety sound of the distant explosions. Sonia put her hands to her ears—the sound was faint. She took them off—it was loud again.

"Mama, Mama, come look at the sky!" she called while jumping from one foot to the other in delight.

But instead of Mama coming, her sister Irina quickly plucked Sonia up into her arms, covered her with a warm, blue shawl, and rushed down to hide under the staircase where they waited for the prolonged sirens to come to an end.

Besides Mama, Irina, and the gorgeous Lucia, there was a German officer named Hans living in their apartment. Hans was given the small, dark, mahogany-panelled library with a tiny, pretty balcony facing the main street.

Lucia was five years older than Irina. In 1938, at age twenty, she was already married to a Polish doctor, Stanislav. Stanislav's mother adored Lucia and showered her with presents. She often traveled to Europe. Lucia's favourite gift was the French perfume, Chanel N°5. For their wedding present, Mama got Lucia a dinner set for twenty-four people from Czechoslovakia. It was light turquoise, sprinkled with small, white flowers accented by burgundy petals. Hugging the turquoise background were two gold rings separated by a deep, cobalt-blue and stamped with red flowers to match a butterfly in the centre of each plate. If you held the plate to the light, one could see an intricate design through the fine Rosenthal. Mama also bought them tall, crystal, wine glasses that reflected the sunny rays in the mornings.

When the Soviets came to Vilna in 1939, they immediately arrested the local intelligentsia. They came for Stanislav and took him away. Lucia returned home to stay with Mama, bringing her wedding presents along. Now all these gorgeous dishes were in a display cabinet to be admired.

It was mostly Lucia who took care of Sonia. She took her for a stroll in a beautiful carriage every day. Neighbours felt sorry for Lucia having to care for her child alone without a husband. They just assumed that Sonia was her daughter.

Lucia always smelled delicious, and Sonia followed her aroma through the rooms of their spacious apartment. Lucia found it amusing when Sonia sniffed her lovingly. She would sprinkle a few drops of her perfume on Sonia's neck and hands, asking how it felt. And she laughed and laughed and sprinkled some more.

When walking on the streets with both girls, Lucia was often stopped by strangers who admired Esther. Esther had huge, sky-blue eyes, long eyelashes, and rosy cheeks.

"What a stunning girl! A real doll!"

They often pinched Esther's cheeks and gave her candies. Hardly anybody looked at Sonia or said anything nice about her. Sonia was skinny with a runny nose. She hated Esther who was plump and loud. Esther screamed if she did not get what she asked for. But she usually did. Mama rarely said no. Sonia knew that both Lucia and Irina preferred to take Esther for a walk, but Mama insisted they take them both at the same time.

Sonia liked to pray the way Mama taught her to pray before going to sleep. She asked God to make Esther disappear one day; to just disappear and never come back.

One afternoon Sonia spotted Hans's gun on the chair. She thought that maybe she could kill Esther. She took the gun and hid under the dining room table.

"Sonia, Sonechka?" Mama was looking for her, but she kept quiet. Lucia, Irina, and even Esther were looking for her but were unsuccessful.

"Oh my God!" Mama saw her crouched under the table.

Sonia never saw Mama so angry. Mama knelt down, grabbed the gun, and quickly pulled Sonia out. Mama's face was red; she looked scared. She took Sonia in her arms and held her very tight to her chest.

"My little baby. Thank God!" Mama said again and again. There were tears in her eyes.

Hans sometimes flew to Berlin to visit his family. He had twin boys who were Sonia's age. Each time Hans came back from Berlin, he brought chocolates for everybody and a new doll for Sonia.

Sonia had difficulty to walk. By the time Sonia was two, Mama was worried that something may be wrong with her legs.

"Don't worry, Matka. I will take care of it," said Hans a few times.

Indeed, Hans brought some miraculous pills. Thanks to the pills, Sonia started running.

By far, the nicest room in their flat was the salon with its parquet floors, grand piano, oak bureau on carved legs, and a large painting of a half-naked Saint Mary Magdalene washing Christ's feet.

It was very quiet in their apartment. Sometimes Lucia would make Sonia and Esther sit silently on the sofa in the big salon while she sang Russian songs like Mama. Other times Lucia would stop singing, get up and dance, twirling Sonia around. Lucia would dress up the girls, put lipstick and powder on their faces, and giggle.

While Lucia danced, Sonia and Esther would glide on the slippery parquet floor and roll on their tummies while admiring their reflections in the gigantic mirror on the wall or in the shiny, black piano. Mama didn't approve of the noise they made. Lucia jumped and laughed like a little girl, bribing Mama with her kisses. Irina just watched them from the sofa. Although Irina was five years younger than Lucia, she was more serious. Most of the time she sat by the window, observing what was happening on the street.

There was a Gestapo office on the upper floor of their building. One of the officers came to talk to Mama. He asked to take Lucia out to see a movie.

"Mama, don't worry. I will not go out with him," Lucia assured Mama. There was no way Mama would let Lucia date a German officer.

Lucia hoped that her Stanislav was alive and would come back to Vilna when the war was over.

It was a sunny day in March, and Mama was preparing a delicious meal when the doorbell rang. Two Gestapo officers walked briskly into the apartment, caught sight of Irina and Lucia in the dining room, and ordered them to follow them.

"Don't take both. Please leave one to help me with my toddlers," Mama pleaded.

They took Lucia.

Mama knew that the Germans gathered young men and women to send to Germany to work in their factories to feed the war machine. That evening, Mama went upstairs to talk to the Gestapo officer who had wanted to date Lucia. His name was Frederik Wolf. Sonia never knew what they talked about, but she understood that this officer was in love with Lucia.

Frederik Wolf went out of his way to find where Lucia was taken, and he got her out. He never came back to his apartment. Instead, they flew to his idyllic country estate somewhere in the depths of the Bavarian Alps. It was as if Lucia disappeared beyond the horizon. For many years, Mama had dreams of a smiling Lucia washing the windows.

Every night before going to sleep, Mama would tell her little girls exciting fairy tales about kind princesses. Sonia liked it when Mama read them stories. Mama had a soft, melodious voice and knew many old songs. When Sonia asked nicely, Mama would sing until they fell asleep. They had a high bed with gigantic goose-feathered pillows.

Mama slept in the middle with the girls on each side. Sonia begged Mama to go to sleep at the same time as she did, but most of the time Mama stayed with them just long enough for the girls to doze off. Then Mama would go to the other room, sit in a big, green velvet fauteuil to read her own heavy books until midnight.

The air raids became more frequent. Irina was frightened most of the time while hiding under the staircase and holding both girls in her arms. Mama decided to go away to the country until things calmed down.

Walking out of town, along the river, they saw some German soldiers eating their meal from a large, round pot in the middle of the field. They recognized Hans who waved from far away. Sonia pulled Mama's hand toward Hans, but Mama shook her head. They slowly continued on their tiring walk.

After a few weeks, when life in the city got back to normal it was time to return home. German officers came to the house to collect Hans's belongings. Hans never came back. He had been killed in one of the battles. Mama cleaned out his room. She found the picture of his wife and his children, looked at it for a second, then promptly threw it into the wastebasket.

Meanwhile, the Germans closed down the city's orphanage letting people to take kids if they wanted them. Since their house was across the street from the orphanage, Mama and Irina stood on the balcony and watched how people grabbed the older, stronger kids. Mama noticed a very skinny girl hiding behind the trees. Nobody seemed to want her. Mama quickly went out to bring this girl into their apartment.

Her name was Nurka. She was dirty and full of lice, with a big, swollen stomach and an unpleasant smell. She looked like a boy with her nearly bald head. The Germans had shaved their heads. All of them. Nurka must have been twelve or thirteen years old.

"What is your name?" Irina asked her

The girl gave Irina long look but didn't answer. She didn't talk. She didn't want to. On her papers her name was Nurka.

Irina felt nauseous and left the room closing her nose.

"Smell will go away soon. Poor girl, she wasn't washed in months," said Mama.

First, Mama together with Helga, our cleaning lady, who happened to be with us this afternoon, took this new creature into the hot tub to wash her head thoroughly in kerosene and scrub lots of the dirt away. Helga was boiling water to make more steam running back and forth from the kitchen to the bathroom.

After that, every evening for a full week, Mama soaked Nurka in a hot bath and put her to sleep in the kitchen for a while.

Mama asked our polish dressmaker Jadviga to move with us and to dress Nurka.

Jadviga made her a wool long coat with sheep curly fur for the collar.

Nurka was skinny, undernourished, but in this coat she looked taller and older.

In no time, Nurka turned into a very healthy, beautiful girl, with green eyes and silky reddish hair. Nurka had long eyelashes and big eyes.

But she hadn't an ounce of gratitude in her bones. She particularly hated to watch Sonia and Esther as she was insanely jealous of them. Irina openly disliked Nurka; she didn't trust her and couldn't figure out why Mama went to all the trouble to bring her home from the street.

Sonia was actually scared of Nurka. One look of Nurka and Sonia would run to hide under the table or in the cupboard. Mama seldom left Sonia with Nurka. But each time she did, Sonia begged her not to go away.

One morning two strange women came to visit and sat in the salon with Mama for a very long time. They took Esther for a walk. That night Mama went to bed with Sonia but without Esther. Sonia was really happy and hugged Mama's big, warm body. Sonia saw Mama crying the next morning.

"Why?" she asked.

"I will miss her," Mama said.

"Mama got used to Esther. She is a sweet, playful girl fun to be with," Irina tried to explain to Sonia.

"I never liked her," Sonia announced. "Is she coming back?"

"I don't think so."

"How lucky we are. Tra-La-La-La. I am really, really happy!" Sonia could hardly believe her good luck.

For a while, their large sunny salon, where Lucia's piano sat silent since she was taken away, was occupied by a sad, weird lady who didn't like Sonia and chased her away whenever Sonia sneaked in. The lady was a bit mean. Her name was Raisa. Sonia was very happy when this lady finally left.

After the war was over, a handsome officer named Dadia Sasha arrived to live in the salon. "Wow! What will I do with such a huge place? Ride horses?" Dadia Sasha put his grey, battered suitcase in the middle of the shiny, parquet floor.

Kind and funny, Dadia Sasha was six feet tall with blond, curly hair. He talked about his family who lived far away, near the Ural Mountains. His mother had taken care of seven children alone in the village. His father was an officer who died near Leningrad.

Dadia Sasha was the eldest son. He had five sisters and one little brother, Misha, who was seven years old. Dadia Sasha showed Mama a lot of respect, and he often brought sweets for Sonia, mostly chocolates. In the evenings, Dadia Sasha stayed home instead of going out to drink with his pals. Apparently, army food was terrible, so Mama frequently invited him for dinner. He adored Mama's *pirozky*, her veal cutlets, her *borsch*, and her delicious *pellmeni*. After helping Mama clear the table and put away the dishes, Dadia Sasha stayed in the dining room to chat with Mama and Irina for a long time. He knew lots of old, romantic songs and played the guitar.

As a rule, Sonia went to bed right after the meal. From their small bedroom, Sonia could hear Irina laughing.

Once Sonia woke up and tiptoed into the dining room, which was next to the little bedroom she shared with Mama. Dadia Sasha was holding Irina's hand. Irina saw Sonia, blushed profusely, and hurried out of the room.

One evening Dadia Sasha asked Mama's permission to play piano one evening. He played and sang old love songs. Then he asked Mama for Irina's hand in marriage. Irina got so excited that she started crying.

"I will be very good to her. Elena Stepanovna, you can trust me. I will be the best husband ever born," he pleaded.

Mama was silent. After dinner, she invited Dadia Sasha to the small study that Hans used to occupy.

Irina knew Mama would say no. Dadia Sasha was a Soviet officer. He might take Irina far away to Siberia or God knows where else. Besides, Mama didn't like Soviets. They were uneducated boors, not our type.

As Mama and Dadia Sasha talked, Irina stayed in the dining room and cried.

Years later, Dadia Kolia told his wife, Irina, that Mama fooled Dadia Sasha that Irina may look healthy, but she was actually sick. Mama lied and said that Irina had tuberculosis and it was a bad idea for him to marry her.

The next evening, Dadia Sasha came home late. He was drunk and wobbled from one side to the other on his way to the dining room where he hugged Mama and begged her to let him marry Irina. At one point, Dadia Sasha took a revolver out of his belt and threatened to kill himself.

Soon after, he was sent by the army to be stationed in Riga, Latvia. There he was promoted to colonel. There were tears in his eyes when he said good-bye. Irina wanted to go with him to the train station, but Mama said no.

Dadia Sasha wrote long letters, six or seven pages. Irina listened to Mama and never answered them. He finally stopped writing, and Irina wondered what happened to him in his life.

Not long after Dadia Sasha left, Dadia Kolia appeared on the scene. Dadia Kolia was a very charming, handsome young man. Mama treated him like an old friend. He was related somehow to the family.

Dadia Kolia was the youngest and healthiest of eleven children. Before he was born, his father decided to go to America to get rich. In America, his mother missed her family and cried a lot.

When Dadia Kolia was barely two years old, his loving father, not able to bear his wife's tears because she missed her family so much, set them out on their journey back to her beloved Ukraine. They were robbed on the train through Germany. They never made it past Vilna where they had some distant cousins.

As a very religious family, parents hoped at least one of their eleven children would serve God by becoming a priest. Dadia Kolia didn't want to be a priest. Nevertheless, he was sent to seminary school although in his heart he dreamed of being a surgeon. Dadia Kolia graduated from the Theological Seminary for Russian Orthodox Priests. After graduation,

Dadia Kolia managed to enrol in a medical school at the University of Vilna, greatly upsetting his mother. They had no money to help him.

When the war was over, Vilna was liberated by the Soviet Army. Dadia Kolia was called for questioning. Why had he been born in America? Why had he been sent to the seminary for Orthodox priests? He was let go, but no longer allowed to study medicine. A person with his background could not cure people who were supposed to build a Communist State. The Soviets didn't want religious doctors. Religion was opium for the masses. If someone believed in God, he couldn't be a decent doctor.

The only thing left for Dadia Kolia was to become a clergyman. But first he had to find a wife. Russian Orthodox priests were not allowed to marry once they were ordained. He had no intentions of being a religious monk. This is when Mama contacted his family to arrange for him to meet Irina.

Dadia Kolia was exceptionally handy. He knew how to fix electricity, plumbing, everything. He loved to take things apart and put them back together. After he was thrown out of University, Dadia Kolia worked as a janitor in the building across the river.

Each time Dadia Kolia was expected to arrive, Mama dressed up, prepared his favourite dishes, and then, upon his arrival, treated him as if he was already her son-in-law. Mama, who normally said very little, found it very easy to talk to Dadia Kolia. Dadia Kolia was educated. He was a true Russian, not a Soviet peasant.

Mama chatted with him about his family, about the horrible war, and about Irina. Irina sat on the edge of her chair listening and not saying much. Mama beamed.

Soon Irina too began to dress up for him, join in on their conversation, and smile a bit. After three months, Irina and Dadia Kolia got married. On their wedding night, Dadia Kolia gave Sonia a drop of vodka. She threw up, making both herself and Mama a mess.

Mama was very pleased with their marriage. She let the young couple live in the big salon. Whenever Sonia walked in, they looked for an excuse to send her out as if she didn't understand that all they wanted was to kiss each other.

After her wedding, Irina stopped wearing braids and instead let the cascade of her chestnut hair hang loose over her shoulders.

Irina took after Mama in her height and her straight posture. Her facial features were more like her father's, whom Sonia had only seen in the photo album. A high, open forehead and bushy, dark arrows for eyebrows emphasized Irina's grey-green eyes that had long, curling eyelashes. Irina had a very straight nose that was a bit on the large side, which Dadia Kolia made a lot of jokes about. She had Mama's delicate, butterfly shaped mouth.

Dadia Kolia was the same height as Irina. He, too, had grey-green eyes. They looked beautiful together. He must have been the handsomest priest in all of Vilna. Everyone liked him except Nurka.

Dadia Kolia wore his heavy, solid-gold cross with a shiny ruby stone in the middle. It had belonged to his great-grandfather, who died in America on the same day Dadia Kolia was born.

When Dadia Kolia got his own parish in the country near Molodechno in 1947, they had to leave Vilna. Mama went along with them to help them settle in their new home. Sonia had to stay at home with Nurka.

Nurka ignored Sonia, instead giggling and whispering with her fat ugly girlfriend Shura, who worked as a maid for the Russian colonel who lived on the third floor above their apartment.

Sonia got bored and said she would complain to Mama. Nurka got mad and kicked her, spilling the glass of milk Sonia was drinking all over her. At that moment, Sonia decided never to stay with Nurka alone.

Mama thought it was a good idea for Sonia to stay with Irina and Dadia Kolia in the summer, to get out of the city and be in the fresh air. It was supposed to be healthy for your lungs.

Sonia loved the countryside. The land stretched as far as the eye could grasp. Green fields were sprinkled with tiny, fluffy dandelions, and patches of yellow wheat swayed with a warm breeze.

Normally, Dadia Kolia left very early in the mornings. Irina didn't want to be home alone all day; she would rather walk to the river to join him.

Irina usually woke up the moment she heard Dadia Kolia move. He prepared the worms, putting some on the hooks in advance. In the beginning Irina found it repulsive. Later Irina volunteered to help. He laughed and let her.

The path Irina walked on was narrow, often disappearing between high stalks of wheat. The air smelled of flowers and moist earth. It gently caressed her nostrils, her arms, her legs. Irina felt secure; she was fulfilled in this tiny village alone with her Kolia.

Six months ago, when they first arrived, the church had been neglected and filthy with broken windows. Dadia Kolia repainted it himself. The local peasants came to help install the windows and floors. Now it is beautiful.

Irina walked slowly, stopping to look at the delicate blue and pink flowers growing wildly around the footpath and wondering how such gentle flowers sprang out of the ground from nowhere.

Dadia Kolia's floppy, yellow hat was the first thing Irina saw behind the bushes down by the river. She slowed her pace so as to not disturb him or alarm the fish. She found a cozy, secluded spot nearby to watch him. Dadia Kolia seemed to be intently concentrating. Maybe a fish was biting. There was something flipping in his bucket on the ground.

Irina laid on the grass and carefully examined the clouds as they tirelessly moved and blended from one form into another. Irina made out a lion, then a chariot with white horses. Before she blinked, the lion turned into a rabbit with two sharp ears on the lookout for danger. She imagined all sorts of creatures just above her head—friendly, smiling, or dangerously stretching their paws.

Irina got up from the grass. Her Kolia pulled her toward him and held her tight. He touched her hair, kissed her nose.

"How did you know I was here?"

"My fish whispered to me." He laughed, pointing to one tiny fish in his pail.

Dadia Kolia took the little fish out and threw it back into the water.

"You didn't catch much."

"I guess you are right. We don't have fish for dinner."

"I don't mind. I hate to clean them."

It got darker. As they crossed the fields, on the way home there was a forest of birches and pine about a mile from their house. He ran ahead and disappeared, expecting Irina to find him. Often, she did, but today she gave up. Dadia Kolia came out from hiding and caught her. His tenderness wrapped Irina's soul with much love.

Five years later, they were with their third congregation and were once again painting, rebuilding, and renovating. The bishop in charge of sending priests to different parishes must have been really impressed with what they had been able to do.

Their little house was the very last on the left side of a paved country road. They had a small garden for vegetables, and many apple trees. It was pretty during the spring and summer. Winters were long and dreary. Dadia Kolia spent most days in his church.

The village church was about a two-mile walk from their home. He chose the side trail behind the houses. Walking on the main street, you met the locals. Many of them walked by as if they didn't see him. The schoolteacher and the administrator of the kolkhoz were particularly rude and nasty. Dadia Kolia took it personally, got upset by their behaviour, and often had nightmares. It was humiliating to know that they considered him an oddball and crossed the street to avoid him. Irina only went to church on Sundays.

When Sonia turned six-and-a-half, Mama managed to register her for grade one. Mama walked Sonia to school every morning and always picked her up after school to go home.

Sonia didn't like school. She did not understand what the teacher was doing on the blackboard with huge numbers. Some children knew to read and to count. She did not. Mama never taught her.

Sonia tried to copy in her notebook the numbers exactly the same she saw on the blackboard, but they didn't fit. Her notebook was much smaller than the enormous blackboard.

Her grade one teacher, Tamara Kornilovna, thought Sonia was stupid. Sonia never received any mark but zero. It was only after Mama brought in a big box of perfume for her that Tamara Kornilovna stopped scratching Sonia's notebook with a red pencil.

Tamara Kornilovna had to be very unhappy, for she was as skinny as a stick. Mama often said that mean, unhappy people were skinny because the nastiness inside them eats them up. Because of the big present Mama gave her for International Women's Day on March 8th, Tamara Kornilovna passed Sonia to grade two. Second grade was not much fun either. There were rough boys who teased and scared her.

Next to Sonia sat a big boy with large ears who pinched her legs during classes. Sonia complained to Mama. The very next day Mama came to the class, lifted the boy by his protruding ears, and asked him if he cared to see Moscow. After that he stopped pinching her, but other boys still scared her. Sonia would run straight home as soon as the bell rang, often meeting Mama halfway.

An army colonel who had a daughter Sonia's age moved into the apartment on the third floor. His daughter, Tatiana, had red hair, and was much taller than Sonia. Tatiana talked very little, but she came over so she and Sonia could play together. Tatiana knew how to make pretty dolls out of grass. She was the best student in her class. Too bad she was going to a different school than Sonia. They spent a lot of time together in the afternoons.

In the middle of the school year, Sonia's class got a new teacher, Klara Ivanovna. The first day she appeared in their class, Sonia knew she was going to like her. Klara Ivanovna had a soft, warm voice. Like Mama.

Klara Ivanovna came to visit Sonia at home when Sonia had to stay in bed with the measles. Nobody else came, but Klara Ivanovna did and brought sweet biscuits. She sat next to Sonia in her bed for a long time. She was not afraid.

Sonia tried very hard for Klara Ivanovna. She finished second grade with excellent marks. The neighbours began to say that Sonia was very clever for her age.

That summer Klara Ivanovna met a handsome pilot from Siberia. He took her with him to Sverdlovsk.

Mama walked her to school each day, carrying her school bag. Mama claimed that it was much too heavy for Sonia. Some kids were mean and made fun of her. One boy hid her school bag and laughed when Sonia cried unable to find it. Sonia couldn't wait until Mama came to pick her up to take her home each day.

Some days Mama couldn't make it. Sonia hated to walk home alone. Mean, older boys from grades four and five followed her and pulled her. She was petrified of them.

There were many reasons why she was scared, and it all started with a chocolate bar a boy from her class, named Oleg had put on Sonia's school desk. The second Sonia took it, Oleg grabbed it back.

"I will give it to you after class," he said.

After class, he walked her home. Oleg teased Sonia with the candy and pushed her toward the garage near their apartment building. She didn't want to go inside the garage, but Oleg and his friends surrounded her and insisted that she pull down her panties and show them her private parts. Sonia started crying and said no.

They promised her more candies.

"Nobody will know. Just take them off fast for a minute."

She tried to get away.

"If you don't, we will tell your mother you did it."

Frightened and ashamed, Sonia quickly pulled down her underwear and then quickly ran out of the dark, dirty garage.

How could she do something like that to her Mama? She hated herself for being scared of them and for taking her panties off. It was her shameful secret. What if one of those nasty, rotten boys told Mama? Just having this thought brought sweat to Sonia's forehead. It wasn't her fault; they had chased her into the garage, pressed her to the wall, and surrounded her.

Sonia heard boys laughing behind her. How many were they? Four? Five?

She was ashamed to meet them at school the next day. She felt dirty, ugly. They laughed when they got close to her and chased her again on the days Mama did not pick her up. Sonia did her best to avoid them so not to go to the garage anymore. But it happened. Big, awful boys managed to catch her at the entrance to her apartment. They surrounded her under the stairs. She resisted. Oleg threatened to tell Mama how she had done it a few days before.

Horrified, she picked up her skirt and pulled down her panties so that they could look for a minute, scared to death that someone would pass by. Then screaming and crying, she ran upstairs.

The cruel boys probably told others. Who knew how many kids knew about it? Sonia had nightmares that Mama would find out; that someone would tell Mama. It was a big stain on her heart. It stayed as her dirty secret for many years.

5

Neighbours didn't believe that Irina and Dadia Kolia supported Mama and Sonia financially. Also Irina tried the best. She knew. First of all, she took Sonia to her country home every summer. Every single visit they brought fresh eggs, butter, large pork chops, wooden sweaters. Sonia got some small change that poor peasants left in the church for them.

Deep in her heart, Sonia loved aunt Irina. (Let her be aunt if she prefers it.) And admired Dadia Kolia. Sonia looked forward to their visits.

Irina wrote often how she is missing Mama, wishes to come, stay with her.

Mama had difficulty with her legs, with her heart, worked very hard all day. Cooking, shopping, cleaning their home. Everything took a lot of time.

But each and every time Irina arrived, she would run to go shopping for herself. Coming home late, exhausted, complaining that stores were empty and there was nothing to buy. In the meantime, Mama had to work harder than ever cooking for them to take yummy food back to the country. Poor Mama never ever complained.

On the days Irina and Dadia Kolia came to visit, Mama served her meals inside their tiny quarters.

Still, Sonia's favourite room in the house was a big dining room, which could not be occupied by a single tenant because to access the kitchen, one had no choice but to cross the dining room. It didn't belong to any one of the families living in their apartment.

Their apartment had two entrances. If you came through the backdoor from the inner courtyard, you would walk directly into the large, neglected kitchen with tiny windows and a small rusted sink in the dark corner. Sonia never ventured into the kitchen. Mama wanted her to read books and study, not wasting time on helping with housework.

Off the kitchen was a big door leading into the large dining room with a balcony to the courtyard. The dining room had two other tall doors, one to the corridor facing the main street and the other to a small bedroom where Mama and Sonia lived.

A long, narrow corridor had four doors in total. The large, heavy one led to the main marble staircase, another one led to the salon with the piano, the third door went to the small library, and the fourth one, the most important for everyone, went to the dining room. One had to pass through the dining room to reach the kitchen. The kitchen had three housewives: Mama, Malka, and Wanda.

A long time ago when Sonia was very little and the house was empty, she could run everywhere. But no more. After the war, the housing committee decided that Mama and Sonia could not occupy so much space alone. They sent a young man named Fedia, a bus driver, to live in the salon. Fedia settled in the same salon where Dadia Sasha used to live. Not long after, he brought his wife, Malka, and lots of furniture.

In the small library lived a young woman named Wanda who was studying to be a nurse. Mama and Sonia had their two little rooms behind the dining room for themselves.

Sonia loved being in the dining room because there was always somebody there.

Everybody had to pay their part of sharing common space. The dining room had, in total, twenty-four square meters. Mama paid for ten. The other two families in their flat paid for fourteen, seven each. There was always a lot of action. By now, Malka and Fedia had two young boys who were growing up. All four of them lived in one room. As big as the salon looked, it got crowded for a family with two kids. The two boys spent most of their time in the dining room around the large, oak table, doing their homework, playing games, listening to the radio, or riding their bicycles.

Most of the furniture belonged to Mama. Mama received the hundred-year-old oak table with the carved lion heads on its heavy legs from her parents. A dark, walnut cupboard near the balcony door used to belong to Mama's husband, Irina's and Lucia's father, who passed away long before Sonia was born.

Dadia Kolia did not want to eat in the dining room. At any given time, there were people busy around the table. He was a real hermit when it came to avoiding strangers.

"Why are you always unhappy? Don't you feel privileged to live in our times when we are building new healthy society, building Communism? We may witness a miracle in our own lifetime." Sonia bugged him many times.

"Mama, I cannot stand it! Sonia gives me a headache!" He would say, annoyed.

"Why do I make you so nervous? I want to understand why you are angry at me? I just don't get it." Sonia was clueless and frustrated.

"Leave me alone. You are so totally brainwashed that I cannot talk to you. You live in a different world. Stay there. Mine is finished. Kaput. Your system is working for you. You don't listen to me. You repeat what they teach you in school. They tell you their truth. Stick to it but leave me alone."

Sonia asked Mama again and again what was wrong with Dadia Kolia. There were days that Dadia Kolia was so much fun—he would tell jokes and play games. Sonia remembered when he and Irina were first married and living in their first parish near Molodechno. They played hide and seek with her and chased one another in the fields. Irina would fall while running, and Dadia Kolia would catch her, kiss her, and tickle her. They would roll in the tall grass and laugh.

But lately, Dadia Kolia had stopped laughing. He even stopped wearing his long cassock when they came to visit. Sonia hoped Dadia Kolia was not ashamed of believing in God. Why should he be ashamed? He was not a Party member. His parents made him believe in God, so he believed.

Dadia Kolia had the misfortune of being born in America. He was often stopped in order to have his papers checked because his place of birth was written in his passport.

"Is that what you call justice? To stop a person on the street and interrogate like a criminal?" Dadia Kolia would say, visibly irritated.

What could be done? People who believed in God represented a move backward, the undeveloped element of society. One had to explain to them, to teach them the truth.

Dadia Kolia was hardly two years old when his family returned from America. He could not possibly be a spy. But the Party officials could not take chances. In these hard times, security was first priority. Everybody had to understand real sacrifice for there to be peace in the world; for building a just Communist society. Sometimes, the innocent people suffered a bit. It was inevitable.

Only Dadia Kolia was stubborn. He refused to see the truth, the noble purpose of it all. Lately, he had lost weight and gotten grey. He even looked shorter; he looked nothing like the handsome man in his wedding photo.

Both Irina and Dadia Kolia complained to Mama that Sonia was lazy, had a big mouth, and didn't help at home.

"Mama, look at your Irina. A mighty queen! What does she want from me? Who is she anyway to criticize me?" Sonia protested.

"Mama, you are spoiling Sonia. Other children of her age do everything at home. You give her too much freedom. She has no discipline whatsoever," Irina said, sounding desperate.

"Ira, I am not getting younger. Times are new, but I am not. I am too old to change. I am doing the same thing with her as I did with you and Lucia. You learned fast. She, too, will learn everything she has to know to do in the house. In time. Let her have her childhood," Mama answered in her calm, soothing voice.

"Did you hear that? And why do you interfere? How can you know anything about children when you don't have any? Don't give Mama advice about what to do with me. She doesn't need your advice!" Sonia interjected.

Clearly, Irina wanted Mama's attention; was jealous of her.

One day, annoyed by Irina's comments, Sonia asked Mama directly, "Can you please tell her that you love me more than her?"

Mama kept quiet for a few seconds, then whispered to Sonia, "You need me more."

Sonia was satisfied with this answer from her laconic Mama. At the same time, she could guess that Irina was not comfortable with Mama's response. Irina would have preferred that Mama had said nothing.

Despite these harsh exchanges, Sonia wished to be more like Irina. She admired her perfect profile, her straight posture, and her slow, melodic voice. Sonia loved when people on the street turned their heads to look at Irina.

Jadviga, a dressmaker, came to the house a few times a year to sew new things and to repair old. She could have been tall, but she was born with a hunched back and walked crookedly. When she came, Jadviga worked in the corner between the kitchen and the dining room where there was a place for the sewing machine. There Mama had a big armoire with drawers full of all sorts of fun threads and fabrics from which Jadviga could choose.

Mama was short on words, and Jadviga loved to tell stories. They were both born in Vilna and grew up on the same street. This was at the time of the Tsar, a very long time ago. Mama went to Russian school. They usually walked together, although Jadviga had to walk much farther to her Polish school. When they were in grade four, Tsar Nicolas came to visit Vilna. There was no school that day. Everyone lined the streets to greet the royal carriage. The Tsar smiled and waved to the cheering crowd. He had a small beard and was very handsome. Jadviga pushed Mama to the front raw so that she could see better.

When Mama graduated from high school, they had a big ball. She wore the most exquisite long gown. It was deep-blue taffeta with three velvety roses of the same colour. One was near the high collar of her neck, one was on the waist holding it tightly, and one was just below the knees gathering the shiny, lacy folds on the bottom of the dress. There was on the piano a beautiful photo of Mama in this dress.

Jadviga told Sonia that Mama had a dream to go to St. Petersburg to visit her aunt Masha who lived there. Mama also loved opera. When she finally got to visit St. Petersburg, aunt Masha took her to the opera. Mama claimed that God had listened to her prayers because the very evening they got the tickets was the premiere of Boris Godunov. Fyodor Chaliapin himself appeared in the main role. Aunt Masha bought the very best tickets. They sat in the first loge at the right of the stage. After the show, they were invited to the reception.

Mama wore her beautiful dress from graduation. Chaliapin walked over and gave her a red rose. Mama kept that rose in her little, gold-trimmed Bible all her life.

Jadviga knew a lot about Mama. She respected and adored her.

"Your mother has a heart bigger than Siberia," Jadviga said many times to Sonia.

When the school year was over, Sonia eagerly waited for Irina to take her to their country place.

Irina and Dadia Kolia lived like hermits seldom having any visitors.

In each new place they moved, Dadia Kolia wasted no time improving his surroundings. He immediately painted the church, fixed broken furniture, and repaired electrical appliances with his capable hands. There was little he could not fix. Dadia Kolia could repair watches, make furniture, install new floors, and build a barn. He could do most anything.

Dadia Kolia tried to start a choir in this new church as he did in his previous parish, but nobody showed up. Young people were afraid to come.

There were days Irina and Dadia Kolia didn't see a person on the street or through the windows. On cold winter days, even when the sun was shining, Irina didn't go out. No gloves were warm enough for her fingers. Gigantic icicles hung from the roof and all around the windows like diamond scones. On sunny days, they sparkled against the blue sky. Everything was covered with white, glistening snow. It made one dream of Greece with its turquoise, cloudless sky, and small, white cottages with red roofs like the pictures in the books. On warmer days, it was thrilling to walk around listening to sound of crackling snow under her boots.

Most days the sky was grey, and the snowflakes were soft and moist. They landed gently on branches, and if there was no wind, they stayed for days. This type of snow was ideal for creating a snowman.

Last year, Irina and Dadia Kolia actually made a nice snowman at the back of their house. It was a lot of fun. This year, Dadia Kolia was not in the mood. Irina was worried about him. Mama said if he continued to take everything to heart, he may get sick. What would Irina do without him?

Their new house, with its cold walls and many empty rooms, was located at the very end of the street. It gazed with one eye to the bare fields and curling river, and with the other eye toward an ancient, tired oak at the end of the unpaved road.

To save on the cost of heating the house during the long winter, Dadia Kolia shut most of the rooms except for two in the front and the gigantic kitchen with the cold, cement floor.

The kitchen had a white, low stove, a heavy, wooden table with long benches, an old, brown couch where Sonia slept during her visits, a tall wall cupboard filled with Dadia Kolia's holy books, and an ancient, metal trunk filled with goose pillows, handmade tablecloths, nightgowns, and lots of warm, embroidered dresses.

When Irina and Dadia Kolia first married, Mama bought them a light-beige, pine bedroom set. But the furniture never arrived at their house. Poor Dadia Kolia had no idea how long he would be allowed to stay in different parishes. Some of the furniture pieces were dismantled, hidden under Mama's bed. The rest were stored in the attic in Vilnius.

Dadia Kolia finally managed to organize a local chorus for young girls who adored Irina. The chorus girls were sweet and respectful. Tall, stunning Irina looked like a queen next to barefoot, peasant girls who covered their hair with flowery scarves. The most devoted of them was Manka. Manka never missed prayers, was grateful for the presents Irina showered on her, and prayed a lot dreaming of becoming a nun.

On Mama's visits to Irina, Sonia refused to stay behind with Nurka. Sonia was scared of her. One look from Nurka sent Sonia running to hide under the table. Mama seldom left Sonia alone with Nurka. Each time she tried, Sonia begged, "Don't go! I am not staying with her!" Thus, Mama usually took Sonia along, leaving Nurka alone at home to take care of the house.

Mama and Sonia took a train from Vilnius to Volozin, then the horse-drawn carriage for many hours before Irina and Dadia Kolia met them. They walked together through open fields, then through a young forest with trees so thin you could almost see through them.

At night, Sonia saw dancing rabbits, and maybe even a big, grey wolf looking through the window with hungry, burning-red eyes.

Mama never stayed for very long. The day they left to go back home was very sunny. Fragile young trees glittered with silver under the warm rays. Walking through the fields, Sonia chased squirrels and wondered if there was a chance of meeting a wolf so early in the morning.

As soon as Sonia and Mama were seated comfortably in the horse-drawn carriage that took them to the train, Irina and Dadia Kolia turned back to go to their house on the little hill by the end of the road. Mama was sad to leave them alone. She waved at them for a quite a long time.

The driver was in cheerful spirits. The horses wore amusing bells around their necks. Encouraged by the whip, they galloped faster. Sonia clung to Mama, yelping with excitement.

Sonia and Mama arrived home earlier than expected. They rang the doorbell a few times, but nobody answered.

"I cannot imagine where Nurka can be at this hour," Mama worried. "Let us try the back entrance."

Sonia ran quickly to the courtyard just in time to see two soldiers leaving their place.

Inside the apartment, on the dining room table, there were empty glasses and a few bottles of vodka.

Later that evening, Mama tried to open the cupboard where she kept her jewelry and important things, but the key wouldn't go in. Mama tried different keys, but to no avail. The next day, she had to call a locksmith.

"Someone broke the lock," he said.

Mama had a lot of wonderful, old pieces of jewelry. Her husband, Lucia and Irina's father, used to buy Mama a piece of jewelry on each anniversary.

"Nurka, what did you look for?" asked Mama when the locksmith left." And why to break the lock?"

"I think my father was a thief."

Stupid girl, thought Sonia. *Nurka didn't know who her father was. Why would she say that? Such a troublemaker! She does not even lie smart.*

Mama worried plenty about Nurka. By now Nurka was almost eighteen. She could learn dressmaking or be a hairdresser, but she was lazy and refused to learn. She didn't say much, and she was never at home. Mama didn't like her friends. She liked to be around all kinds of maids and soldiers. Nurka was not too mean, but you couldn't trust her.

But it was the way she walked that was most embarrassing. Her blouses and skirts hugged her body so tight that Nurka looked naked and vulgar in whatever she put on. Men always looked at her and whistled. She liked it; she wanted them to whistle and to look at her. She moved her hips slowly. Every step promised something that men lusted for. Irina and Dadia Kolia found it repulsive and disgusting.

"Mama, Nurka is asking for trouble. Watch out."

"Kolenka, Nurka is still very young. She will grow out of it, have patience." Mama obviously had patience.

One time, Mama suggested coming to visit them with Nurka. Irina never said no to Mama, but she could not have Nurka in their house. If the parishioners thought she was Irina's relative, Irina wouldn't know where to hide from the shame.

Mama was different. Everything was okay with Mama. She never worried about what the neighbours said or what they thought. The neighbours talked between themselves, and they talked to Nurka. They told her about Lucia and about the beautiful dresses and expensive jewelry she wore before the war.

Mama often asked Nurka to watch Sonia. The neighbours whispered that Mama treated her like a maid.

In order to have enough milk, Mama bought a brown cow, which had to be kept on the outskirts of town. Usually, Nurka went there in the mornings. At noon, Mama and Sonia walked over along the river to bring Nurka a lunch.

On some days when Mama was busy, Sonia went with Nurka for the whole day. There were always a lot of soldiers in the fields. Mama strictly forbade Nurka to make friends with the soldiers, but Nurka ignored what Mama said and disappeared for hours, leaving Sonia alone to watch the cow.

One day, Mama caught Sonia playing with a metal spoon like the ones that soldiers tuck inside their boots. Mama got the message.

"Nurka, trust me. You are a big girl. It is time to think about your future. Looks are not everything. I would like you to learn dressmaking. You could be very good at it."

Nurka kept silent. There were days she didn't come home to sleep.

On winter evenings Mama kept the fire in the chimney going. Neat, rectangular fireplace rose from floor to ceiling covered with smooth, white and blue tiles except for where a square opening was for the coals or maybe for the stork to bring newborn babies in.

One evening, Mama sat by the fireplace reading a thick, medical book. Sonia glanced at the pictures trying to figure out which was the healthiest way to sleep at night. According to the book, the right way was to lie on the right side in order not to disturb the heart.

"Sonechka, it is getting late. It is bedtime. Go!"

"I don't want to go to bed by myself. I wait for you."

"It is so dark outside. I am worried about Nurka."

Just then they heard the front door open. Mama sighed with relief. Nurka was home safe.

Nurka, her face red with fury, stormed into the room, pulled off her new Persian-lamb winter coat Mama had made for her, and threw it straight into Mama's face.

"When you drop dead, cover yourself with it!" she screamed and ran out, slamming the heavy front door.

A week later, Mama got a notice to appear in court. Nurka was suing Mama for years of hard labor washing dishes, taking care of Sonia, and pasturing a cow.

"Somebody put her up to it. I feel sorry for her," Mama tried to defend Nurka.

While people gossiped, Sonia kept her ears wide open.

"Precocious young lady. How long she should take this abuse? I am surprised they didn't send Elena Stepanovna to Siberia," said Maruska talking to her neighbour on the balcony one floor below theirs.

The following day the same tall, bony Maruska with her thin, bleached hair and blood-coloured lipstick talked completely differently to Mama.

"Oh my God, dear Elena Stepanovna, you are a real angel. You definitely don't deserve such villainy. Who would imagine that Nurka could behave like that after all you have done for her? Obviously, she runs with the wrong crowd. What can you expect? I really feel for you. Such an ungrateful bitch!"

The courtroom was filled with people. Many were sitting on the window ledges, and some sat on the floor. The noisy crowd waited. Nurka never showed up. When Nurka didn't show up for the second and the third time, the case was dismissed.

One year later, Sonia met Nurka walking a baby carriage and trying to hide the fact that she was working as a maid.

"How is Mama? How is Irina?" Nurka asked eagerly

"It is none of your business. My Mama isn't your anymore." Sonia walked away angrily.

By now, there was only the two of them. Sonia had her Mama all for herself. Nurka was out of their life by her own choice. Irina lived far away in the country with her husband taking care of their parish.

Sonia and Mama took long walks in the afternoon along the riverbank. Big, tall Mama walked slowly but very straight for her age. Mama had small, grey eyes, practically no eyebrows, a sharp, little nose, and an elegantly shaped, raspberry-coloured mouth that never knew lipstick. Mama didn't use any make up. She said lipstick ate up natural colour. Some neighbours considered Mama an old woman. Sonia thought Mama was beautiful. Her thinning hair was a silvery grey.

Sonia loved to go with Mama to the bazaar to look at tomatoes and apples and to meander through the busy, messy, second-hand market. It was joined next to the bazaar waste ground, filled with her own shifting busy crowd. Through the gates of the fence separating the two streams of people unceasingly poured inside. One was only allowed to sell personal, used clothing. Buyers moved freely, touching merchandize, snorting at prices, bargaining, and quickly filling their large bags.

One could spot a ten-year-old girl selling her dresses, her shoes, or even her baby carriage, as well as to see an old drunk in a dirty shirt who was hardly able to stand on his widespread legs while holding his trousers in his right hand and his jacket with his left.

Deaf, mutes had permanent spots. They were the only ones not bothered by the police. They sold pictures with swimming swans and kissing lovers with a broken heart between them. It all looked very exciting for Sonia, particularly when she saw those people who pretended to be buyers but who were actually looking for customers to sell their hidden possessions: nylon stockings, men's shirts, jersey sweaters, good shoes, and other items one could not find in the stores.

6

Their class had begun getting a different teacher every year, and the worst of them all happened to be Lydia Alexandrovna. Sonia liked her at first. Lydia Alexandrovna was a big woman who lived next door to them. She would ask Sonia to help her to carry heavy books on the way home from school because she was much too fat. She walked slowly, breathing heavily while carrying her load.

One afternoon, Lydia Alexandrovna invited Sonia to her place to do the dishes and to wash the floor in her kitchen. Country kids, where Lydia Alexandrovna came from, were used to cleaning their teacher's house; they were proud to please. But Sonia didn't know how to clean, and she didn't want to. Mama never asked Sonia to help with the housework. Mama clearly wanted Sonia to read books, to study, and to be a diligent student.

After that invitation, Sonia didn't want to carry her books anymore. Then something really terrible happened.

As Sonia walked into her class—at the last minute as usual—every head turned to look at her.

"Why are you looking at me? What is wrong with me?"

"Read your article, smart aleck!" snapped Svetlana, who was one of the friendlier girls.

"What article? I didn't write any article." Sonia ran to look at the weekly class newspaper displayed on the wall.

The main editorial titled, "HOW I PREPARE MYSELF FOR THE COMING EXAMS," screamed at her in big, bold letters. Silly article. It boasted about how clever and industrious student she was, how hard she worked, and how gratifying it was for her to answer the teacher's questions faster and better than anybody else in her class. To Sonia's surprise, the article was signed with her name.

It was true that Sonia was always prepared for questions. But how dare Lydia Alexandrovna write this column in her name! At that moment, Sonia hated her teacher's fat face, and her soft, chameleon-like voice. Furious, Sonia wanted to shout that it was a big lie. She had not written the article.

There was little she could say. In her heart, Sonia knew that nobody would believe that Lydia Alexandrovna wrote the article herself without talking to her about it. She had to swallow it.

Sonia loved all subjects except math. She forced herself to do all the problems in her book since Mama encouraged her. Mama sat next to her to check Sonia's answers before she could put her exercise book away. Sonia was amazed that Mama knew all the answers to every single problem in her book.

Sonia never went shopping for herself. Jadviga still came once a year to sew, to fix whatever was needed. Sonia enjoyed Jadviga's company. She had many interesting stories to tell. She had no family and was never married. Jadviga wasn't grouchy like an old spinster. She was cheerful, full of jokes, and never said a bad word about the neighbours.

Sometimes Jadviga took Sonia for a walk through the little crooked streets in the old part of town. They would pass the main prospect to examine beautiful displays of dresses and jewelry in the windows of expensive stores.

"Enjoy looking. I hope you are not jealous, my beautiful princess," Jadviga would say to Sonia in her cheerful voice.

"Pretend for a minute that it is all yours. Close your eyes and see it all in your mind. Shiny pearls feel cool on your neck and a silky scarf caresses your arms. Feel good?"

"Actually, it does." Sonia would join Jadviga in her fantasy.

"You see, my little treasure, one does not have to buy these things. Admire them; pretend they are yours for ten minutes. It is enough. You cannot kiss gems or love them or dance with them." Jadviga looked happy and beautiful.

One could forget she was born with a hunched back.

"Tomorrow is my birthday," she whispered as if sharing a secret.

Wow! Sonia had no idea how old Jadviga was. A birthday? Birthdays were special for Sonia. Mama always made a big fuss for her on her birthday, April 1st. She was determined to get Jadviga something to surprise her.

After dinner Sonia sat at the dining room table drawing a funny birthday card and writing a poem for Jadviga. She then looked at their antique display cabinet next to the fireplace. Her eyes stopped on pretty English tea cups. They were turquoise with tiny gold leaves and exquisite pink roses. Sonia gently pulled one out of the cabinet. As far as she remembered, they were always sitting on the shelf. Mama never used this cup. In the drawers Sonia found two nicely embroidered, lace napkins, wrapped the tea cup with saucer in them, and hid the bundle in her school bag before going to bed.

Sonia had a strange dream that night. They were living on an island surrounded by turquoise water. Jadviga was Sonia's sister. She taught Sonia how to swim because she swam as well as a fish. They were both naked in the clear water. Jadviga was holding Sonia and they were laughing. Her back was not hunched.

Sonia woke up early and got ready quickly. Jadviga lived on the fifth floor of an old, grey building without an elevator. Sonia ran up the stairs wondering how difficult it was for Jadviga to climb these worn-out steps every day. What would it be like when Jadviga got really old?

Sonia rang the bell.

"Oh my God, what happened? Nobody ever came to visit me so early."

"Happy Birthday, dear Jadviga, Happy Birthday to you!" Sonia sang.

"My sweet girl, you remembered! Come in, come inside."

Once inside, Sonia gave her the card with the poem.

"I made it myself."

"So sweet, so kind of you!"

As Jadviga admired her card and read the poem, Sonia unwrapped the starched napkins and placed the tea cup and saucer on the round papier mâché table by the window.

Was Jadviga surprised? She jumped, she danced, and she hugged and kissed Sonia again and again while asking,

"Are you sure it is okay with Elena Stepanovna? Did you ask for permission?"

"Absolutely. 100% It is from both of us." Sonia didn't blink an eye.

She lied with a straight face, enjoying Jadviga's excitement.

"The nicest gift I have ever received in my entire life. In our family, nobody has ever had something so beautiful. I can't believe my eyes. Now I can close my eyes and dream, look at my cup of tea, sip some, and dream again. Every day for the rest of my life! You are an angel. "There were tears in Jadviga's eyes.

Mama was upset with Sonia long after she discovered that the teacup was gone. It was the only time Mama was ever cross with her.

Three weeks of school were left. Sonia could hardly wait to go to a new school next year. She would be attending grade five in a middle school in a beautiful, pink building next to the main square.

"You need some fresh air. Jerusalimka has a pine forest, good for the lungs. We will find a place for you to stay."

Sonia was delighted. This summer she was not going to Irina They were going to rent a dacha. Her and Mama together.

Sonia was still asleep on Sunday morning when Mama got up at dawn, prepared a lunch for the road, and ironed her new dress. A festive breakfast was ready on the table when Sonia got up. Sonia enjoyed her hot chocolate drink while Mama patiently braided her long, thick hair. Sonia had tried to do it herself many times, but her braids never came out as neatly as when Mama did them for her.

Mama always wore teardrop diamonds in her earlobes. Sonia was very proud of Mama. She was proud to walk next to her while holding Mama's finger with her hand and to see how neighbours looked at Mama with respect and some envy.

On this particular crisp morning they took a bus to a little village in the thick forest called Jerusalimka, strolled along the river, picked flowers, and looked at little houses with signs for rent. One-and-a-half thousand rubles for one room with a common porch for the summer seemed a steep price. Apparently, most locals vacated their homes for the summer. The most desirable and expensive rooms were by the river. Mama was afraid of water; she was more inclined to look for a room inside the pine forest.

Here and there, vacationers who came early were putting out hammocks and setting up volleyball nets. Many families arrived here from as far away as Leningrad, Kiev, and even Moscow.

Mrs. Saveleva, who Mama knew from before the war, owned a big place away from the river but still within walking distance if Sonia wished to go swimming. Mama had decided to stay in the city to look after their flat. She rented a tiny room with a miniature balcony for Sonia. Mrs. Saveleva would look after Sonia when Mama was not around.

A few days after school was over, Sonia left for Jerusalimka.

She spent her mornings in the forest reading books and picking wild blueberries. Three times a week at exactly at one o'clock, Sonia ran to the road to meet the bus bringing Mama to visit her. Most of the time, she spotted Mama already climbing the hill that approached the house.

"Maybe tonight you stay with me," Sonia begged after grabbing Mama's heavy parcel.

"Don't touch. It is too heavy."

Mrs. Saveleva usually received Mama with hot tea, fresh raspberry jam, and home-baked cookies. Mrs. Saveleva was old, used a lot of red lipstick, powdered her face, and bleached her hair.

"Do you have a lot of trouble with my girl?" Mama asked her each visit.

What trouble? Every single day, Mama carried delicious food from the city. The only thing for Mrs. Saveleva to do was to warm it up and put it on the table.

Sonia didn't like staying with her.

"Mamochka, it is so boring. She won't let me go anywhere by myself. She never goes to the beach, even when it is boiling hot outside," Sonia whispered. "Stay with me, we will have fun."

"Sonechka, I cannot stay. I have to hurry now so I don't miss the last bus. Mrs. Saveleva is an older person. Show her respect. She means well. I don't want you to go to the water by yourself."

Sonia held tightly to Mama, not wanting her to leave.

"I'll be back tomorrow at exactly the same time. Be a good girl. What should I bring you? Do you want some *pirozky*? I'll get you fresh strawberries. We will have them together with milk and sugar."

"Tomorrow is Sunday. Can you stay overnight with me? My bed only looks small, but it is actually very wide." Sonia could hardly keep up with Mama on the way to the bus stop.

The bus stop wasn't near the house. Twice a day, Mama walked up and down the hill carrying heavy bags so that Sonia could have a fresh food.

Mrs. Saveleva was a widow. She owned five acres of land with a vegetable garden, lots of cherry trees, and a large, pine forest. The only house one could see from her property was a white cottage with pretty columns behind the cherry trees.

By the end of June Sonia noticed the arrival of a grandmother with two boys and a parrot. Curious, Sonia peeped through the white fence. Granny was sitting on the veranda in a painted, wooden, rocking chair holding a tiny, red parrot in a palm of her hand while two boys circled around her jumping and laughing. Granny's eyes caught Sonia's. Still holding the parrot, she motioned Sonia with free hand to come over through the gate.

"What is your name?"

"My name is Sonia. I live on the second floor," Sonia whispered, afraid that Mrs. Saveleva would come and fetch her back immediately.

"Please join us for an afternoon tea. Sema and Jasha are first cousins. They are my grandchildren."

This time Sonia didn't stay long because she had to meet Mama. She never mentioned the boys to Mrs. Saveleva.

Whenever she could sneak away, Sonia ran to the neighbours to play with Sema and Jasha. They had many books and were happy to see her. They showed her the paper airplanes they were building.

During these warm summer days Sonia wore mostly shorts, letting the sun brown her skinny chest and back. But she started getting embarrassed wearing just shorts. She put on her new red T-shirt.

When the cherry trees ripened and the fruit was safe to eat, Mrs. Saveleva let Sonia try a few.

"Would you like to help me pick the cherries?" she asked Sonia.

"Sure," Sonia said, agreeing immediately.

She took an empty pail and ran to the trees. Ripe, sweet cherries were falling very fast. Sonia, holding herself on the ladder, had fun seeing the red fruit clustered thickly above her.

"Look, I have two full pails." She proudly brought them to the house.

"You're a good girl with young, fast fingers. Continue picking, but don't eat them. I will give you your portion later."

For a split-second Sonia was insulted. She felt like stopping picking cherries for the mean woman, but she liked to look at the luscious, inviting cherries.

Sonia didn't put any into her mouth. She wanted to show how fast she could fill the pail.

Sonia saw her friends from the top of the tree. She got a great idea. Sonia had never invited the boys over to her side because Mrs. Saveleva hated noise and Sonia was afraid that the boys would annoy her. But the cherry trees were away from the house. It would be a lot of fun to pick cherries together.

"Sema!" she called softly.

Sema heard her and turned to look up. Sonia waved to him, inviting him to join her. In a few seconds, the boys were in front of the cherry trees. Sonia's heart skipped happily.

"Sonia, what if she won't let us? Shouldn't we ask her?" Sema pointed to the house.

"Why? It is for her benefit. Three of us can pick much more. She should be thrilled you are helping."

The boys promptly climbed up different trees. Their little fingers danced, competing with each other. Sonia was the happiest girl in the world seeing how much fun her friends were having. The busy kids didn't notice Mrs. Saveleva approaching them with a big stick.

"Who let you into my garden? Get out! I'll break your necks before you break my precious trees!"

The boys jumped down and disappeared in an instant. Embarrassed, Sonia ran after them to apologize, but stopped because she was ashamed of herself and of Mrs. Saveleva.

Mrs. Saveleva victoriously carried the big pails of cherries that three of them picked into the house. Sonia hid behind the old tree trunk crying. She could hear loud, excited voices. The boys were probably explaining to the granny what had happened. Sonia hated Mrs. Saveleva. She didn't want to go inside the house; she didn't want to see her cruel, old, stupid face.

Some time passed. It became chilly. She was willing to go to the white cottage to apologize.

"Sonia, supper is on the table," she heard her enemy say.

There was silence behind the fence. Maybe the boys had left for the beach with their granny. Sonia went inside the house to have her dinner.

"Mamochka, please take me home. I hate her!" Sonia said to Mama the next day as she walked her back to the bus stop.

"School starts soon. Next week you are coming home.

Sonechka, please be nice to them. They are old people and very nervous. They don't have patience with children. Don't aggravate them. Don't invite these boys over. The country air, pine trees is very healthy for you."

"Mamochka, is Ludka back home from visiting her grandparents?"

"Not yet. Here is my bus. I must go if I want to have a seat."

"Go, mama. Go. I don't want you to stand in a bus all the way to the city."

"It has happened many times. I must go." Mama kissed Sonia and waved goodbye.

On the other side of the road Sonia saw the same boy she had seen the day before yesterday. He looked straight at her with a shy smile. He must be local boy, looked like a shepherd.

Bleached by the sun his hair was really yellow. And clear blue eyes.

Sonia walked slowly aware the young boy followed her but was too shy to come closer.

Suddenly Sonia turned around, he stepped forward giving her a small bunch of wild blue and yellow flowers. Before she could thank him, the boy run away into the children camp across the road.

Sonia couldn't see inside the camp but she was envious of the children in the summer camp.

Mama would never send her to the camp. When Sonia asked Mama why not, she said there was not enough supervision to take care properly of so many youngsters. Besides Mama didn't belong to any institution that organize summer camps.

Sonia walked on with her little bunch of flowers and suddenly, without any particular reason she felt like singing.

She wished to pass the white cottage to see Sema and Jasha. The closer she got, the more anxious she became. She wanted to see Sema, especially, to know that he wasn't angry with her for yesterday.

"They all left for the city this afternoon. Grandmother sends you warm regards. And they left a present for you. It is a book," the owner of the house told Sonia.

Sonia didn't know their last name or their address in the city. But she was determined to find them. Sonia would walk on the main street in Vilnius as long as it took to meet them. Even if it took years, they would meet eventually. Sonia imagined that Sema wouldn't recognize her. Then Sonia would tell him about the white cottage in the pine forest, about the cherry trees, and about the red parrot with blue feathers. Sonia would confess to Sema that she had a crush on him. She wasn't exactly sure what she would say. But it would happen.

7

At her new school Sonia shared her seat with Larisa whose family recently moved to the apartment upstairs from Sonia's. Larisa was spoiled and moody. When they fought, they drew a line on their desk in order to not touch each other by mistake. Larisa had red hair like her colonel father. She was shorter than Sonia. Her small eyes and sharp nose made her look like a little fox.

On the days when they were friends, Sonia and Larisa could talk for hours under the stairs of their house until one of their mothers asked them to come home for dinner.

"Tomorrow will be another day, Sonechka," Mama would call from the open door on the second floor.

In the dining room where someone was always eating their meals, hungry Sonia would burn her tongue on hot chicken soup, relish fat, juicy cutlets while Mama warmed up her favourite roasted potatoes for the third time.

"Poor Elena Stepanovna stands on her feet all day cooking for her princess. She has to warm her meals ten times until the princess is ready to eat," Malka scolded Sonia.

Sonia knew Mama was not angry with her. Mama wanted Sonia to have good friends. Mama actually liked Larisa. After dinner Sonia would hug and kiss Mama, thanking her for the yummy food.

"Mamochka, can I go to Larisa?" Sonia asked immediately before running upstairs for the rest of the evening.

"Go, go already." Mama gently pretended to push her away.

"Mama, please show me how much you really love me!" Sonia insisted, not letting go.

"Okay, love."

Theirs seemed to be the last girl's High School in all of the Soviet Union. Girls came from all over the city. Only the best were accepted. Sonia was at the top of her class. Since they were friends, Larisa asked to copy her homework every day. It wasn't fair, but Sonia felt as if she had no choice.

Zenia was a new girl in school, about two years older than the other girls in their class. She had arrived from Ural to stay with her aunt who lived in the same courtyard as Sonia and Larisa. She was very pretty with big, grey eyes and a ready smile. Full of good humour and open for mischief, Zenia was quickly accepted and liked by most of the girls in the class.

Zenia walked on the streets of Vilnius amazed by how well people were dressed, how beautiful the stores were, and by how many goods there were inside them.

When Mama got Sonia a new blouse with a turtleneck collar, puffed sleeves, and shiny gold buttons in the back, Zenia was afraid to touch the semitransparent fabric. Mama had gotten it from Jadviga, who occasionally received parcels from Poland.

"Can you get something like it back home?" Sonia asked Zenia.

"Are you crazy? I have never even seen taffeta or nylon." Zenia became very serious. "I wish my mother could see it. Mother knew that life here would be better for me. She cried when I left."

"Why did you leave?"

"I didn't want to. My mother begged me to leave. She said that life in Vilnius is like in Paris, that stores have goods, that there is respect for our officers, that I would have nice dresses. Mother was right."

Sonia liked Zenia's musical voice, her willingness to share about her life in Ural, and her talent for imitating famous personalities. Sonia wanted to be friends with Zenia until she overheard Zenia and Larisa making fun of Dadia Kolia, saying he was retarded and looked stupid with his long cassock and cross.

In grade six, Sonia was elected leader of one of the three groups that were supposed to organize social activities for the rest of the class. They chose which films to see, then they would analyze them together. Sonia suggested a trip to the nearest kolkhoz. They also read books about much-admired heroes like Oleg Koshevoj and Zoya Kosmedianskaja who had sacrificed their young lives for their beloved country. The girls studied their heroes' lives carefully, striving to emulate their values.

At the end of the group discussions, they talked about the importance of friendships, agreed on the need for solidarity, and planned how to improve their character. The girls sincerely promised to be more attentive to each other and more helpful to those in the class who were behind in their homework. They would be a good example to other students in their school.

That year, Sonia began to spend some time looking in the mirror. Mama said thin lips were a sign of meanness. She tried hard to stretch her lower lip to make it appear larger.

The New Year was approaching, and the excitement for the coming masquerade swelled. On the eve of the masquerade, January 31st, while Mama braided her hair, Sonia asked her to leave the left side undone. On the same side, on the top of her new pretty dress, she asked Mama to sew an old, shabby rag. She put a torn stocking on her left foot with an old dirty shoe. Sonia then smudged her left cheek with Indian ink and attached a band on her head that read: TWO WORLDS—TWO CHILDHOODS.

Other children had more interesting costumes, but Sonia got a first prize for her original idea of representing the contrast between Soviet Union and America. Sonia received lots of praise from her classmates and from teachers as well. Everyone seemed to be proud of her.

Everything in Sonia's life suddenly had a meaningful purpose. If something was forbidden, it had to be forbidden. Peasants came to the city to buy loaves of bread. Mama felt sorry for them, but not Sonia. These peasants didn't want to work in the fields. They didn't like the kolkhoz. They didn't want to share with society. They were selfish and not interested in the future of their country. Brainwashed by a Capitalistic system for many years, simple uneducated peasants held on tight to their property, then dared to complain that Soviet Law cheated them. What Law were they talking about? The Law was not written for them. The Law was for people who wanted to build Communism, for those who loved their country and were willing to make sacrifices. The Law was not for the people who were concerned only with themselves and who didn't care what was going to happen in the rest of the world. It was about time that peasants stopped crying and complaining. They needed to be educated.

Each time that eggs, sugar, and flour were sold in the stores, long lines would form early in the morning. As a rule, there was a quota of six eggs and one bag of flour per person. Sonia could see from her balcony that people were standing in the same line again and again to triple their quota. Their skirts waving in the wind, women searched their braziers for hidden bundles of money.

It was surprising how much tolerance the Party had for local farmers. Most of the Lithuanian farmers were against the Soviet regime. Many of them were bold enough to praise the times of Smetona before the Soviets took over. They would talk about how many goods there were and how there was no need to freeze in the lines waiting all night for the store to open.

Big deal, they had goods in the stores! What else did they have besides material goods? What purpose in life did they have? Did they have any industry? Did the world know about a little country called Lithuania? Could they afford to send their children to university? It was a pity that ignorant peasants didn't understand priorities in life, were not able to be proud of the Soviet Union, and could not comprehend with depth what it was trying to do!

Sonia often dreamed about how proud she would be if her father was an army officer like Larisa's. Sonia looked at military men with special respect. Mama said that most of them were uneducated, rude, and alcoholics. So what? They were strong, patriotic, and ready to give their lives for their country if need be. This was courage to be admired!

One of Sonia's real heroes was Pavlic Morozov. Sonia had read and reread how the twelve-year-old boy couldn't bear to witness the dishonesty of his grandfather and his wicked uncles who tried to cheat the people of their village by secretly storing goods away. Pavlic made the only choice he could make; he told the village people the painful truth about his family. Sonia had learned to admire Pavlic Morozov and to hate his grandfather who had murdered such a wonderful human being.

While lying in bed, Sonia liked talking to the old, friendly moon and always pondered the same question: could she be as strong and courageous as Pavlic; would she have the mental strength to go through the tortures that others went through for their country?

Sonia was clearly aware that the Americans, Germans, and Frenchmen were constantly preparing for war with the Soviet Union because they made their Capitalistic profits out of wars. The Soviet Union had to be strong to keep peace in the world; it had to be determined to not let these criminals fan new fires to destroy the world.

Sonia's task was to do well in school, to strengthen her character, to grow up courageous, to be ready at any moment for an attack from the

West, and to protect her good people. Everyone around her believed that nobody would be able to defeat the great Soviet Union. It was impossible because whatever happened, justice would win in the end.

Sonia didn't remember the Second World War, but she knew about heroes who had sacrificed their lives for her and her generation. She knew about cunning, wicked Americans who pretended to help when Soviet forces chased the Germans to Berlin.

Sonia felt fortunate to have been born in this privileged time; that she would be one of those to build Communism. She hoped to live long enough to witness the day when the dream of all those who had fought for Communism and perished, the dream of all mankind would be realized.

At times, Sonia woke up afraid that something would happen to her and she would not be able to participate. She prayed to God to be alive and to deserve to build it. Sometimes they had a discussion in class about how they imagined life would be when Communism became a reality all over the world. No one could imagine what life would really be like, but one thing was guaranteed: everybody would be extremely happy.

Sonia loved to read and to learn more each day. She cried while reading about black children in America who were beaten, insulted, and not allowed to go to the same school as white children. Sonia couldn't understand how it was possible; how people could live with such humiliation and not rebel against it.

Sonia had never seen a black person in her life. She read books, saw movies, and could picture their lives in her mind. Sonia could imagine an old, exhausted, black person in a factory carrying a heavy load on his bent back. Suddenly in would walk a white American with a fat stomach, in a tweed-checkered jacket, exactly like the ones she had seen in the Crocodile journal. Between his teeth would be a stinky cigar. He clearly detested these dirty, overworked, poor people. His eyes would catch the old, tired man. The old man would be trembling with fear.

"Move faster!" the American would yell, kicking the man in the stomach. The old man would sway on the floor and fall.

"Out! Fired!" The capitalist would order his aides around, then briskly leave the plant.

The old man would be ashamed to go home. At home, his son, a hungry boy named Tom, would be waiting for a crust of bread with a little warm water. There would be water, but no bread. His mother would tell Tom a fairy tale about happy children in a beautiful, rich country where children ate fresh buns and loved him. The name of the far away country was the USSR. Tom would lick his lips and then fall asleep with an empty stomach.

Sonia and Larisa saw these scenes so vividly that they decided to put on a play for the school.

Everyone hated the Americans who were preparing for new wars, kept people in fear, and made huge profits on their sweat. There were some rich people in America who ordered gold chains for their dogs, cooked special food for them, and beat their maids if the maids were not gentle enough to their animals.

The girls appreciated having a worry-free childhood, living in a country where the kindest and the smartest people sat in the Kremlin and thought about their future; thought about everybody's future. Sonia wanted to love her country as much as her friends did, as much as Pavlic Morozov did.

The crippled barber who lived in their courtyard was patiently awaiting orders what to do. All little kids meddled around asking for the thousandth time what exactly is going to happen and what kind of trees and flowers they are supposed to plant.

Sonia watched from behind a little corner of the heavy drapes in the dining room. She could hear a lot of noise, laughter. Nobody seemed to be very tired.

"Whoever heard about it? Let them bring peasants from the country, not young kids to dig the ground and work so hard.

My Sonka is too weak. She is staying home. I don't let her to dig the ground and plant their flowers."- mama was telling Malka in the kitchen.

"Our Sonia is a big girl. Elena Stepanovna, it is not such a hard labour. She doesn't have to dig the ground, just plant some seeds with other kids. The youngsters love it. It makes them feel good to participate with grownups. Elena Stepanovna, please let Sonia come down and join us," the neighbour on the first floor tried to convince Mama.

Mama never taught Irina to cook or to clean the house, just like she never taught Sonia. Mama also did not teach Irina to brush her teeth every morning. It was Irina's Polish teacher who insisted that the girls in her class brush their teeth. Now Irina forced Sonia to brush her teeth for three minutes every morning.

Summer or winter, Manka loved to be in Irina's kitchen. She was coming to teach her to make borsch and to cook meat. Every day, Manka cleaned the kitchen, the outside toilet, and did laundry. Sonia liked to watch her move swiftly through the house, folding bedding, sweaters, and dresses. Manka had passed thirty, but she looked much younger.

Manka's family had their crooked old hut exactly opposite from Irina's house. Early in the mornings, Sonia could hear Manka's father slowly getting up from the top of the stove where he slept most of the time, choking from chronic asthma. Prochor, Manka's father, wouldn't part with his heavy, sheepskin jacket in the winter or summer.

During the day from the top of the warm stove, Prochor cursed his wife, Paraska, for not being able to manage their household and for keeping them poor. Short, vigorously moving Paraska ignored his blabber. She answered back at times, though, with the most colourful Russian curses. Embarrassed, Sonia blushed a lot in their presence. But at the same time, Sonia enjoyed sitting on a big bed, eating hot, baked potatoes with salty herring, and listening to them reminisce about their youth; their hot romance.

Shyly smiling at her distant memories, Paraska remembered how popular and well-liked by the other girls in the village her handsome husband was many years ago. Once Prochor had bought her red leather boots for Christmas, soft as butter. Young Prochor was a fabulous dancer. His strong voice was as good as an opera singer.

"He also knew how to kiss, my bold devil." Paraska's thoughts took her far away.

But the chest-tearing cough of her husband promptly brought her to reality.

"Lazy bastard, everyone left for work and you're still warming your stinking bones. Cough, choke yourself. I am fed up. I don't care anymore," Paraska would say angrily, waving her red, hardworking hands.

Prochor paid no attention to her words. More often than not, he turned over onto his other side and went back to sleep.

Some days, he would slip down from his warm abode, take a fishing rod, a small box of flies, and disappear for the whole day. In the evening, Prochor would return with a few skinny fish for Paraska to fry for supper.

After sunset, most villagers would emerge from their huts to gather near the fence, sit on the benches facing the unpaved road, and watch those who were slowly returning home from the fields.

Irina's big, empty house was the very last in the row of houses. Next to them was a newly build, white home with a metal roof and iron shutters.

It was the biggest and nicest house in the village. It belonged to Alexander Sergeyev. Every summer, his niece, Dunka, would arrive from Minsk to stay with them. A high, wire fence divided the properties with red raspberry bushes sprouting on both sides. In addition, Sergeyev put four beehives next to the fence. Sergeyev was a known atheist. He intentionally ignored Dadia Kolia and Irina. He wouldn't even say hello when meeting them on the street.

It would be extremely boring for Sonia to stay with Irina and Dadia Kolia if not for the colourful weddings. Dadia Kolia was invited to all of them. Each time the groom's party came to pick up Dadia Kolia, he would take Sonia along for the ride. It was so much fun to sit in a decorated pretty carriage behind trotting horses, with an accordionist beside her and jingle bells dancing around the horses' necks.

Everyone in the village would come out to greet the couple. The church would be packed, leaving a small space for Dadia Kolia to bless bride and groom. Dadia Kolia had forbidden children to come inside the church during the actual ceremony because kids laughed, made funny faces, and a lot of noise.

After the ceremony, Sonia and Dadia Kolia would walk back home, but not through the main street. Dadia Kolia rushed home past the cemetery and through the fields, glad not to have met anybody on his way. He was deeply hurt by the local so-called intelligentsia: teachers, a veterinarian, and a nurse who would not say hello to him. In the past, they at least nodded when passing by. Lately, however, they actually pretended not to see him.

The KGB was snooping around trying to persuade some people to spy on their neighbours. They got through with their friend in the next parish. It looked like he cooperated with them. Irina didn't want him to visit anymore. They tried to draft Dadia Kolia. He would beg before he would work for the KGB, spying on his congregants.

Apparently, they succeeded in enlisting the majority of clergy. It was very sad and scary too. They came often to intimidate Dadia Kolia. He wasn't afraid of them, but Irina was. They could beat him up or take him away if he didn't cooperate.

When they arrived, Dadia Kolia usually drank vodka with them, fed them, and told them jokes. Afterwards, he would have a severe headache and dizziness for weeks and weeks. It was bad for his nerves.

Sonia could invent her own truth. For her, the truth was what she wanted it to be. Every night before going to sleep, Sonia prayed to God for almost an hour thanking him for her good fortune in life, asking God to give Irina and Dadia Kolia at least one child, to make Dadia Kolia less nervous, and not to have troubles with the government. Sonia also prayed for Mama not to have pain in her legs, and to get some good news about Lucia.

Recently, Mama had had a dream about Lucia.

"I saw an icon of Virgin Mary. Lucia was standing behind the icon cleaning the dining room windows and smiling. I saw her face as clear as I see you now. Soon we will get some news." Mama's face was radiant with hope.

Soon after that dream on one sunny spring morning, Mama received a few photographs showing a royal-blue, plush sofa with fancy pillows embroidered with gold thread and two well-groomed poodles looking into the camera. Nothing was written on the back of the pictures, but they were supposed to be from Lucia's apartment.

"Where does Lucia live?" Sonia asked.

"Nobody can tell us. She cannot tell us. Thank God for the pictures."

Sonia just turned twelve when she got a letter addressed to her personally. Mama said that it was a special invitation. She groomed and washed Sonia until her normally pale cheeks turned red.

The people who had invited them must be very important if Mama dressed in her best, like when going to church.

They came into an old building near Cathedral. A tall, handsome officer took Sonia by the hand and gently walked her inside a very fancy, large room. He asked Mama to wait outside. Sonia was surprised and begged Mama to come with her. Mama reassured Sonia and told her that she better follow the officer.

Sonia sat down on the dark leather chair and examined with amazement the heavy, leather doors with metal knobs that were in four corners of the room. The dark-green drapes, mahogany-panelled walls, and dark, wooden furniture looked impressive. The officer had a soft voice and a kind smile.

"What can I offer you?" He opened a box of chocolates.

"Thank you," said Sonia, taking the largest piece.

Sonia's eyes followed his hand as he pulled out some papers from the desk's drawers. Sonia had never been so curious before.

"How do you like this photo?" He leaned across his desk and showed Sonia a picture of a woman with wide eyes and long hair with curls over her shoulders.

Yes, she did look familiar. A long time ago, this woman lived with them in the salon and chased her out each time Sonia walked in.

"Why do you show it to me?" asked Sonia impatiently.

"You have a family who wants you to join them. This beautiful woman is your biological mother who survived the war."

"What are you talking about? I don't understand."

"This is a photograph of your real mother. She lives in Israel. She asks you to go to live with her."

"I don't believe one word you are saying. I don't get it." Sonia interrupted him. "Let me go to Mama."

Sonia literally jumped from her seat.

"Don't get upset. Nobody is going to force you to go. It is up to you. I am here to help. It is completely your choice. You can go home and think about it."

"There is nothing to think about. I have only one mother, the best in the whole world."

"Do you want put it in writing?"

"Write what?"

"Write how you feel about it, write what you said to me."

"I want to go."

"Would you like to sign it, please?" The officer put some kind of letter on the table in front of her.

Sonia would sign a thousand papers saying that never, in a million, in a zillion, years would she leave her loving Mama to go to live with this unpleasant stranger who slapped her and send her away from her room. Sonia was already worried what had happened to Mama who was waiting outside. It had taken so long. Mama gets worried too. She had to tell her all of this nonsense. Mama would be so surprised!

Mama was there, sitting and waiting for Sonia. Sonia gripped her hand tightly. One of the officers opened the front door to let them out of the red-brick building. He smiled at Sonia.

"Mamochka, I thought that police never lied. Here they are such liars."

Mama walked slowly and said nothing.

"Mama, I don't know how to tell you. You may not believe me," Sonia said as they continued to walk on the street.

"My sweet girl, they did tell you the truth."

"How do you know what they told me?"

"Sonechka, sooner or later you had to find out. Raisa is your real mother. She gave you birth. She brought you to me as a baby. Now she wants you back. Sooner or later, you have to know the truth. I am not young. One day when I am not here anymore, you may want to go to be with her."

"Don't talk like that." Sonia stopped, hugged Mama, and whispered in her ear. "Whatever it is, I don't want to know. I don't want to hear about it. Never."

Mama said nothing. Her small, grey eyes blurred with tears.

8

The neighbours were ready to go to bed, but their lights were still on. Sonia was reading Gogol's *Dead Souls* while Mama was drinking her last cup of tea. The bell rang—surprisingly, for such a late hour. Two strangers in trench coats charged in, asking for Mama. They promptly pushed themselves into the bedroom. In a split moment, books, dresses, and towels were flying in all directions, landing on the parquet floors of their tiny two rooms.

Sonia had no idea what they were looking for, but one thing she was sure of was that it was all a mistake. These unpleasant men had better leave Mama alone immediately instead of ordering her around and making a mess of the entire house.

"Stop it! Stop it!" Sonia screamed. They ignored her.

The two men, the kind that walk in dark suspiciously sneaking on the streets, commanded Mama to put on her coat and follow them.

"Mama, I am going with you! Don't leave!" Sonia cried.

"It is late. Go to bed. I'll be back soon."

But when Sonia woke up, Mama was not back. She left for school perplexed. There was no one to ask any questions. On this particular day, as though they had planned it advance, all her teachers called her to the blackboard.

She stayed in her seat during recess, trying to comprehend why they had taken Mama. She felt like vomiting.

"What's wrong? Are you sick?" The girls gathered around her.

"I am all right, but my Mama got lost." Sonia burst out crying.

"What? How?"

"Last night. She went for a walk and never came back."

"Did you call the police?" The girls were sincerely alarmed.

"They could not find her."

Sonia didn't think about what would happen when the girls found out she had lied. She wanted attention. If she told them the police had come and taken Mama away, no one in the class would talk to her. They would think Mama did something wrong.

Irina was waiting for her when Sonia got home from school. She had arrived with Dadia Kolia from their parish that morning. They had spent all day running from one place to another, trying to figure out why Mama was arrested.

The next day her classmates ignored Sonia gossiping that her mother had some criminal connections abroad and was dangerous. Girls made fun of Sonia for making up the stupid story that her mother had gotten lost.

Irina and her husband hired a lawyer, Mr. Ermolaev. The lawyer was a huge man with a protruding belly. Sonia did not like him.

Mama was kept in the city jail at Lukishki until the trial. Sonia and Irina were allowed to bring Mama parcels. The waiting room was always full of people begging the guards to take their parcels of food and letters from families to the inmates.

It was an open trial. Somebody said Mama had received letters from Germany from her relatives. Another woman claimed she overheard Mama saying that she didn't trust Soviets. Mama sat very straight in her seat and tried to smile a few times at Sonia.

Sonia wished to move closer to Mama, to stand next to her, but the policeman roughly grabbed Sonia's hand, actually hurting her, and pushed her aside.

Sonia didn't understand much what anybody was saying, and she was annoyed by the dull, unconvincing voice of Mr. Ermolaev.

In the end, Mama got four years in jail. For what?

Back home, Malka was teaching her sons to play the accordion while Sonia wrote "four years" in her notebook twelve times, trying to resolve in her mind who to blame for this unjust shame which had befallen her proud, kind, harmless Mama.

The golden rays of the afternoon sun spread generously over the Persian carpet hanging next to the icon of the Three Holy Saints. Their cold, flat faces stared at Sonia in the glowing red light, saying nothing, meaning nothing. Sonia forced herself to pray in case it helped get Mama back. And if not to the Three Holy Saints, then to dear Stalin who saw every person with their big and small sorrows through the grey smoke rings of his pipe. And as long as Stalin watched over all, as long as Stalin lived, every citizen could sleep peacefully. Sonia had to find a way to let him know about Mama.

Sonia was in grade seven. When Mama comes back, she would be graduating from high school. It seemed like such a long time. An eternity.

Irina and Dadia Kolia lived a few hours away by train. On their previous visits, they had never stayed overnight. Now they did, using Mama and Sonia's bed, forcing Sonia to sleep on a sofa next to the piano in an adjacent small room.

"Maybe we should place her into a foster home for the time being," Sonia heard Dadia Kolia whisper.

"I heard you last night. I'll tell Mama what you are planning to do with me," Sonia announced before they left to go back to their new parish.

"It is all in your imagination." Irina was visibly shaken. "Please don't upset Mama. She has enough worries."

They left for the country, supplying Sonia with cans of food and leaving her with a small electric plate to warm up the food or to fry potatoes. In addition, Irina also had made arrangements with a waitress at the corner restaurant to prepare meals for Sonia after school.

Visits were allowed once a week and it was allowed to bring Mama a parcel. Lukishki, the prison where Mama was held, was located across the river. The river peacefully carried its warm-for-the winter but pitch-black waters. Covered with unstable ice patches, it indifferently observed the world with its dark, half-closed eyes.

The right bank of the river where they lived was dotted with cozy houses, promising gardens in the spring, and a little church where children gathered on long summer nights to tell frightening stories. Most of the time after hearing one of these horror tales, Sonia had a difficult time falling asleep in the room alone. She kept imaging someone's bloody hands stretching out from under the bed. Mama warned her many times not to listen to those scary stories. But this what was happening in spring and summer. Now they were in the middle of winter.

The prison side of the river was sparsely settled. The soft earth was barely covered with snow, promising an early spring. Last year at this time Sonia, walked home from school while jumping with joy, soaking up the warm sunshine, and picking the first snowdrops for her mother. Spring and Easter were her favourite times of the year when she coloured eggs with Mama, painting them like a rainbow.

Sonia began to run, counting the minutes and hugging her heavy parcel. Once she reached the prison's gate, the guards made her wait and wait.

Her name was called at last. Sonia walked into the long, narrow room. She saw Mama walking slowly, straight toward the double-netted, metal wall. The guard was dragging his squeaky, heavy boots back and forth between the double bars.

"Please let me talk to my mother," Sonia said to him. "I cannot talk if you shuffle between us all the time."

He stopped for a few moments at the other end of the corridor that divided prisoners and visitors.

"What is new in school?" Mama asked. "How are you doing? Is Irina good to you?"

Sonia wanted to touch Mama. She stood there with both her hands stretched through the bars.

"Turn around, please," Mama whispered. "Take off your hat."

Sonia couldn't take care of her long hair that Mama always braided for her. She had cut off her braids.

"Mamochka, don't get upset. By the time you come home, my braids will have grown back. Looking into Mama's wet eyes, she started to sob. Sonia didn't care about her braids; she cried because her proud Mama had to stand behind bars, because her loving Mama couldn't kiss or even touch her. Mama tried to say something, but her thin lips trembled and tears melted on her cheeks.

"Mama? Mamochka, it is okay."

"Citizen, your time is over." The guard appeared between them.

"Please, one more minute!" Sonia begged.

As Mama followed the man, Sonia noticed her usually straight figure looked a bit bent. Mama moved backwards waving to her. The huge, double-metal door silently locked behind her.

Two weeks later, Mama was transferred to another jail. Sonia was not given the address. She could only correspond through Irina. It was not fair.

There was not much new in school or at home. Fedia and Malka tried to take away one room from Sonia. No wonder. Their two boys were growing up. It was too crowded in one room for four of them.

One day, Fedia arrived home drunk and threatened Sonia that he would throw all her belongings into the street. But he did nothing.

Sonia and Mama always had two small rooms for themselves and now Sonia lived there alone. The Housing Committee decided that four years was much too long a time for Sonia to occupy so many square meters by herself. So they sent Luba to live with her.

Luba was a tall, extremely skinny woman who looked like a toothpick. You could almost see through her. Luba worked as a dressmaker and knew lots of jokes. She had a husband who served in the army far away in Siberia and a little boy who lived in the country with her mother.

Lying in her high bed and talking to Mama's portrait overhead, Sonia daydreamed of going to Moscow to meet Stalin. She knew that Stalin was not God Almighty, but she also knew that the justice of the entire world was in his hands. If she could only see him once, Stalin would understand. She planned her trip silently.

Sonia truly believed that every day while she was still asleep, Stalin went to his balcony to smoke his pipe. At that early hour, he would think about all the children in the country and all the problems to be solved that day. He was the only one who could understand it all and would be able to make the right decisions. Sonia decided that she would go to Moscow the coming summer. She would leave the day after school was over.

When no one expected it, tragedy struck. The whole country was shattered. People listened hungrily to every word on the radio, refusing to believe that the most precious heart in the whole universe might stop beating. It happened on the fifth of March. With that announcement, Sonia's last hope for justice died. What would happen to the world?

For the first two periods of school, the students all gathered in the gym. The principal, Elena Nikolaevna, tried to give a speech. Normally, one look at her meticulously dressed figure and strong carved features was enough to put anyone in their place. Elena Nikolaevna started the speech in her familiar authoritarian voice, but something got stuck in her throat and, before finishing the first sentence, she burst into tears.

The head counsellor of the school, Galina Ivanovna, swallowing her own tears, took over, and tried to express in simple words the need to have courage while facing this unbearable loss that hurt so deeply. Her words touched every heart, and students responded with uncontrollable sobs. Even the history teacher, an old, strong man, was unable to hold back his tears of grief.

Sonia hated herself for not being able to cry with the others at this most appropriate moment. Ashamed and utterly confused, she went to the washroom to wet her face and to rub her eyes a bit so that her classmates would think that she, too, had cried as she was supposed to.

Irina and Dadia Kolia arrived in the afternoon.

"So, what will happen now that your dear Father is dead?" Irina asked, sarcastically.

Sonia went to bed early, now unable to plan her trip to Moscow to complain to Stalin about the injustice done to Mama. She felt angry and hopeless.

After Irina and Dadia Kolia left for their parish, Sonia got a fever. She had to stay in bed. Luba brought her food from the restaurant, but Sonia had no appetite. She remembered reading about healthy Siberian porridge made from crushed bread, boiled water, and some sugar. She tried it and liked it a lot.

Sick in bed, Sonia felt sorry for herself. She missed her Mama and actually started to like Irina who left her a hundred rubles for her food. There was quite a supply of canned food on the windowsill, and having already spent seven rubles on medicine, Sonia decided to skip the restaurant and live on canned food and Siberian porridge. Irina would be so proud of her! She would be surprised that Sonia had saved ninety-three rubles.

When Irina arrived two weeks later and discovered that Sonia had only eaten porridge of bread with water and had lost six kilos, she was furious.

"Dear God, what did I do to deserve such a punishment? This girl can get sick and die. Mama would never forgive me!" cried Irina, facing the icon of the Three Holy Saints.

Deep in her heart, Sonia felt guilty. She wanted to hug Irina and ask for forgiveness for disappointing her. Irina was truly mad at Sonia. Maybe after all Irina liked her a bit.

High, high up, tiny stars twinkled and angels danced. Maybe at this very moment Mama was awake looking at the same stars and thinking of her. What if Mama's room had no windows? How many people were there in the room? Was Mama alone? In the darkness, the cold, silly moon had no answers.

Luba, her cheerful roommate was a kind and caring person. She happily cleaned Sonia's room and did her laundry. Together, they fried eggs and drank tea in the afternoon. Sonia slowly got used to her new lifestyle.

One late afternoon, Sonia was alone waiting for Luba who usually came home right after work.

Tzinh-tzinh-tzinh. Ring, ring, ring. Luba had forgotten her key again. Sonia got up to open the door. It was... Mama! Mama!

"Mama?" Sonia screamed, holding her as closely as she could. "I knew you would be back soon! I knew it!"

Sonia looked into her eyes and kissed Mama's face and hands.

"Mamochka, you are here! How was it, how was it?"

Mama sat in her favourite armchair, still holding Sonia's hands.

"What would you like to know? I made friends with two professors. Thanks to the Soviets, I know that you can find a lot of good, educated people in jail. You have a big choice now: doctors, lawyers, engineers, painters. People from every walk of life."

It was her old Mama with her confident smile. For the next hundred years Sonia could sit on the carpeted floor next to her Mama, hugging her knees and hiding her face in the folds of Mama's light grey coat, the same one she had put on when she left the house.

Mama took off her scarf. Her once-grey hair had a lot of white.

"I don't remember you having so much white hair."

"My silly girl, don't worry so much. Better, tell me how you managed all by yourself?"

"Mamochka, I don't want to talk about me. It is boring. I want to know everything about you."

"After Stalin died, they granted us amnesty." Mama said. "Just like that, thank God!"

Her big, warm Mama was talking and patting Sonia's hair. A beautiful new world was gently, but surely, taking the place of the old.

9

In the evenings, boys and girls from her school took a promenade on the main street from the Cathedral all the way to the Russian church on the top of the hill. They would walk in two rows in both directions. Mostly, the boys would be on the left side and the girls on the right. They were excited with anticipation. Most of them knew exactly who they were looking for, hoping to catch a smile or to exchange a few words. They were a pleasantly noisy group of young people who knew each other, if not by the name, then by seeing each other in school.

Sonia did not enjoy these walks, but her friends pushed her to join them. Rosa and Larisa would often ask Sonia if they should agree to go to the movies if asked by a boy, or even better, to go skating. But there was nobody Sonia would admit that she liked enough to try to meet on these evening promenades. Walking calmly on the main street with boys and girls steaming with unpronounced passions, silent confessions, and dreams, made Sonia visualize fairy tales with monsters falling in love with young beauties.

"Sonechka, you seem lost. I understand you. Look, nobody will fall in love with you at first sight, but once someone takes the time to know you, they will love you back,"- Rosa said kindly many times. Comments like these spoiled Sonia's mood. She would go home sad and disappointed.

"I told you many times, don't go with them," said Mama. "They are older; they are interested in boys. You are still a kid. Too young."

It was the end of March, Sonia's favourite month. Fresh grass stretched through melted patches of white snow glittering under the warm, spring sun.

Sonia walked home from school, jumping from left foot to right foot, anticipating something wonderful happening at any minute. She spotted the first fragile lilies of the valley, inhaled the aroma of spring, and was eager to bring a few of them home. Their velvety slim violet petals stretched gracefully from under the soft glistering patches of snow. Sonia leaned to smell the yellow dot in the centre of delicate flowers. The earth was moist inviting to touch promising warm spring.

When Mama opened the door, Sonia jumped with joy, embraced Mama's neck, and kissed her cheeks.

"Mama, look, look, look! Aren't they amazingly beautiful? Smell them!"

As usual, Mama said very little, just smiled her hardly noticeable Mona Lisa smile, which was Sonia's biggest reward.

Sonia felt that the whole universe was around her. She was at its centre. Sonia could not envisage the world functioning without her. Deep in her heart, she knew she was special; she was destined to do some extremely important mission in life. There were some fleeting moments, but they managed to colour the rest of her life; to keep the reality of every day at a safe distance as if there were two of her. Or even more.

"You are my precious gift from God," Mama often said.

Mama never said that she loved Sonia. She never said the actual words, but she didn't have to. As far as Sonia felt, there was nothing in Mama's life more important than she was. Mama's life revolved around taking care of her. Sonia was a child of high maintenance. Only she didn't know it for a long time.

It was amazing how little Sonia knew about her Mama's personal history. Mama was always next to her, walking streets of their medieval town while holding Sonia's little finger. Sonia clearly expected Mama to do whatever Sonia felt like.

Sonia never had a key to the house. Instead, Mama would wait for her to get home and let her in. As a teenager, Sonia had to be home before ten o'clock. because it was Mama's time to go to bed.

Neighbours often commented that Mama spoiled her rotten, but Mama just smiled gently and dismissed their comments by saying, "This is how I brought up my girls, Lucia and Irina. I am too old to do it differently now."

Mama spoiled Sonia with love, and Sonia loved every minute of it.

There wasn't a shower in the apartment, but they had an old, porcelain bathtub. Bathing was a big job. Mama would scrub the tub, boil the water, pour it in, and soak Sonia for a long time while washing her arms, legs, and her entire body. Sonia would just lie there giggling, enjoying feeling pampered by Mama massaging her body.

Their dark, neglected kitchen was dreary, drab, and unappealing. Sonia never ventured inside.

"There will be plenty of time for you to be in the kitchen once you get married," Mama would say. "For now, just read books. Don't worry about the housework or cooking. You will take in somebody to clean. I want you to have a good life, to do what you like to do. You will get your pay and you can give it to a peasant girl to take care of the house."

That idea sounded very good to Sonia. There was no need to learn to cook and to clean, although this wasn't exactly the way her school wanted the girls to think.

Everything was okay with Mama. She never worried about what neighbours said or thought. And they talked and gossiped between themselves.

Mama had a lot of wonderful, old pieces of jewelry that her husband had bought for her.

"Gold and diamonds outlive us, my darling. I never want you to worry about money after I am gone. I want you to always be my princess," he would say to her. "Before I met you, my life was like a night, and with you, my life is like a day full of sunshine."

Irina was nine when he died in Mama's hands. Mama was only forty-one. Irina never thought much of Sonia, not like Dadia Kolia who tried hard to figure her out. Sonia was quick, smart, and a very good student, but she was very bony and not very pretty as a kid. It was a big struggle for Mama to fatten her up, to put some meat on her bones.

Mama let her sleep in until the very last minute. Mama made her braids as Sonia ate her breakfast. Sonia was always in a hurry and had to run to school. Mama stayed home to clean the house, to shop, and to cook. Sonia's meal was ready and on the table no matter when she showed up.

Sonia never rushed to get home. She had fun chatting in their doorway with her girlfriends. As usual, the moment she walked in, hot food would be waiting on the dining room table.

"Elena Stepanovna, you are spoiling her rotten," Malka would lament while passing through dining room at the exact time that Mama served dinner.

"I am too old to change. This is the way I brought up my daughters," Mama would say, again and again.

"Those were different times. Sonia will not be able to take care of herself."

"Sonechka will have plenty of time in the kitchen when she gets married. Let me spoil her now."

"Sonia will have a hard time finding a husband. She is no beauty and will not be able to keep the house. You will have problems with her. I warn you."

This stupid Malka didn't know how to stop, thought Sonia.

Sonia knew her Mama was right. Mama did everything right. She couldn't care less what other people said. Nobody could change her mind. Sonia felt so proud of her Mama. Her Mama was more than a Mama to her. She was her mother, her father, her grandmother, and her aunts. Mama was Sonia's whole family because there was nobody else on the entire planet for her. Definitely not Irina. Sonia liked Irina very much, and she wished to love her, but Irina didn't want to love her back. She wasn't Sonia's sister. Sonia was simply her mother's daughter.

"Blood is not water," Irina had said too many times.

Life was so uncomplicated. Sonia had no worries, and she dreamed about what surprises tomorrow would bring. Maybe she would meet the right handsome man worthy of Mama.

Mama did not teach her to brush her teeth every morning, nor did she teach her to cook or to use cutlery in any particular way. Mama did not have any rules for Sonia. She did not say much either. Mama mostly listened, occasionally smiling at Sonia's rambling. Sonia wanted Mama to know everything. Mama was her entire world.

The only reason Sonia looked for a husband for her mother was so Mama would have someone to love her; someone who was not a child. For herself, Sonia did not need a father. She had Mama.

Mama normally send Sonia to the office to pay bills for their apartment to the House Committee. The last person in line with Sonia waiting to pay bills for his flat seemed almost perfect for Mama. Sonia liked him a lot. He was handsome, friendly and asked a lot of questions. He even admired that a girl was alone in line paying the rent. He asked Sonia about her father. Sonia told him that her father had passed away a long time ago and that her mother was a widow.

"How long ago?" he asked.

"A long time…maybe fifteen or even more years ago," Sonia said.

Then he laughed and laughed. A pretty dumb man. Not for her Mama.

Lately Sara, Larisa, and Sonia became best friends while walking home from their school every day.

They had difficulty parting. There was so much to talk about, to share. Sara and Larisa lived in the same building on two different floors, a few blocks away. Sonia's place was halfway home for the two girls. They would stop under the marble staircase at the entrance to Sonia's house, chatting sometimes for a whole hour until Mama finally called Sonia in to have dinner. The girls were never hungry. There was so much to discuss.

All three talked fast, interrupting each other about the books they had read, the movies they had seen, and about what was happening in the world at large.

"Sonia, I sometimes forget that you are not Jewish. It feels like you are one of us," Sara said once.

"We forget to be careful with you," Larisa remarked.

"What do you mean, careful? We are like sisters!" Sonia protested.

"Not really. We are Jewish. You are not. Nobody likes Jews. We really cannot be like sisters."

"I don't understand the difference."

"You don't understand the difference because you don't understand what it means to be a Jew, or what it means that your brother wants to marry a Russian girl so that his children will have an easier life…maybe get accepted to university." Larisa tried to explain.

"Let us not talk about it, not with Sonia. I always feel that being Jewish is some kind of a crime. It is written in your passport forever, like a stain." Sara sounded pretty sad.

"Watch her, Mama. A wolf always looks to the forest. Sonka will leave you before you know it," Dadia Kolia had been telling Mama on their visits from the country.

"I don't know what you are talking about," Sonia said, trying to interrupt him.

"Isn't it obvious? Look at your friends. You are gravitating to Jews. Blood is not water. You smell your own."

"Kolia, leave her alone. Sonechka doesn't get what you are talking about. You are confusing her," Mama would say calmly.

"Mama, you must be blind. Don't you see how she has changed her friends? Before it was Svetlana, Luba, and Zenia. Now she hangs out with Sara and Larisa. Only Jewish girls."

It was painful to admit that her dear, kind, wonderful Mama didn't want other people to find out that Sonia was born to Jewish parents, not because Mama would love Sonia less, but because people would look down on Sonia as an inferior human being. Mama wanted to spare her that pain. Sonia felt like telling everyone that she was born Jewish and that she was still the same person. Sonia wanted to tell, but she didn't. Was she ashamed of it? What was it that kept her silent? Was she protecting her Mama so that Mama would not endure gossipy comments about saving Jewish babies? No, it wasn't Mama. It was her future; it was herself she was protecting if she planned on living in Vilnius for the rest of her life.

But the seed of personal pride was planted. Sonia had one life. She wished it to be meaningful. If Sonia had plans to improve this world, she had to find a way to live the truth. Being Jewish is pretty complicated. Once you are born Jewish, there is no choice. The world will not let you not to be Jewish.

Most people have their sense of identity in their blood. It comes with the mother's milk, with holding and touching a baby who is an extension of the family. It goes into your every cell. There should never be questions about it.

Sonia didn't have it so simple. The people she was around the very first few months of her life had disappeared from this planet. She would never meet them. She had no idea what they looked like, what they thought about, what they wanted from her, for her. She was simply uprooted. Sonia had neither feelings for nor knowledge about her family's past. Basically, she had no past to feel about.

So, what does it mean to be Jewish if the only truth about it is that you were born into a Jewish family that you have no ties to and no feelings about? Is it possible to forget about your heritage, to ignore it? To start like a new tree with a new beginning? Could she figure out who she would like to be and pretend to be that person? Could she imagine some interesting past, some captivating ancestors for herself, and pretend it to be the truth?

Could she create her own ancestry in her fantasy? Was it possible? If she shared it with others, did that make her a liar?

Sonia had recently read a book about a Jewish man who escaped the miserable shtetl life in Poland and ended up in Berlin. He got married, started a business, and became quite successful. He educated his children in the best schools and settled into a very comfortable new life.

But when the Nazis came into power, his life slowly became more and more confusing and miserable. He feared for his livelihood; feared for his children's future. Frustrated, he went to his Rabbi to ask what was happening in his life.

"My dear friend," the Rabbi started. "You wanted to be a Jew inside your house and a German on the street. But what happened is that you ended being German inside your house and still a Jew on the street."

Mama was actually a saint. To take in a Jewish baby and risk her own life, and then to take Nurka and try to help her? Sonia wondered if she could ever give herself so many problems for strangers. Most definitely not. One didn't take a baby for a few hours. It was a commitment for a long time.

"Mamochka, did you expect to give me back?" Sonia asked her one evening.

Elena Stepanovna touched her soft face, gently kissed Sonia's forehead, and kept quiet for a few seconds.

"I expected nothing. But if your mother survived, yes, I thought she will take you back."

"But I don't want to go back to her. She left me once."

"Sonechka, your mother didn't leave you. She brought you to me to save you from the Germans. It was a question of life or death. She saved your life."

"I have no feelings for her. You are my mother, and I love you more than anybody on the entire planet!"

Sonia didn't particularly like the Jews she knew. Sonia didn't like the way they looked. She didn't like the way they spoke Russian with a funny accent. She did not want to be part of them. But even more than that, Sonia didn't want to live a lie. Sonia wanted the truth in her life.

Sonia had her mother, the best in the world. But what about her father? How did not knowing her father affect her life until now?

Mama asked Jadviga to make a new dress for Sonia's High school graduation. It was a fairly modest dress, chocolate in colour. She draped a yellow shawl with a velvety yellow rose attached to it around her bony shoulders. Ruffles of brown satin hid her flat chest. Sonia was actually shy to wear it assuming yellow rose was too showy, too fancy.

Sonia stopped on the stairs, embarrassed to walk into the large, bright ballroom in her new dress. Would everyone look at her? Was she overdressed?

Boys and girls gathered on opposite sides of the rectangular hall and looked at each other. Musicians started playing the tango. Boys moved rapidly toward the girls they had been choosing with their eyes for last half an hour. Within seconds, the walls were empty, with most of the young people swaying clumsily on the shiny parquet. Sonia stood frozen behind a wide, ornate, wooden pole. Nobody invited her to dance.

Sonia graduated with a gold medal. She didn't have to pass the entrance exams to university. She wanted to study Russian Literature or maybe Law, but she also thought that these two subjects would be pointless if she decided to leave the Soviet Union. There was no way Sonia wished to be a teacher. Studying something scientific that was not dependent on language, like engineering, made more sense. There were no engineering schools in Vilnius, however, so she planned to go to Kaunas.

It was summer and she had plenty of free time. For years, Sonia had belonged to a drama group with a wonderful instructor named Alexander Ivanovich from Leningrad. Every summer they put on a play by Chekhov. This year was special. For the first time, there would be an International World Festival of Youth in Moscow. Alexander Ivanovich said to their drama group, "I am planning to go. Would anyone wish to join me?"

"How many people will be there?" asked Sonia.

"They expect forty thousand from more than o countries."

Wow! It sounded very tempting to go to the festival. For the first time, foreigners could come to the Soviet Union thanks to Nikita Khrushchev's new Party policy. Besides, in Moscow, Sonia could go to the Israeli Consulate and ask them questions about life in Israel. It sounded like terrific idea, but she still didn't want anyone to know about her interest in Israel.

In the end, nobody else from her drama group was interested in going to Moscow. It was too far and too much trouble. But Sonia told Mama that Alexander Ivanovich was taking them as a group for a field trip to the Moscow Youth Festival.

"Where are you going to stay?" Mama wanted to know.

Sonia got an address from Larisa who had an aunt living in Moscow.

"Tell her you are my best friend. Sara Petrovna will receive you as she would receive me. She is a Professor of Russian History at Moscow University."

Sonia bought a train ticket to Moscow. The train arrived late at night. By the time Sonia reached the apartment building with Sara Petrovna's address, it was almost midnight. She knocked on the door and rang the bell in vain.

A bright light woke Sonia up.

"Where am I?"

Nothing looked familiar.

"Young lady, I came home last night from the Opera to find you sleeping by my door," said an older woman sitting by the window. "What is your name?"

"Sonia. My name is Sonia. Larisa is my best friend. She suggested that I stay with you. I came for the International Youth festival."

"Good idea. I am pleased to have you stay with me. This International Youth Festival is an amazing event. The streets are full of young people. Thirty-four thousand from 131 countries dancing and holding hands with each other. Everywhere there is music."

"Where?"

"Actually, everywhere. Look what I have here. A complete, detailed program for all events. I am afraid by now it will be hard to get tickets for most of them."

"Sara Petrovna, it doesn't matter. The festival is not the main reason I came to Moscow."

"Really, what else?"

"I would like to visit the Israeli Consulate, to see the Ambassador."

Sara Petrovna literally jumped from her chair. She quickly pulled down the window drapes.

"Sha, sha, wait a minute. This is a very different story." She turned her now-pale face to Sonia.

"I would appreciate if you could help me find their address."

"Dear girl, I have no idea where the Israeli Consulate is in Moscow. It will not be listed in telephone directory. But we will try to find it. I will go with you."

After a nice, warm breakfast that Sara Petrovna prepared herself, she and Sonia went outside to try to identify Jewish persons on the street in order to find out the location of the Israeli Consulate. Most of the people they asked had no idea. Someone suggested walking toward the Ministry of Foreign Affairs. The Israeli Consulate was supposed to be near that building.

Sara Petrovna only asked those people who definitely looked Jewish. She was always dead on.

"The address is Vesnina 16," an old man with a white beard and bushy eyebrows finally told them.

Sara Petrovna and Sonia stopped at the corner and looked straight at the fancy-looking building with a guard in a sparkling uniform and white gloves.

"Okay. Go. I will stay on this corner waiting patiently for you," said Sara Petrovna.

"I will inquire what the visiting hours are so I can come back another time by myself. It will only take a minute." Sonia didn't wish to keep Sara Petrovna waiting.

The guard looked pleasantly at Sonia while she approached him from across the street.

"Can I help you?" He politely bent toward her.

"Thank you. I just want to know what the office hours are at the Consulate."

"Let's check." The guard took Sonia's hand and moved away from the door.

"I can come tomorrow. Don't hold me." Sonia tried to free her hand. He tightened his grip, not letting her go. He literally pushed her around the block into a building attached in the back that was almost invisible from the street.

On the second floor, there was another uniformed guard by the door of the large hall. He placed Sonia on the bench by the window. There were four more strangers in the room: a young gentleman in a tweed suit wearing large glasses with brown plastic frames, a painter in his working clothes, an older, well-dressed man in a dark-green suit, and a middle-aged lady with a flowery scarf around her neck. Sonia tried to leave the room after a few minutes, but the guard by the door stopped her, silently motioning to sit down.

She sat next to the man in the tweed jacket, certain he was an English tourist by the way he looked and dressed.

"Why are you here?" Sonia asked him.

"That is what I would like to know as well. This is your free democratic country. You walk on the street and suddenly someone grabs you, forces you into a car, and brings you here," he said in Russian.

"Don't worry, if you are innocent, they will let you go free in no time. Everything will be okay."

"What are you talking about? Nothing will be okay. They will not let me go." The foreigner seemed to be a bit frightened.

"Trust me, don't worry, you will go home soon," Sonia insisted, trying to calm him down.

"Call this number tomorrow. You will see I am right." The tall, skinny Englishmen took the festival program from Sonia's hand and scribbled his telephone number for her.

But before he could finish writing it, the guard jumped in front of Sonia and snatched the festival program.

"Please give me my program back. I need it," Sonia asked.

He silently walked back to his position near the door.

It was getting late. How long was Sonia supposed to sit here, and why? What would Sara Petrovna think? How long could she wait? Sara Petrovna probably left a long time ago.

Someone came in after a few hours and asked Sonia to follow him.

The room she was taken to reminded her of the one in Vilnius where the officer informed her about Raisa living in Israel more than five years ago. There were the same heavy, leather doors on four sides of the room.

Once Sonia was told that all police stations had heavy, leather doors in case they torture you nobody could hear the screams.

A few strange round faces stared at her from an enormous circular table.

"Your passport?"

"I don't have one yet."

"Your address?"

"I am not telling you."

"What is your name? Where are you staying?"

Sonia said nothing. As little as she understood, one thing was clear: it would not be good for Mama or for Sara Petrovna that she was interested in visiting the Israeli Consulate. It was not clear why, but it may harm them. She would not let anybody harm them because of her.

"Where are you staying in Moscow?"

"I am not going to answer your questions."

"Young lady, I am asking to protect you. Come with me to the window."

Sonia walked over to look down through the window. The officer pointed at a very busy intersection.

"There is a lot of traffic in our big city. Imagine if you had an accident. You have no documents on you. How will your family find out what happened?"

"If I have an accident, I would prefer that my family doesn't find out what has happened to me."

"You seem to be very stubborn, young lady; very naïve. Why did you want to see the Israeli Consul?"

"I have my personal reasons." Sonia tried to answer in a calm, flat voice.

"Don't be afraid. You can discuss with us everything you wished to discuss with a consul."

"You are just a policeman. I wanted to see the Ambassador."

"We are here to help the Ambassador. The Israeli Ambassador is a busy man. He cannot see everyone who wants to see him. We can answer your questions."

Sonia was asked who she lived with in Vilna, her exact address, and what family she had in Israel. Sonia was determined not to divulge any information except for the city she came from. They asked the same questions one, two, three…ten times. Suddenly she couldn't stand their repeating of questions any longer. Large, uninvited tears choked Sonia. She burst into loud, uncontrollable sobbing.

"So young and so anxious!" One of the officers got up from his chair and walked over toward her, offering a white, starched handkerchief.

"I am not anxious. You make me anxious!" Sonia screamed. "I didn't come to you. You fooled me, dragging me by force to this place." Still sobbing, Sonia hardly noticed when the others left the room. Before long she was alone with one man.

"I want to help you, young lady. Would you like me to call an expert from Ministry of Foreign Affairs?" he asked in a pleasant voice.

Sonia nodded. The officer disappeared for a short while, then came back with a much younger person.

"This man is the Deputy Minister of Foreign Affairs. You can tell him everything about yourself and ask any questions."

"Don't try to fool me. Do you think I am so stupid as to believe that this person you just brought in is really the Deputy of Foreign Ministry?" Tears of frustration overwhelmed Sonia. "I already have spent all day here. When will you let me go?"

"Have a little patience. I would like to talk to you some more."

"It is very annoying. There is nothing more to talk about. I am not going to tell you anything about myself."

Sonia clearly realized that even if she stood on her head and spit nickels, they would not let her go inside the Consulate. The simple discovery of her helplessness brought new tears. Sara Petrovna need not worry. Sonia would never divulge her name, even if these people put her in jail.

"You arrived to Moscow at most exciting period. There is so much happening every day, every night. What would you like to attend?"

Sonia understood how difficult it was to get tickets at this late date. She would love to see the Druzba Ensemble from Leningrad, listen to three singers performing "Moscow Nights," and many more.

After two more hours of waiting, Sonia got tickets for the performances she had her heart set on for three nights in a row for two people.

Sonia was finally allowed to leave the ugly building in a blue limousine accompanied by two uniformed policemen. She had the precious tickets in her pocket. When the gate opened wide for their large car, Sonia felt the warm breeze of freedom.

"Please leave me at the metro. I know my way," she said to the driver.

Sonia rode on the underground metro for a very long time, getting on and off at different stations until she was totally convinced nobody was following her.

Early in the morning, she dared taking the train to Mayakovsky Square.

Pale, frightened Sara Petrovna opened her door.

"Are you alone? Thank God, they let you out. It is all my fault. I should have known better than to let you go to the Israeli Consulate."

"Sara Petrovna, I couldn't imagine you would be so upset."

"When I saw the guard taking you to the back of the building, I ran home as fast as I could. The first thing I did was burn all the photographs and letters I happened to have from Israel over the years."

"But why, why?"

"Why? I was certain that police would arrive at my apartment any minute."

"I would never in a million years tell them a word about you or where you live."

"You wouldn't have to; they would know how to find out."

"They couldn't. I took many trains in different directions for hours. They also gave me wonderful tickets for performances, sure that I would attend. I'll throw them out. I will not go."

"All right, let us forget about it all. I am glad you are back."

"Sara Petrovna, please forgive me. I am so sorry for the commotion I caused you. Do you want me to leave your apartment and go somewhere else?"

"Don't be silly. You have to forgive me. It is my fault. I took you there. I should have known better."

Exhausted, Sonia slept like a baby. Sara Petrovna lay awake quivering with the slightest rustle of the doors.

10

With a gold medal, Sonia was exempt from taking entrance exams to university. Sara and Larisa were busy applying to different universities outside of Vilnius.

She had plenty of free time before classes started in September. One day Sonia decided to see a movie by herself for the first time in her life. But the movie theatre happened to be full; there were no tickets left. Disappointed, Sonia walked down the stairs wondering what to do. A latecomer in a straw hat passed by her.

"No tickets?" he asked. Sonia silently moved away. She didn't like talking to strangers. She stopped to look at an advertisement with nice pictures. The young man with the straw hat appeared beside her.

"Pity all tickets are sold out," he complained.

He was very tall and slim with olive skin; he was really handsome. Sonia said nothing and walked away. The man with a straw hat followed.

"If you wish to talk to me, let's sit on the bench. I am not comfortable with you following me. As a rule, I don't talk to people I don't know."

They sat down on the bench across from the theatre. There was a twinkle in his eyes.

"Do you often start talking to strangers on the street?" Sonia asked.

"This is my first time."

"So why did you start with me?"

Could it be that he found her very attractive? If yes, Sonia was surprised. Sonia talked a lot about what was on her mind at the moment, her future and about the purpose and meaning of life. The young man, whose name was Vytas, listen and smiled, smiled and listened. They talked for quite a while.

It was getting dark. Sonia gave Vytas permission to walk her home so they could continue their conversation.

"What are your plans for tomorrow?" Vytas asked as they were crossing the bridge close to her home.

"Tomorrow I am leaving for Poland," Sonia lied, suddenly.

After a few minutes she remembered that tomorrow she had to return her book to the library, and she had to buy a present for Irina's coming birthday.

The next day, in the afternoon, Sonia met Vytas on her way home from the library. Again, they walked to her house together, then she quickly said good-bye and ran upstairs.

The following morning, Vytas was waiting for her outside their apartment building near the entrance.

"Some gentleman in a straw hat is standing below my balcony. Is he waiting for me? Seems you have an admirer out there, on the street waiting for you." Teased Malka.

Embarrassed, Sonia ran quickly downstairs to meet Vytas. They went to the river where they walked and talked for hours.

The next morning Sonia wished Vytas to be under the balcony in front of her house. Sure enough, he arrived at the same time and patiently waited for her. Every day that week Sonia woke up excited to see Vytas, to go for a walk with him and to talk.

That particular Friday she planned to pick out the photos she had taken at a professional studio after her graduation. Vytas came along with her. Sonia stared at the photos. She wished to look more beautiful; not to have such a bony neck, large eyes, and a serious, long face.

"These photos are terrible. I don't look like that. I don't want them."

Sonia was not as angry as she sounded. She wanted Vytas to like her pictures, he said nothing.

"Too bad you don't like them. Much better than in life," quipped the photographer.

Upset with his answer, Sonia stormed out. Vytas walked quietly behind her. Maybe he objected to the way she behaved? If he really liked her, it should not matter.

"I am sorry, but I have to go," Vytas said, breaking the silence. Sonia wished to say she was sorry too.

"Go, nobody is keeping you," she said instead, shrugging her shoulders.

Vytas did not show up the next morning. Nor the day after, or the day after that. Sonia tried hard to talk herself into forgetting him.

"Stop thinking about him. He is not worth it," Mama said when Sonia could not fall asleep late at night.

Sonia had no idea where Vytas lived. All she knew was that his place was at the other end of the city. She knew his brother was a surgeon. Vytas shared a flat with his mother and his married brother and their two children. His father lived with another woman. Maybe this was the main reason Vytas was sad most of the time. In her head, Sonia plotted how to find him, how to meet him again, and how to capture his heart.

One night Sonia dreamed she was a bride covered with spring flowers. Next to her sat her groom in a black tuxedo. Sonia held his hand, knowing he was hers. She could not see his face, but she knew he was extremely handsome. Suddenly a stream of blood spurted between them. The groom bent over and Sonia saw it was Vytas. Sonia jumped for joy, letting his hand go. But Vytas was not a groom anymore; he was just another guest at her wedding. She saw the groom at the other end of a very long table drinking with his friends. Sonia could not care less. She looked at Vytas. He smiled at her. She woke up with a smile, hiding her face in her downy-soft pillow.

Sonia knew that Vytas worked in a Kino studio. She found the address and invited Larisa to come along for a bus ride.

On a rainy, summer day, the half-empty, old bus lazily left Vilnius behind as it headed toward a large, lonely building in the middle of green fields. By the time they reached studio, there were only two boys left on the bus with them. It was the last stop.

"Do you work in the studio?" Sonia asked one of the young boys.

"Yes, we both do." He was friendly, and obviously Russian.

"We are looking for someone who is studying in Leningrad. He works here only during the summer."

"Maybe Vytas?"

"Yes, yes. It is Vytas."

"Vytas Valinskas. Who does not know him? Very likeable chap."

Vytas Valinskas. Now Sonia knew his family name. One day it would be hers.

It was raining cats and dogs. They ran to hide inside the building.

"Look, there is your friend," the Russian boy said, pointing to Vytas who was leaving the building.

He did not seem surprised to see Sonia. Did Vytas understand that she had come all this way just to find him? She looked at her feet, not daring to meet his smiling, hazel eyes. They took a bus back to the city, and Vytas walked her home. He promised to come the next day at six o'clock in the evening to visit her.

At five minutes after six o'clock, Sonia felt anxious and began biting her fingernails. She went in and out of the house several times. Vytas arrived at eight o'clock with the excuse that he had helped some old lady with her shopping bags all around the city.

His favourite place to sit was on the La-Z-Boy near the radio. Vytas would turn on classical music while Sonia crawled cosily into another armchair, admiring how handsome, kind, and wonderful he was.

He came by a lot, almost every day. They did not talk much. Vytas mostly listened to the music. In the meantime, Mama stayed in the dining room reading most nights. Sonia wondered why Mama stayed there until Vytas left instead of going to bed. It took Sonia a while to figure out that Mama did not wish to pass through the tiny room where Vytas and Sonia were sitting. But why not? What did she think they were doing?

Vytas took a leave of absence from Leningrad's Institute of Cinematography. The climate in Vilnius was much better for his health than Leningrad's. Still, he often suffered from migraines. On particularly rainy days, the unbearable pain in his bones was killing him.

When the antique grandfather clock struck ten o'clock, Vytas would get up to leave.

"Stay a few more minutes." Sonia would whisper, knowing that he had to walk far across the town. Vytas would sit another half an hour. Then he would gently take her skinny, trembling fingers into his large, hot palms, kiss her burning cheeks, gently touch her lips, and leave.

Before going to sleep, Sonia would look in the mirror for a long time, touching her lips and cheeks in the same spots his lips touched them. She did not look different, but she felt different. The thought that Vytas may love her one day filled her heart with happiness.

That year on March 25, 1957, there was a signed agreement between the Soviet Union and Poland that all individuals who held Polish citizenship before September 17, 1939, were allowed to leave for Poland. By that summer there were long lines in front of the AVIR Agency, that was in charge of giving visas to leave the country, from early morning until late in the evening. Within five years 245,501 Polish citizens left.

Young people of marriageable age could name a high price for marriage in exchange for an exit VISA if their parents were born in Poland before

1939. Money was paid, young couples got married, got permit and left with their parents and in-laws. It was all handled with a lot of experience and very discreetly.

"Would you go to Israel?" Sonia asked Malka.

"Me? I would run in my nightgown yesterday and never look back. But we are not so lucky. All we can do is dream. We are Lithuanian Jews; we have no chance."

At the School of Engineering where Sonia was in her first year, many Jewish students arrived from Kiev. Misha was in Sonia's class. His friend and his parents had come from the Ukraine to Vilna to find a young girl who wanted to leave for Poland and would agree, for certain amount of money, to take their family with her. They did find a girl and soon left.

"Those who leave our country are real traitors. I could never leave." Misha was angry at his friend's decision.

Misha had originally tried to get into the Institute of Aviation and Nuclear Physics in Leningrad, but he had not been accepted. His father, a staunch Communist, had his buddy from the army appointed as the Dean of the Institute of Nuclear Physics.

"We get guidance from a higher level to keep our student body in proportion to our population. We should accept seventy percent Russian students, twenty-eight percent Ukrainian, and not more than two percent Jews," he was told by his old friend.

"Misha graduated with a gold medal from high school and was a Ukrainian champion in every math competition. Check him out; don't ignore his application," Misha's father begged.

"Dear friend, you are right, but it doesn't depend on me. I only follow the orders."

In Lithuania at this time, nobody had yet received orders restricting entrance to the Jews. In their group of thirty students, twenty-two were Jewish. Misha was happy to be involved in many activities, and he was chosen to be the president of the student union. Misha also took charge of the publication of the student newspaper.

As much as Misha didn't miss an opportunity to condemn the Jewish *petit bourgeois* who were eager to leave for Poland, Sonia, on the other hand, had met some interesting, fine people among them. She did wonder why so many Jews from Baltic countries were eager to leave, however.

More and more often, Sonia had a feeling that she wasn't really as Russian as everyone thought her to be. What if she got married and her husband found out that she was born Jewish? What if he called her a

Zidovka, a kike? Sonia wished to be like other Russian girls, but she wasn't. At times, she felt like a white crow.

The refrigerator, the washing machine, and a fur coat would mysteriously disappear from Malka's room for some time and would be returned a few days later in their regular place. Strange people would come to the apartment and search Fedia and Malka's room. Nervous, Malka would run back and forth with goodies and vodka to please them. Mama tried to explain to Sonia that Fedia was buying and selling cars illegally. Someone had probably reported him to the authorities. But not to worry, everything would be settled.

Sonia was aware that in her free Socialist world bribery was hanging in the air, invisibly penetrating every pour of one's skin, becoming an undetachable part of one's existence. The dictatorship of the proletariat tried to silence its tongue, but bribery flourished among the people. Everyone was afraid of it, but they needed it to get a job, desperately needed it to get an apartment.

It wasn't easy for Sonia to accept that bureaucracy, lies, and bribery lived in full harmony with the goal of building a new perfect society. One had to believe in equality, even if the director of any enterprise could never be seen talking to a simple worker.

Okay, great academics, doctors in Kremlin, and rectors of universities were paid astronomical figures. Maybe they deserved it. But why did a major in the army get seven times more than an engineer or a teacher? Why did directors have private chauffeurs waiting on their wives' orders to drive them around? Everyone who had an opportunity to steal at work was stealing. Cheating the government was not shameful; it was a normal part of life.

Sonia was Jewish. But what did that mean? She was not brought up Jewish. Sonia did not think she had much in common with Jews. Sonia did not particularly want to be one of them, if she had a choice.

Sonia walked on her familiar streets but felt very differently from before. If she revealed that she is actually Jewish, people would like her less and would look down on her as if they were superior.

The more she thought about it, the more it hurt. She wished to identify with the crowd on the street, but they were not her brothers. Through no fault of her own, they might suddenly turn into her enemies. Their culture, their heritage, their traditions of past generations were not hers. So, what was really hers?

Sonia no longer despised the short, fat men and women with long noses, curly black hair, and restless eyes. They walked fast, whispered, and moved their hands a lot, clearly accepting their inferiority to others. The ones she knew to be Jewish were mostly tailors, drivers, and store managers. They kept to each other, laughed a lot, and were pretty loud. Sonia realized that identifying as Jewish would expose her to negative emotions from others around her, cut down her privileges, swallow numerous possibilities in the future, and basically deprive her of the good things she took for granted at this point in her life. She would be singled out as a stranger, as not belonging.

Sonia did not wish that. On the other hand, she felt almost dirty inside her heart. She was a hypocrite for pretending to be someone else than what she was born to be.

What did it mean for her to be Jewish? Sonia felt spiritual; she felt the presence of all those she loved protecting her in the most difficult situations. *Hashem* was there always, even if she didn't understand Him.

Born Jewish, stay Jewish, there is not much to it. Instinctively, without knowing much about it, Sonia felt that being Jewish was not just about religion. There were Jewish people around her who were atheists from the day they were born. They could not pretend otherwise, even if they wished to.

Basically, Sonia had no choice. Like it or not, she had to cross the road to join her people, the people she belonged to. On the other hand, Vilnius was not a good place to be Jewish. Nowhere in the Soviet Union was a good place to be Jewish. She had to get out. The most logical, most suitable place to be Jewish was Israel because it was a Jewish State, a Jewish country. Nothing could be clearer or simpler. She was also ready for a change. Sonia was curious to see another world. It may be cruel, unjust, and full of contradictions, but it would be free.

Many people were saying that after the 20 Party Congress, the government was trying to repair the damages inflicted in Stalin's time. Most people still lived in fear. Peasants refused to work in fields, just the same as before. If it weren't for thousands of students sent to the kolkhoz, more than half of the wheat and potatoes would rot uncollected. Students could not afford not to go to help. They would not get their grades or scholarships.

Obviously, Sonia was not yet ready to admit being Jewish publicly. It did not sound very attractive. Sadly, deep in her heart she knew she had to admit that it was time to part with her old self; it was time to say good-bye to the young, patriotic girl she had been. There was a time when she had loved her country very much. She believed that she could have died for it. That young girl had had a purpose in life—to help build a Communist society for the entire world. She had had a feeling of belonging; had been proud to be Russian. But since she knew that she wasn't exactly Russian, Sonia could not sincerely remain true to these feelings anymore. Living in Vilnius, she wasn't Russian, Polish, or Lithuanian. She was just Jewish.

Maybe she should go to Israel where everybody was Jewish, where she would not be a second-class citizen. There was no risk in going for a visit to find out what there was in the tiny country with kibbutzim, hot sun, and beautiful girls. Sonia heard that in Israel, there were no potatoes or salami. In the market sellers would stuff bags with oranges on the bottom with a few potatoes on the top to sell potatoes.

There were rumours that in Israel, there was a shortage of girls to marry. Young men had to go to America to find a bride. The ugliest girls had a choice of handsome, young, clever men. All the widows and old maids who left for Israel got married there almost immediately. Apparently, when ships with immigrants arrived in the port of Haifa, many eligible men waited nearby. It did sound like a lot of fun. Sonia fantasized about finding out more about it.

"Who speaks Yiddish today? Nobody. It is only here in the Baltic States that some remember Yiddish from her parents. Look at me. I like Jewish songs. This doesn't make me Jewish. I like all kinds of music: Polish, Georgian… Jews are not a nation." Misha insisted on their walks.

"Misha, what are you talking about? Jews are a special, brilliant nation. There is a Jewish State—Israel."

"Jews are highly educated people, but who needs a country filled with intelligentsia? A young country needs workers to build roads and houses."

"So, who builds them in Israel? Jews do. Israel must be the only place in the world without any anti-Semitism."

"Sonia, there is no such place. There have been plenty of fights between Jews and Arabs from the very beginning. Besides, the Jews who have lived there for a long time don't like newcomers. It is a kind of anti-Semitism. They don't like Soviet Jews. They are suspicious that they are spies. Israelis segregate them in special places."

"You are brainwashed. It is not anti-Semitism. In your passport it is clearly written that you are a Jew. In Israel, it isn't."

"You are silly. In America, nationality is not written as 'Jew.' They write 'American.' Do you believe there is no anti-Semitism in America?"

Jewish people in Vilnius had a certain look that you can recognize them on the street. True, it could be a bit boring to live in a place where everybody was Jewish and looked alike. Sonia had heard that Jews in Israel looked different from Jews in Vilnius. The French lived in France, the English in England, and Jews should live in Israel. Sounds logical.

It was her luck that her wonderful Mama did not adopt Sonia when she took her as six-month-old baby from the ghetto. Now she could apply for exit Visa as an orphan who wants to join her mother who survived the war and ended up to live in Israel. AVIR should grant her permission to leave.

It was amazing how when her identity was threatened, Sonia rebelled fiercely from inside with emotional force, almost like an animal. She had to leave! Where to go? Only to Israel where she could be like everybody else; where she could actually be herself. Can a leopard change his spots? Can one change the colour of their eyes? So how could she pretend or believe she was Russian once she knew she was born Jewish?

Where to start? The only way to apply was through the AVIR Agency. It seemed to be very tiresome and not promising. Sonia needed a notary, or a lawyer, or another professional person to walk her through the maze.

It was important as well not to talk to Mama about it. With Mama's pain of losing Lucia, of being arrested for having connections with the West, and her always being on guard for something bad to happen, Sonia knew that Mama would not believe she would be allowed to leave the Soviet Union for Israel.

In her heart, though, she was determined to try. It was her only way to truth, to freedom, to be herself!

In the Soviet society, Jews were inferior to Russians the same way as they had been before the revolution. Nothing had changed. By being born Jewish, Jews had to bear the stain of their existence, accepting and expecting that in a moment of slightest ideological crisis, they would be the scape goats, the first to be blamed. If Jews managed financially better than others, they were envied, accused of speculation, corruption, and greed.

Jewish children were always encouraged by their parents to obtain higher education, but at the same time, were aware of the quota imposed on accepting Jews to universities. Despite being heavily involved in local politics, and some even ready to die for party lines, Jews carried a legitimate fear of being dismissed and pushed aside for just being born Jewish.

There was no way Sonia wished to tolerate to breathe the air of despicable contempt or shame that would befall on her as soon as she would disclose her Jewishness. Besides, Sonia did not want to live in fear like Mama, Irina, and Dadia Kolia.

Often, Dadia Kolia was stopped by ugly, little men with fedoras covering their bald heads, wearing grey, khaki raincoats below their knees. Sonia found them scary and repulsive. They would harass him, question him for hours, then let him go. This happened again and again. For years!

Dadia Kolia loved to visit Mama with Irina, but he hated traveling not knowing what to anticipate. Irina cried a lot. She missed Mama, but it was expensive to travel by train. They never had any money. Parishioners brought them eggs, and sometimes chicken and pork, but very little money. Irina was afraid of everything. Any little noise outside the window made her tremble like an autumn leaf.

Sonia had to make a careful plan to organize her application to leave for Israel. It had to be very discreet. She would not tell a soul in case it did not work. First of all, she could not jeopardize Mama's life.

To start the legal process, Sonia decided the safest bet would be to go to the notary in Kaunas where she studied.

She put on a new dress, collected her documents, and bravely walked into the nondescript, grey building with a sign on the door advertising notaries. It was dark inside the front room. The very high ceiling was peeling.

There were about five different tables placed closely to each other in a large rectangular room, which had probably served as a ballroom before the Second World War. A fat, elderly woman sat in front before you could approach any of the people hiding behind their old, wooden desks.

"What is it that you want? What is your story?" Her voice was harsh and masculine.

"Mine is a very delicate matter. I don't want to discuss it now. I need to see a professional."

"You have to pay first."

Sonia hated the tone of her voice. The idea of paying someone she wasn't sure she could talk to about her personal issue gave her uneasy feeling. She left.

The next week, Sonia tried another office building that was close to her dormitory. Again, there was no way anyone would talk to her before she paid. Sonia decided to wait until she got back home to Vilnius and try her luck there.

It was winter break for students; exams had finished. The first snow was covering naked branches, roofs, streets, and crunched under your feet.

Sonia wasn't cold, only her face was tickled by fresh, crispy air. It would be fun to pick up the fluffy, white snow and to thrust it playfully down someone's neck. As the cold caressed her rosy cheeks, Sonia was conscious that far away, in Israel, it never snowed. So, let it snow now and make her cold. Maybe it would be her last winter here, in the Soviet Union. She thought about the strange woman whose heart cried for Sonia, whom at this moment, Sonia would like to hug and comfort.

The past week, Sonia had written her a long, warm letter. It was more a poem than a letter. Sonia was pleased to spread a healing salve on the wounds of her Israeli mother, let her know that her grown-up daughter had finally made up her mind to go and live with her.

Sonia stopped at the red-brick building with a sign outside that read "NOTARY HOUSE." She had passed by it on numerous occasions, but this time she planned to go inside.

Right at the entrance started an enormous hall filled with tables, each one being occupied by what looked like a professional expert. Unsure as to what to do, Sonia sat in the corner on a wooden bench observing what was going on and hoping that some sensitive, understanding person would notice her and ask her what she was waiting for all by herself for the last hour.

Her eyes caught sight of a pale man with grey temples leaning toward a broad-shouldered peasant man uneasily fidgeting in his chair. The poorly dressed peasant was waving an old, yellow paper and was talking fast in a halting voice while nervously wiping his forehead with a big, grey handkerchief.

Sonia moved to another chair nearer to them to try to figure out what was causing such a heated discussion. Sitting just a few feet away, she understood that it was all about an old fence on the farm between the peasant and his brother-in-law. Too boring to be excited about. The notary sympathetically nodded his head, never interrupted, and occasionally wrote notes on his paper pad. Impressed by his patience, Sonia waited until the peasant left. She immediately rushed to take his place at the table.

"Excuse me, I have something very important to discuss. It is exceptionally confidential. Nobody can ever find out," Sonia blurted out hurriedly, afraid he would not listen before sending her to pay the cashier in the office. He introduced himself as Notary Peres and assured her of complete secrecy on his part.

"What is your name?"

"Sonia."

"Sonia, please slowly explain how you want me to help you."

Sonia gushed about everything. First about Mama, then about Irina and Dadia Kolia and their misfortunes with authorities, and then about her Israeli mother whom she refused to acknowledge for many years.

"Now I want to leave to go to Israel. My Mama, whom I adore, who is the best mother on the planet, has no idea that I want to go to Israel. Mama doesn't believe that I will ever get permission. In no way can she find out about my decision. I cannot hurt her. It absolutely has to be a top secret."

Sonia talked very fast, talked and talked more. Almost three hours passed. It was already dark outside. Notary Peres didn't interrupt her once and didn't ask any questions, but he did take notes.

After that visit, Sonia went to his office every time she was in town. She never had to register in the reception or wait in line. Notary Peres was there for her, preparing her file for application. He always seemed to be glad to see Sonia. He wanted to know about her everyday life, her classes, her friends, and the books she read.

They had to get her birth certificate from the archives. They had to compose a letter explaining how Sonia got the family name Ostianko. Notary Peres got her birth certificate and prepared her application to go abroad to join her birth mother. Sonia sat across the table on the very edge on her chair in full trust and appreciation of her new, reliable friend. She couldn't honestly claim that she was an orphan. She never felt like an orphan.

Notary Peres understood everything. He didn't write anything negative about Mama. He leaned forward to read her application, asking if she agreed with what he put on the paper and if there was anything she would like to change or to add.

"Maybe it is dishonest not to mention how good Mama was to me over all these years," said Sonia.

"My opinion is that it is not a good idea to talk about the wonderful qualities of Elena Stepanovna. After sending this letter, you will not love her less. It is only a piece of paper. But it is an extremely important piece of paper."

Listening to his gentle voice, Sonia wondered why during all these numerous and time-consuming visits Notary Peres had never asked her about payments for his service. For a long time now, she had been noticing his old, worn-out briefcase. She planned to buy him a beautiful, new, leather one.

"Here is everything that is needed according to regulations. Be brave. Deliver it to AVIR." He put the thick folder in front of Sonia.

"Now?"

"Why not? Good luck." His kind eyes smiled reassuringly at her.

Is that all? When and how would she thank him? How should she pay? Sonia hadn't found a new, leather briefcase, but she had saved her scholarship money for him.

The AVIR office was open until three o'clock. She would hurry and go there first, go home, get the money and then return to his office to report how it went.

The AVIR building was open, but nobody was in the reception. Sonia walked into the next open room.

"Excuse me, please." She approached a serious-looking man sitting by a heavy, oak table near the window. "I have my documents to deliver."

"For Poland?"

"Not for Poland. For Israel."

"Oh? Wait a minute." He looked at her and disappeared swiftly to the next room.

After about half an hour, he came back with another very tall, skinny man with large, brown glasses.

"My name is Comrade Sokolov." He invited Sonia to another room, which looked like his private office. "How old are you?"

"I am already eighteen," Sonia answered proudly, making herself comfortable in a deep, leather armchair.

"Already eighteen," he repeated, slowly. "Sonia, please tell me. Did you give enough consideration when making such a serious decision? Israel is not the Soviet Union. It is a tiny, poor country in the desert, completely dependent on America. You may not like it there. What if they don't let you come back? People in Israel are very different from our people. You are very young and don't know much. You may regret this decision for the rest of your life."

"Maybe. I understand, but there I have my birth mother. Here I am completely alone." Sonia blushed at this unkind lie. She was never alone. She had Mama.

Comrade Sokolov asked if Sonia read newspapers about the situation in the Middle East, whether she realized that in Israel there are persistent and dangerous fights between Jews and Arabs. Women are forced to join the army.

"Israel is a desert with unbearable heat, a miserable climate, and a very low standard of living. I have a good piece of advice." He poured some lemonade for her from nice pitcher. "Apply to visit for a month or two. See everything with your own eyes. This way you don't close the doors on yourself. You seem to be puzzled by my suggestion. Maybe we should discuss it with your friends to hear their opinion."

"Never, never. I don't want other students to know about my application. Please, nobody should find out!" Sonia blurted out.

"Sha, sha. I didn't mean to upset you; I'm just trying to be helpful with my advice." There was something about him she trusted.

When she went back to see Notary Peres, he has left for the day.

Sonia felt uneasy that Notary Peres would think she was ungrateful for all his efforts by not coming back to share with him how her application was received at AVIR.

The next day was Sunday, and the office would be closed. Sonia decided to find his address and to see him at his home.

A tall, comely woman with hair curled in little pieces of newspaper opened the front door.

"Please come in," she said in a low voice. "I am sorry my husband is not home yet. He usually plays chess on Sunday mornings."

Sonia walked in, sat down, and searched for the right place to put an envelope she prepared for Notary Peres. When Mrs. Peres—the woman with curls who was obviously his wife—disappeared for a moment into the kitchen, Sonia quickly put her envelope under the ceramic bowl on the table and left.

The next day started new semester in Kaunas.

When she came back to Vilnius after two weeks, the first thing Sonia did was visit Notary Peres to tell him about her adventure at the AVIR office.

"How long do you think it will take to get an answer?" she asked him.

"Nobody knows. You have to be patient. We did our best. At least we can hope. If they refuse, we will start all over again."

For the moment, Notary Peres had done everything he could. He was a busy notary. She should get up and leave and thank him again. But it was sad to say good-bye. They sat opposite each other, separated by the narrow table. Sonia held her school bag tightly on her knees. He would never know how grateful she was. Notary Peres leaned a bit over the desk and gently opened the zipper of her school bag.

"You forgot this in my house." His eyes twinkled as he dropped the white envelope inside her school bag. Sonia tried to protest, to say she meant to leave it for him. It was her small token of appreciation. She tried to take the envelope out of her bag, then shame and guilt came crushing at once. Tears she couldn't control rolled down her cheeks. She was embarrassed to look at him, to meet his eyes. She swallowed her sobs. Notary Peres got up, walked over to her, and took out his white handkerchief to wipe her cheeks. Sonia gathered all her strength and rushed out to the street, desperate to hide.

The first flowers of spring were struggling through patches of snow, smiling with their tiny, blue eyes and warming the soul by bringing sunshine. After classes, students walked through the main street. Boys were on the left side; girls were on the right. They looked at each other. The girls held hands, giggling.

Lithuanian men, as a rule, are much more attractive than the girls who are tall, athletic, and broad-shouldered. Lithuanian girls lack femininity; they are too tall, too muscular and rough looking. Sonia felt petite next to them; she felt prettier than most. She became popular after realizing that some girls wanted to be with her to attract young men. It was a very new feeling being attractive and being looked at.

Sonia finally received an answer from the AVIR office. Her application to go to Israel was considered "misguided" and "irresponsible." Reading this short reply, Sonia felt a sharp, uncomfortable pain in her chest. There was nothing to do but wait the three-month period stated in the rules and then reapply. It was hurtful not to tell a single soul, so Sonia whispered to herself about her secret desire to leave this hypocritical place of her birth that was full of lies and brainwashing. Misha may have guessed from their many conversations that Sonia was really troubled by something.

Misha's mother worked as a store manager, but they seemed to live very well. How and where did they get money? Misha explained to Sonia that the store got additional products not registered in the books. These goods could be distributed under the table with profits divided by the people in charge, his mother included.

"It is actually cheating!" Sonia said, surprised.

"Where did you come from? Sonia, it isn't Chinese grammar. These are facts of normal life that everyone knows exist but are afraid to talk about."

Misha confided in Sonia that last summer when he worked at a big electrical plant, every engineer got a special bonus envelope on the top of their pay at the end of each month. Why? From the private sales of illegal products.

"I don't believe there is a factory in the Soviet Union where one couldn't make an extra ruble. One has to understand human psychology. You say it is cheating. Bullshit. This is how a country operates. The nicest, the most honest people, I know, do it. There is no crime in cheating the government."

On her following visit to Vilnius, Sonia was surprised to see Mama sitting with a stranger in their little room. She immediately didn't like his looks. The strange man sat on the edge of an armchair wearing a beige raincoat inside the house. Not only did he not take off his raincoat inside the flat, he actually wore an old, wrinkled fedora covering his forehead.

"We were waiting for you." Mama said as Sonia walked in.

"What is this all about?" Sonia asked.

"I came to inform you that you are going to receive an invitation from the Israeli Consulate."

"Pardon me? I don't understand what you are talking about."

The man's presence made Sonia anxious.

"Sonechka, sit down," Mama said, calmly.

"I don't get it. Can you please explain to me, slowly and clearly, what this is all about?" Sonia sat in her favourite green, Louis 15-style, French fauteuil next to piano.

"I came to inform you that you will receive a letter from the Israeli Consulate inviting you to visit them."

"Are you serious? Where? In Moscow?"

"Yes, in Moscow."

"So, what should I do when I get the letter?"

"I cannot tell you what to do. We are a free country. It is up to you to decide to go or not to go."

The actual invitation arrived two days later. While holding the letter, Sonia suddenly reexperienced all that happened two years before in Moscow when she went to the International Youth Festival and couldn't get into the Consulate.

With the letter in her pocket and without saying a word to Mama, Sonia ran out of the house to the train station. She didn't want to waste one-second in case something changed.

"When is the next train leaving for Moscow?" she asked in the ticket office.

"There is no train today...."

Sonia didn't wait for the end of her sentence. If there was no more train today, there may be a plane. She would fly. Sonia had never flown, but she knew now that she had to get to the airport.

She had taken money for tickets before leaving home, and luckily for her, there was a plane leaving from Vilnius to Moscow in two hours' time. First, she bought herself a ticket, then she went to the post office to send a telegram to the address written on the envelope she had received this morning.

Vesnina 16.
Arriving at 5 pm today. Sonia.

The flight was uneventful and rather short, about one-and-a-half hours. Just as the plane landed, a stewardess came and asked her, "Are you Sonia? If yes, follow me."

Sonia jumped up from her seat and was escorted to the exit. She was the very first person to leave the plane.

As Sonia walked down the stairs, she saw a handsome elegantly dressed gentleman waiting for her. He brought her to a large, blue limousine. An older, noble-looking lady about fifty years old with two adorable boys dressed in the same sailor outfits, like in storybooks, sat in the back seat.

It was already late afternoon and the streets were almost empty. Their long car glided like a big, free eagle through the centre of Moscow. The moment they approached Vesnina 16, Sonia saw a guard, similar to the one who had grabbed her hand two years ago, standing by the main door. This time he was motionless. They drove smoothly through open, iron gates.

The handsome gentleman opened Sonia's door and helped her out of the car. Sonia understood that she was actually inside the Israeli Consulate. She pinched herself not really believing that this time she walked in so easily.

"Thank you for sending us the telegram about your arrival. It was very helpful," the older lady said while leading Sonia to a large, beautiful staircase full of people.

At the very top of the staircase stood a tall, distinguished-looking man holding a glass of wine. His other hand was wearing black glove. *It must be a prosthetic arm*, thought Sonia. The stately looking man stepped down two stairs and offered Sonia a glass of red wine.

"Welcome to our home. We are very honoured that you accepted our invitation." It was obvious that he was the Ambassador.

"Thank you very much for inviting me." Sonia had never drunk wine in her entire life. She took her glass and gulped it down in one sip. There were lots of people at this reception.

"We invited everyone to come tonight to meet you," said the same sweet lady who had brought Sonia into the reception room. Touched, Sonia had never felt more privileged or more important.

After most of the people left the Embassy for their residences, the lady with soft intelligent eyes took Sonia to the top floor. It was a cheerful room with lace curtains, a tall, big bed covered with a Chinese bedspread embroidered with peacocks and large, pink peonies. A young, pretty woman with a white apron walked in.

"This is Maria. We brought her from Italy. She is going to prepare your bed."

By now Sonia figured out that the woman who was in the car at the airport and who brought her to this charming guest room was the Ambassador's wife. Her name was Jamima Chernowitz. Maria was their maid who they had brought to Moscow. Maria didn't speak Russian. Jamima said something to her and Maria immediately left the room, quickly returning within five minutes.

"Sonia, since you came with no baggage, I believe that Maria can give you some of her dresses. You are about the same size."

Sonia touched the soft, velvety fabrics. There was a beautiful, navy-blue dress, a yellow, silk blouse with white polka dots, and a green, suede jacket. Obviously, they were brought from Italy or France.

"Which dress do you want me to have?" Sonia asked.

"Try them all. They are for you." Jamima smiled.

It was so much fun. Everything fit like a glove. Sonia turned around and around in front of the mirror, admiring her own reflection, encouraged on by Jamima and Maria.

When she went to bed, she noticed that there were poems by Esenin and Pushkin on her night table. Everything looked so exquisitely elegant. She had never seen nicer room. How sensitive was that of Jamima to prepare

Russian poems for her to read. How could Jamima have known that Sonia liked Esenin?

Sonia woke up the next morning with bright sunshine seeping through lacy, pink window drapes. Her high bed with crisp pillows and a white, fluffy duvet embraced her like a royal princess. Sonia had her own bathroom with a big, shiny bathtub, and her own toilet. They only had one toilet at home, and one old, rusted bathtub for four different families. Mama never allowed her to take a bath before scrubbing the tub thoroughly.

Sonia put on a new dress that Maria had given her, enjoying how well it hugged her body. There was a nice, French-style desk near the window. She saw the telephone. She must call Sara Petrovna to surprise her about being inside the Israeli Consulate in Moscow as an invited guest.

"Hello?"

"Who is speaking?"

"Sara Petrovna, it is Sonia. Remember me?"

"Sonechka, I am glad to hear your voice. Where are you calling from?"

"Sara Petrovna, you will not believe it if I tell you. You will be so happy for me."

"Nu, tell me please, tell me where are you?"

"You will be so surprised. I am sitting in a very comfortable, burgundy-coloured, leather chair by the window in the Israeli Consulate! Hello? Hello?"

Not a sound.

"Hello, can you hear me?"

Sara Petrovna immediately had put down her receiver. Why? Clearly, she was afraid to talk to Sonia. Now Sonia felt stupid, guilty, and insensitive. Sara Petrovna was a member of the Communist Party. She taught History at Moscow University. Sara Petrovna may have problems regarding this telephone call from the Israeli Consulate. But it was too late. Sonia's cheerful mood changed drastically.

After a delicious breakfast prepared by Jamima and served by Maria, Sonia was taken to the office of Joseph Avidar, Ambassador to the Soviet Union from Israel since 1955.floor.

The room had a large, Israeli flag on one side and a big desk in the middle. There was a photo of a gorgeous, young girl with a long, thick, reddish braid over her shoulder. She looked straight at the camera with her wide, intelligent eyes.

"That is my daughter, Dana. She is about your age. If you ever decide to live in Israel, she will be your friend," said Joseph Avidar when he noticed that Sonia was fascinated by the beautiful photo. "Now let us talk about why you want to go to Israel."

"First of all, I have a family in Israel. My biological mother."

"What do you know about Israel?"

"Not much. I expect you to tell me more about your country."

There was an enormous map of the Soviet Union from Baltic Sea to Pacific Ocean spread across the wall facing the desk.

"Sonia, please look carefully at this map. There is your big, beautiful country with so much to offer. Israel is a very tiny sliver of land with no place to put its name on the map. It is a poor country. Life is difficult. We have 1.9 million people living in all of Israel. You have more than 200 million people. You have to think it over carefully before making a drastic change in your life. You are young; you may have been influenced by your friends and will regret it later."

"I don't understand you talking like this to me. I expected you to strengthen my desire to go to Israel, not to discourage me."

"We are here to tell you the facts; to give you the right information."

Sonia was completely befuddled by this encounter. It was only later, when talking to Jamima and other people working at the Consulate, she understood that Joseph Avidar was not free to say what he really wanted to say. There were microphones in the ceilings of every room. Many Russians employed at the Consulate were actually spies for the Soviet Union. This was the reason that whenever it was possible, Israelis tried to bring their own people to work at the Embassy. Sonia was mesmerized by these two beautiful people; she was completely in awe how warm and wonderful Jamima was to her. After all these years, Jamima was still clearly in love with Joseph. Sonia could tell just by the way she looked at him.

"Was it a love at first sight?"

"It was. The moment I saw his missing hand, I wanted to take care of him." There was a mischievous smile on Jamima's gentle face.

"How did Joseph lose his hand?" Sonia was extremely curious.

"Sonechka, Joseph was an officer instructing his soldiers to use hand grenades. He saved the lives by covering a bomb that exploded prematurely."

"Wow!"

"I think so too. He is my hero. Always has been. Now, my dear, it is almost midnight. Sweet dreams." Jamima kissed Sonia and left.

The next evening one of the Israeli diplomats took Sonia to see the Russian ballet at the Bolshoi theatre. During intermission they were selling slices of tangerines.

"Try it." Sonia was offered a full tangerine.

She had never tasted one.

Jamima took her to the Pushkin Museum to see Russian landscape painters. Jamima introduced Sonia to the Jewish-Russian painters Ilya Yefimovitch Repin and Isaak Levitan.

"Levitan was an exceptionally talented Jewish painter. He did maybe a thousand paintings. He came from a very poor *shtetl*, and he suffered from anti-Semitism. But he continued painting magnificent landscapes. It was his passion."

Jamima Chernowitz came from Ukraine's small town of Chernowitz where Jews settled in the fifteenth century. In 1919, there were more than 43 thousand Jews living in Chernowitz. They made up nearly fifty percent of the total population.

Jamima and Joseph wanted to know everything about Sonia, about her friends, her school, her life.

Sonia was keen to tell Jamima and Joseph what a wonderful Mama she had in Vilnius, but, at the same time, Sonia was reluctant to praise Mama since she was planning to leave for Israel to be with her birth mother. The truth was that by now Sonia dreamed of leaving the Soviet Union, a country full of lies and injustice. She didn't want to leave Mama, but she longed to be truly who she was, to be Jewish. But how could she explain all that to Jamima and Joseph whom she admired and who treated her like family?

On the third day of Sonia's visit, Jamima announced, "My dear girl, I have a big surprise for you!"

Sonia could not imagine what it could be.

"We are trying to arrange a telephone conversation with your mother Raisa in Israel."

At home in Vilnius, they didn't have a phone. Here at the Consulate, there were many phones.

"Hello? Hello?" Sonia said, loudly.

She couldn't hear a word.

"Sonia, can you hear me. It is me, your mother," she heard, finally.

Joseph, Jamima, Maria, and few employees of the Consulate were in the room around the table listening to conversation.

"I hear you. Can you hear me?" Sonia actually had to scream.

Sonia looked around. The room was very quiet. Jamima and Maria were crying softly. Sonia didn't feel emotional, but the woman on the other end of the line spoke in a trembling voice.

"Sonia, you have to come live with me. Everything will be different, much better for you.... Do you hear me?" The connection was interrupted.

Everyone was silent, looking at Sonia. She stood there, not knowing what to do or to say.

"I understand that you are confused. It is the very first time your mother and you spoke to each other. I cannot believe it happened just now, in this room." Jamima was holding both of Sonia's hands, crying.

So, what was going to happen now? Sonia did not feel as emotional as the people in the room. Raisa was her mother. Raisa remembers her as a baby. Sonia had no such memories. Her Mama is in Vilnius. Her Mama is Elena Stepanovna Grigorjeva.

Sonia was curious about Raisa, about the real family she was born into, about her father. Whatever happened to him? How did he die? Who knows, who can tell her? Only Raisa. Why did she remember her as a mean lady living in their salon, chasing her out of the room?

Looking at the people next to her who were so moved by her conversation with Raisa, Sonia felt bewildered and ashamed about her lack of feelings toward her biological mother. What was wrong with her?

"How do you feel?" Jamima asked, in a soft, caring voice while still holding Sonia's hands. Sonia had nothing to say.

Her stay at the Consulate was over. Jamima took her to the airport to fly to Vilna.

"Sonia, we did enjoy having you. I believe we will manage to bring you home, to deliver you to your mother." She gave her a big, warm hug and kissed her cheeks.

What a beautiful person, thought Sonia while looking through the window at the city spread forever below the clouds. She could not wait to tell Mama about this amazing visit.

11

The refrigerator, washing machine, surcoats would sometimes disappear from Malka's room and after few days come back placed in their regular corners.

But in the meantime, some strangers would come for a visit. Rough, usually vulgar Fedia treated them nicely offering cakes and drinks. The best vodka. Mama explained to Sonia that Fedia buys and sells cars illegally and most probably got caught. It will cost him few thousand rubles. Everything will be settled by drinks and bribery.

Wow, it was a real surprise for Sonia. At least now Sonia understood how they could afford to travel every summer to Palanga, eat tangerines, grapes. Malka was always nervous living in fear. Fedia seemed to be less bothered, probably got used to it over the years.

They used to have guests for dinners. But lately many of their friends left to Israel through Poland.

"Would you like to go to Israel?"-Sonia asked Malka sitting on her couch, eating full juicy tangerine. Malka offered her so generously.

"Me? I would run in my nightgown. I would never look back. But why to talk about it, why to dream? I. Have no chance. You, it is another story.

Sonechka, don't miss your chance. It is also a sin to torture your real mother. Yiddishe mother.

"No, my child, you cannot understand—" Malka stopped talking, waved her hand, giving up.

"I will never leave," said Sonia, but in her heart hoping the sooner, the better.

It wasn't sheer curiosity or a sense of adventure. Sonia passionately dreams about living in a world where she can be like everyone else, where she will not be afraid to speak her mind, leave without fear.

The fact that Israel was a capitalistic country didn't worry her at all. Everywhere there are nice people. With time she will be able to learn new language, make friends. She will meet her family, tell them about her wonderful Mama. Then they will understand why it was so difficult for her to take a decision to leave.

By now, Sonia understood that in her free socialistic world, bribery and corruption were hanging in the air, invisible, penetrating into every pore of one's skin, becoming necessary parts of one's existence. You needed to bribe to get a job, to get an apartment, to get into university.

Bribery and cheating a government were a part of normal life. Everyone was saying that journal *truth* had no news, and the journal *news* had no truth in it.

Sonia did not kill herself studying, but she spent enough time to earn a scholarship. She was able to memorize in two or three days before exams all the boring material lectured during the semester. Honestly, Sonia liked the examination day. She was one of the first to draw her ticket, eager to answer her questions.

She also liked being in the dormitory with four other girls. They knew how to cook and how to wash the floors. Sonia found it difficult to hide her inability to perform any physical chores. On the other hand, she knew how to share her time, money, dresses, and helped others with their assignments in school. Next to her slept a hard-working, shy girl from a remote Lithuanian village. No one ever talked to her or called her by her first name; she was called only by her last—Kudirkaite.

Her first name was Laima. When Sonia's turn came for housecleaning, Laima happily took over. She would buy her bread, copy her notebook, and make her eggs in the evening. Next to skinny, quick, restless Sonia, Laima Kudirkaite looked clumsy and heavy, but she tried to imitate Sonia in everything she did.

Laima allowed Sonia to cut her hair and dress her up. When Sonia got a cold and had to miss school, Laima cried and didn't want to leave her alone in the room. Laima warmed some water and washed Sonia's feet.

Laima talked with Sonia about her romances back home in her country village. She talked about sleeping with boys. Sonia felt she was in love with Vytas and cherished their gentle romance, but she never thought about going to bed with him or any other man.

Laima confessed to Sonia that when sitting next to their classmate Thomas, she almost faints from excitement. Sonia never experienced these feelings. She was still shy about wearing nylon stockings and exposing her legs.

The students in her class, mostly country boys, asked Sonia out, but she was loyal to Vytas. Her sudden popularity with boys did not turn her head. There were a hundred boys and seven girls in their engineering class. She didn't consider herself pretty, but that was an advantage in her favour. Sonia believed, as Dadia Kolia often claimed, that men didn't trust pretty women. Most of them were silly and empty headed.

Besides Laima, Sonia was friendly with Alla. Alla was the only Russian girl in her class. She was very different. Alla read Polish magazines, bought her dresses from foreign parcels, went to restaurants with her friends, and slept naked.

"Sometimes, I am bored to tears living here. Look around. Show me someone who has a bit of brain and knows how to dress properly. I wish I could escape from here," Alla confessed to Sonia.

Sonia desperately tried to figure out what exactly disturbed Alla so much.

"Sonia, do you think I don't know what other girls say about me? What kind of crime is it to dine in a nice restaurant, to listen to good music?" Alla asked lazily, swinging her gorgeous, long legs sheathed in transparent nylon. "Look at what they call art. Peasants like cows with silly smiles glued to their silly faces. Sickening. I feel like I am choking and short of fresh air, while you seem to be quite content with the stupidity that surrounds us with these stupid peasants from the country?"

"Alla, I don't get it. What really bothers you? You will graduate, became an engineer, get married, build a family. You can be very happy here."

"I want to own my soul. I don't want the government to decide what is good for me. I like to sleep naked, but girls gossip behind my back. It does not go well with their high, Communist morals. To hell with them. I want to do what I want to do. What harm does it do to anyone?"

"You are right."

Sonia wished to share with Alla that she, too, was dreaming of leaving this place if she ever got permission. Her interest in student activities and their social life was greatly diminishing. She ate at the same cafeteria as everyone else and listened to their jokes, but her mind was floating. Sonia wondered if her classmates would despise or disown her if she admitted her Jewish heritage.

Once, while running to lectures together with her classmate Andrew, Sonia drew his attention to a beautiful, young girl crossing the street.

"Andrew, look at her. She is gorgeous!"

"I don't think so."

"How can you say that?"

"Zidovka," Andrew said, indifferently shrugging his shoulders.

Disgusted and visibly disturbed by this comment, Sonia felt cold butterflies on her spine, but said nothing.

When winter break came, Vytas arrived from Leningrad. He had written her ninety-seven letters since August when he left to continue his studies.

They went dancing the first night he was back. Sonia wished she could move her hips, her shoulders, all her body in the same gracious, seductive way as the other girls around her on the dance floor. Instead, she danced stiffly, not knowing what to do with her hands and trying to involve Vytas in a conversation. She looked down at the linoleum floor, too embarrassed to meet his penetrating, dark eyes.

The next day she day dreamed about the night before and her clumsiness. She felt sorry for herself and thought that Vytas must be disappointed in her. But when the bell rang and Vytas arrived at their house, Sonia immediately changed into a young, yearning puppy. Unknown joy flooded her trembling body like a heat wave, reached her heart and stopped there.

They walked toward the river, their favourite walk during the summer. Now their benches were hidden under winter white. Tingling, downy snow fell gently on their shoulders and on her fur hat, melting on her eyelashes and lips. Sonia's wet cheeks got pink from the cold, her small hand resting cozily in his big hand. Cuddling up to Vytas' shaggy coat, Sonia put her fingers inside his pocket, met his smiling eyes, and laughed happily. They walked gingerly, smiled at each other tenderly, listened to the crisp snow as it glittered under the street lights, and creaked rhythmically under their feet.

"Let us take a ride on the bus," Vytas suggested.

"Where to?"

"Nowhere in particular, wherever it chooses to go."

The city seemed to stop short at the last stop. Modest wooden houses with starched window curtains, painted shutters, and multicoloured lampshades nestled on narrow streets. Nothing seemed to move, and silence guarded the air.

"What if we knock on someone's door to say we got lost?" Sonia suggested.

"Let's try," Vytas agreed, standing near a slim pine tree and leaning against its trunk. He studied her large, lowered eyes with fresh snowflakes melting on her eyelashes. Sonia blushed, but she managed to hide her face inside the rough collar of his coat.

"Will you marry me?" he asked softly, his eyes smiling.

"You have to talk to Mama about it," Sonia answered in disbelief.

They boarded the bus to go back home to her apartment. The driver was waiting for more people, and it was so full in the end that one couldn't turn around. When the bus finally moved, it bounced around, throwing passengers in all directions. Sonia was protected from the pushing crowd by Vytas. She was delighted to feel his strong arms holding her.

"What is your answer to my question?" Vytas asked in front of her door.

"Let's talk to Mama first."

Mama was waiting in their little room.

"Mamochka, Vytas wants to talk to you." Sonia could not hide her excitement.

"Please, sit down."

"Elena Stepanovna, I came today to ask Sonia to be my wife."

Mama was visible startled.

"Sonechka, please go to the dining room. I would like to discuss this with Vytas alone," she said, finally.

In the dining room, Sonia sat as close as possible to the door to hear their conversation.

"Vytas, she is very, very young. Too young, I would say, to marry. You have to finish your studies in Leningrad. She is studying in Kaunas. Let her continue. You will be back in the summer. Then we will discuss it again." Mama spoke slowly and softly, but not as enthusiastically as Sonia anticipated.

Vytas left for Leningrad but continued to write twice a week, addressing her as "my precious wife" in every letter. He said that most of the time he felt miserable, and he had to stay in bed a lot. He told Sonia to study seriously and to not forget her unlucky friend.

12

Over the years Raisa wrote numerous letters to the Ministry of Foreign Affairs, to the Russian Consulate in Israel, to everyone she could think of to help her to go to Vilnius to meet Sonia, to get her daughter back, but nothing seemed to help, more like trying to penetrate a thick, brick wall. She made a promise to herself, and to Israel, that she would never give up.

Then to every one's amazement, Raisa got a permission to be the first tourist allowed into Vilnius after the Second World War. She was actually going to meet Sonia.

Sonia came to airport to wait for Raisa's arrival. She waited patiently watching people step out of the plane. There weren't too many. Then, she saw Raisa walking briskly toward her. Their eyes met, and it was like looking into a mirror. Their eyes were exactly the same colour, the same shape. Sonia felt shivers, a strange tingling sensation. This was her, her biological mother, the mother she never knew, the mother she talked on the phone to, the one who gave her life, the woman who knows her past.

"Sonia, Sonechka, it is me, your mother."

It was awkward hugging her. Who is this stranger? What memories did she have of Sonia? It wasn't easy having a conversation. They took a taxi to see Mama before going to the hotel where Raisa was supposed to stay.

Mama was waiting. Sonia and Raisa crossed the dining room where quite a few people were eating their evening meal. Sonia brought Raisa into their tiny room where Mama and she spent most of their time together.

The small, round table was nicely set like Sonia had never seen it before. The turquoise plates were out as were the shimmering crystal glasses. There was a bewildered look on Raisa's face. Raisa would not have recognized the apartment; it looked so different when she left. The furniture was displayed like in the store, and the magnificent drapes and the carpets on the walls were gone.

"It had to be sold," Mama remarked, noticing Raisa's surprise. "Many tenants went through this house over the years. I cannot have so much space anymore. It is a little more crowded than what you remember. In the salon that you stayed in after the war now lives a couple with two children. Lucia's big piano had to be moved here, to our little room."

"Elena Stepanovna, I still don't believe I am here. I dreamed about it so many times. Now I have to pinch myself."

"Do you want Sonia to play something on the piano for you?"

"Mama, do you want me to?"

Sonia obediently sat down, started a nice piece by Chopin, a piece she knew well and knew that Mama liked. All of a sudden Raisa got up and joined her in playing the music. It was a strange sensation to play together with this completely knew person in her life, her new-found mother. Sonia was afraid to move. Occasionally she glanced at Mama to see if it was okay to sit and play this intimate piece with this strange person. Mama smiled and listened attentively. She was proud of Sonia. Sonia recognized that Mama wanted her to make a good impression on Raisa.

Mama prepared sandwiches with smoked pork and after offered fine, dark chocolate. They started chatting. Raisa told Mama a lot of things that Sonia didn't understand. Sonia wished to leave them alone, but Mama asked her to stay in the room. Mama asked Raisa many questions. It was strange for Sonia to watch Raisa and Mama talking to each other. She tried to figure out in her head what they were thinking about. Her two mothers. Two mothers, really? Not really. Mama was her mother. Raisa gave birth to her. What should she call her? She could not call her "mother." Would she ever? What if Sonia left for Israel and stayed with her? How would she address her? By name? It didn't sound right. Is it possible to live with someone and not call them by any name?

"You must be exhausted after such a long trip,"

"It is all still like a dream to me. Can Sonia come stay with me in the hotel?"

"Definitely. Sonia should go with you. Where are you staying?"

"Neringa."

Hotel Neringa was the only one available for tourists.

"It should be a special thrill for Sonia to stay in the hotel."

The room in the hotel was fancy like in the movies, but Sonia didn't want to stay overnight. There wasn't too much to talk about with Raisa. She didn't know what to call her. Raisa took off her jacket. Her blouse looked old and worn out. There was something pathetic about her, something that made Sonia feel sorry for her. She wanted to go back home.

"You better rest tonight. I will come to see you tomorrow," Sonia said, and left, fast.

Was she supposed to give her a kiss? She didn't want to.

Sonia ran home. Mama was already in bed reading. Sonia undressed, put on her new, flowery, flannel nightgown, crawled in next to her, and held tightly to her warm and familiar body, kissing her beautiful, precious hands.

"Why did she come, Mama? What am I supposed to do with her? Mama, why do you look so sad? Tell me something! I want to know what is on your mind."

When Vytas arrived home that winter, Sonia no longer hid the fact that she was very much in love. She had enough trust in him to share her thoughts about Israel, about her mother wanting her to join her in Haifa.

"My sweet, beautiful Sonechka, I want to marry you, to build family with you, but that is very selfish. You have to consider your future." Sonia was touched by his sincere attempt to think about what would be better for her. Maybe by this time next year, she would be in sunny, warm Israel.

In the meantime, Vytas needed her devoted love. They spent quiet evenings in her room, her little radio tuned to his familiar symphonies that were conducive to him complaining about his miserable life. His brother's wife treated his mother like a maid. Vytas had no money for his medicine to treat arthritis causing so much pain in his bones.

"Vytas, will it ever bother you that I was born Jewish?"

"Nobody will ever know. I will not tell my mother or my brother."

"Mama, I feel you don't want me to marry Vytas."

"Why would you put a healthy head into a sick bed? Vytas needs a good nurse, not a wife."

Vytas left soon for Leningrad.

The spring semester went by very fast. At LIKI, the semester finished much later than in Kaunas. Besides, Vytas was not well, he had to defer his exams. Sonia didn't see Vytas for seven months.

He arrived at their house only at the end of August, late at night, exhausted.

"Why didn't you send me a telegram? I would have met you at the train station," Sonia asked, her open arms welcoming him lovingly.

"I felt very weak. Sonechka, I didn't want you to see me in such poor shape. I had to stay in bed for a few days. Even my father does not know that I am here already."

"You were in town for a week and I had no idea?" Sonia almost cried in total disbelief.

Leningrad was a large and exciting city. Vytas could have brought her a little souvenir. Sonia was truly frustrated. On the other hand, she understood that for Vytas, every penny counted. It pained him to depend on his mother and brother. Vytas had no idea that presents meant a lot to Sonia. She accepted and admired that Vytas was very different from other men in many ways. Warm and sensitive by nature, Vytas never grabbed at or squeezed Sonia. Many times, however, she wished to be squeezed, grabbed, and kissed, but thank God Vytas could not read her mind.

Vytas called her nothing but his "wifey" in all his letters. He had not changed since she had last seen him in January. He had the same kind, smiling, dark eyes and warm, huge hands. Feeling tiny next to him, Sonia could not take her eyes off him. She held both his hands, confused as to what to say first.

She was keen to tell him about her new friends, about how much she missed him, about the strange dreams she had been having, and about her latest rejections from AVIR. Instead, she asked how he felt, how his exams were, and if he was tired. Sonia was interested in every detail about his life in Leningrad without her. If Vytas could read her thoughts, he would know how much he meant to her and how she longed for his visits. She wanted to be with him, to finally be his.

Time stopped for Sonia. She did not care anymore about AVIR, about her studies, about anti-Semitic faces in her classroom. If her handsome, clever, and amazing Vytas wanted her to go with him to Leningrad, Sonia would follow him without hesitation. They would never part again.

"Vytas, what we should do now?"

"My dear girl, I am still so weak. I want to go back to bed to have a good rest." Vytas had not even kissed her yet. He left to go home. Sonia went dancing that night by herself. She felt sorry for her dreams about this meeting with Vytas, for her talking to and looking at his photo for hours, for her long faithfulness.

Before Vytas had arrived, Sonia had purchased two tickets to a concert for the following week. But Vytas did not feel like going to the concert either.

"Sonechka, my headache is killing me. I would rather stay in the room. There is a very good program on the radio."

After the concert Sonia could not fall asleep. She tossed from one side of her bed to other till 5 a.m. and then dozed off. The first thing Sonia did the moment her eyes were open was to open her window to look at the clear blue sky and green tree outside her window. Nothing moved, the world seemed frozen. She surprised herself by writing a note for Vytas.

Goodbye, dear Vytas. Enough is enough. I don't want your love any more. The magic is gone. Goodbye!

Then Sonia removed his photo from the piano. She was nineteen. She was free.

When Vytas arrived two days later, he noticed his photo was missing.

"Don't sit down. I want to talk to you, but not here."

Sonia suggested a walk. They walked silently along the river for a few minutes, then stopped at their favourite sunken bench. Sonia tried to explain herself, asked him not to be angry with her, to forgive her if he could. The truth was, her love was gone. She could do nothing about it. It was not only her fault. Vytas had acted very coldly toward her at times, while at the same time calling her his bride, his "wife."

"Love is like flowers. If you don't water them, the roots dry up."

She had already received five rejections for her application to leave for Israel. At the same time, Sonia sincerely hoped she would eventually be allowed to leave for the free west.

In the very beginning of her third year, Sonia was again called to AVIR. What else did they want to know?

Sonia had walked past the yellowish, five story building opposite Kutuzov Square many times. Security affairs and police headquarters were concentrated in this one building with its dark windows. For Sonia, it was like an old acquaintance. There she had met all types of old, young, hairy, bald, impatient, and friendly officers over last few years. She arrived expecting to hear the same answer. Their favourite words were, "Your request is unreasonable."

But for Sonia, it was very reasonable to leave the Soviet Union. After crossing the border, she could go wherever she wished; she could say whatever was on her mind. She could even buy an expensive fur coat without explaining where she got money to buy it. What a shitty country. Unreasonable to leave!?

Sonia sat impatiently in the waiting room, frustrated about wasting her time. Sonia asked,

"Did I have to sit there for so many hours to hear the same answer again?" Sonia asked when finally called in. "Why did you call me?"

"Sonia Ostianko, we have received permission for you to go to live with your mother in Haifa. You can leave and go to Israel," the handsome officer with grey hair told her.

"When?"

"Anytime you wish. Is there any particular country you would like to visit before arriving in Israel?"

Sonia didn't understand his question.

"You require visa for the places you are interested in visiting." Seeing that she had nothing to say, he said, "What about France, Italy, England?"

"Am I allowed to go to all those countries?"

"Sure. We want you to be happy, to have a good time. And if you ever want to come back, you are always welcome."

Sonia felt a tingle through her spine. Her heart stopped for a split second, then began to bounce and jump.

"Please bring us six photos, and we will issue you a passport with visas."

Sonia flew through the streets. Her big eyes were trying to register every corner she saw in order to hold it in her memory. She would never come back. Never! Ever! There was so much joy in her heart but also the fear that it was only a fantasy or a bad joke someone was playing on her. What if something prevented it from happening? She had a secret in her heart, but there was nobody with whom she could share it. Now, how to tell it to Mama? Was it true? What if there was a mistake? What if they got different instructions tomorrow?

The day turned into a song; turned stones to flowers. Sonia was flying, hardly touching the ground, holding in her heart this fragile thread of belief that it was true.

She took a trolley ride in both directions, bursting with joy and full of the selfish desire to keep her secret private. If only the other passengers knew how lucky she was to be leaving soon, while they could only fantasize about it for the rest of their lives.

"I am leaving, I am going, I am lucky, I am happy…" her heart sang.

From this very moment, Sonia no longer belonged to this city anymore. She was jubilantly saying good-bye to the familiar buildings, streets, sidewalks, bridges, the snaking river, and to everything her eyes could catch. None of the people looking at the young girl with a twinkle in her eyes could guess that her lungs inhaled different air, the fresh, unfamiliar, seductive, enticing air of anticipated freedom.

Sonia calmed down a bit as she approached her house, knowing that Mama was waiting with a delicious meal. Mama had never interfered with Sonia's applications and her dream of leaving the Soviet Union. Mama understood the Soviet system, did not trust it, and didn't believe Sonia would ever be given permission to leave, no matter how many times she tried. Mama felt sad for Sonia who she thought was spoiling her own chances for a promising career with her efforts to leave. How could Sonia face Mama at this instant with her ravishing joy over receiving permission to leave?

Unable to face Mama right now, Sonia turned around and slowly walked toward the bewitching narrow streets where one could see from one apartment into another, where only horse-drawn carriages could squeeze through. Good-bye my Vilna, good-bye my Vilnius, good-bye my childhood, good-bye my adolescence. Unexpected sadness crept inside her chest, chasing away her bubbling joy and making her nervous. Now how to tell Mama?

In a few days Sonia received her passport. Still fresh in her memory was her visit to the Israeli Consulate in Moscow. Sonia had been told that if she ever got her exit VISA, immediately come to them. Go to Moscow? It was much farther to travel from Vilnius to Moscow than from Vilnius to the border at Chop. What if there was a war tomorrow? Oh God, please not now, not when she was still here in the Soviet Union.

Maybe Dadia Kolia was right. The train would not take her to Vienna, but to Siberia. Whatever scenario it presented, Sonia was in a hurry to choose the shortest itinerary needed to leave the Soviet Union. Sonia did not want to take any chances. She wanted to leave as soon as possible!

Sonia purchased her ticket to cross at the nearest and only border one was allowed to cross into Eastern Europe: Vilnius to Chop in the Ukraine, then Chop to Budapest, then Budapest to Vienna. She would contact the Israeli authorities from Vienna to bring her to Israel.

Sonia was beaming awaiting something wonderful, unknown, and enticing ahead of her. What was left behind would stay only as a memory. She was choosing the other side of the border for the rest of her life.

Sonia tried to convince Mama how much she loved her and would always love her. She talked late into the night and Mama listened. Eventually Sonia fell asleep in the armchair. Mama moved her into a clean, starchy bed with a downy quilt.

Sonia heard Dadia Kolia wake up at the crack of dawn. She heard Irina going to the toilet and Malka talking to her kids in the dining room. Sonia stretched lazily in her tall bed, then went back to sleep.

"Mamochka, what time it is?" Sonia asked, a few hours later.

"Sleep, sleep. It is only noon."

"So late! Mama, you should have woken me up."

Sonia hurriedly put on her new, silk, Chinese housecoat Mama had bought her for her twentieth birthday. From the kitchen came the aroma of fried potatoes and sizzling veal cutlets. Hiding in a low, green, velvet armchair, Dadia Kolia was finishing his first pack of cigarettes for the day. Sonia tried to read from his sour face how he felt about her leaving for Israel. He did not seem to believe that she had a passport and could just go.

"What if the train takes you to Siberia instead of Vienna?" said Dadia Kolia, provoking her.

"Kolia, leave her alone. Don't scare her," Mama interfered.

What if he is right, crossed Sonia's mind.

"I'm not leaving because I need another mother. You are my only real mother. I love everything about you Mama, Mamochka, you have to try to understand. If not you, then who else would understand? It is me, your Sonka, whom you love. Nobody ever is going to replace you. I am leaving because I want to be free. I want to live in truth, without fear. I want to be Jewish, but in a way that neither you nor I should feel ashamed about."

Mama kept quiet.

"What are you thinking? Mamochka, say something."

"You should be prepared to say good-bye to your studies, to your brilliant career."

"Mamochka, I never wanted to be an engineer in the first place. I don't like science. The only reason I studied engineering is because it does not depend on language. I would rather study law or literature."

"In Israel, they will find you a tailor or a shoemaker for a husband."

"Mama, look at me. You know me. You know that I would never allow anyone to arrange my marriage. I want to be in love with my husband. I want a soulmate for a partner."

Mama came with Sonia to the train station. Three-storied cement buildings undistinguishable from one another boringly lined the skinny river that separated the old, medieval part of the city with its Gothic St. Anne Cathedral, admired by Napoleon himself, from the new, cheaply constructed buildings according to Stalin's five-year plan. One couldn't see the faded pastel colours of the old, mansions built in the beginning of the twentieth century behind the grey, washed-out apartment houses and office structures.

At the train station, just before Sonia was ready to go inside her coach, Mama started to cry. Mama had worn her best, all-season, black, cashmere coat and a silky, burgundy scarf. She wore her black shoes with the little heel that she saved for special occasions, usually for going to church.

"Mama, mamochka, please understand that I am not leaving because I don't love you. It is better for both of us. I will be able to help you more from there. Believe me." Sonia was hugging her Mama and crying together with her.

"Sonechka, I don't think we will ever meet again."

"Mamochka, what are you saying? I will come back to visit many times."

"Don't. If you do, they may not let you out again. Go already. Your train is leaving soon."

"Not yet. How can I go if you are crying?" Sonia kissed Mama's salty cheeks and hands. She had always wondered how those hard-working hands stayed so beautiful and so soft, showing only one little, blue, swollen vein pulsating close to the skin.

"Go already. Don't worry about me."

As the warning whistle cut the air, Sonia saw more tears on Mama's stoic face.

"Mama, why do you cry?"

"One gets used even to a dog. You are going far away. I will never see you again."

The last whistle of the train sounded. Sonia climbed inside the train and stopped on the stairs.

"Mama! Mamochka!" Sonia shouted, violently waving her hands.

The last glimpse she caught was of Mama waving back with her right hand and wiping away her tears with her left.

Mama was right. Sonia never saw her again.

The Chop–Budapest train was old and shabby. A middle-aged army major sat across from Sonia, enjoying his salami sandwich with homemade, sour pickles. Sonia was suspicious whether he was sent to follow her.

"Would you like some?" the man offered to share his food.

"No, thank you. I am not hungry."

Sonia really was hungry but very much afraid in case it was poison he planned to offer.

In the next compartment, a noisy group of Georgian students, definitely tourists, were laughing loudly and taking up a lot of space. Sonia thought of walking over to join them, but they may despise her for leaving the Soviet Union for good.

The train finally arrived to Budapest. Sonia had to change stations to transfer to the train heading toward Vienna. Afraid of being followed, she hid in the bathroom until everyone left the station. Sonia stayed there for more than two hours before venturing out. She then hailed a taxi to take her to the other end of the city.

"Where are you from?" asked the young taxi driver as he zoomed expertly through the narrow streets.

"I am from Vilnius, Soviet Union."

"Oh, I like the Soviet Union. I am Communist too," the young man confessed, proudly.

My God, thought Sonia, *this was all she needed. A real Communist to drive her.*

"How much am I to pay?" Sonia asked, giving him her only bill of a hundred rubles.

It was all she had been allowed to take with her.

"Keep it, I don't have a change for so much money."

"Don't joke. I want to pay you."

"It is my present. I am a Communist, you are a Communist. We are comrades. It is on me," he said with a sincere smile.

The train to Vienna was empty. It was very elegant with green, leather seats. At the next stop, an older gentleman walked over and sat across from Sonia. He was dressed in funny shorts and knee-length socks.

They sat in silence. When the frontier patrol appeared in front of Sonia and asked for her documents, Sonia, not sure what they were asking for, grabbed her suitcase. In the confusion, she dropped it on the floor and was mortified to see her stuff fly out.

The older gentleman helped her put it all back, quickly and orderly, to her complete embarrassment. Sonia figured out that she needed to show her passport. She had to excuse herself to go to the bathroom to fetch it from her brassiere.

When they arrived in Vienna, Sonia walked off the train and was amazed that a train station could be so spectacular. It was already dark outside. She walked slowly down the stairs. On her lips, her shoulders, and even her ankles, Sonia felt the aromatic breath of light, free air. She closed her eyes to cherish this spellbinding moment.

"Excuse me." Someone gently touched her shoulder. It was the gentleman from her compartment. He was holding her tattered, brown suitcase.

"You actually left this behind."

Sonia had no idea what to do next. She was free, in a free world. There was nothing to be afraid of anymore. She showed the older gentleman her passport. He opened it to the page stamped by the Israeli Consulate in Moscow and then led her to a public phone. Apparently, he intended to make a phone call on her behalf.

Sonia was very grateful that he took his time to look for numbers. Unfortunately, no one picked up the phone. What neither of them realized was that it was the evening of Yom Kippur, the holiest day in the Jewish calendar.

The gentleman hailed a taxi and brought Sonia to a beautiful building in the centre of Vienna. He went inside to talk to reception and came back with a key. Sonia understood that this was where she was supposed to stay for the night. He left without saying his name.

Sonia was literally standing in the threshold from old world to new. Stunned by the many ravishing women in the lobby and the opulence of the hotel, Sonia relished her luxurious room with the big, soft bed. The evening coolness touched the shutters, the heavy, crimson drapes with gold tassels, and her burning, pink cheeks.

Bang, bang, bang! Loud noise. Sonia was woken up.

When she opened the door, there was a man talking extremely fast in a language she had never heard before. She began to understand that he was Israeli and that they had to leave this gorgeous hotel. He was taking her somewhere else, maybe to a plane going to Israel. Sonia was ready in five minutes. There was nothing to pack.

The Israeli looked like an athlete. He was a broad-shouldered, six-foot-tall man, with curly black hair, straight, white teeth, and a rough voice. He brought her to a messy office on the second floor of a modest building. Apparently, her strange friend from the train had managed to reach someone from the Jewish Agency who was working in his office on Yom Kippur. He was a secular Israeli from a *kibbutz*. He seemed to be agitated that the hotel she was brought to was much too expensive to stay.

"What do you want me to do?"

He didn't understand Russian. Sonia didn't know any other language besides a bit of Polish and some Lithuanian, but not Hebrew or German.

He allowed her to go out for a few hours as long as she came back on time and did not talk to any strangers. She was going to stay here until he organized her journey to Israel.

Sonia walked for hours, admiring the richness of window displays, the magnificent, well-kept parks, and the stunning buildings. The park benches were used by young mothers, older men, and grey-haired grandmothers with light metal frames resting on the tips of their noses who were busy knitting.

The next day Sonia was put on the train to Trieste, and from there on the boat going to Haifa.

On the boat, there were many decks and many people, mostly tourists from Israel returning home, but also groups of people from Rumania immigrating to Israel. There was nobody to whom she could speak. Some officers tried to start a conversation with her in Greek or English, but Sonia just smiled and said nothing.

She met a tall, handsome, Greek Orthodox priest wearing a long, black cassock with a large, gold cross on top of it. He looked so much like Dadia Kolia.

"Why are you going to Israel?" Sonia said, approaching him on the deck.

He looked straight at her and smiled, answering in his native Greek. It was pretty frustrating.

Sonia walked from deck to deck, looking at all the interesting strangers. An elegant, older couple was sitting outside getting a suntan. The woman wore a red dress. They looked English. A much older couple was settled cozily on long, comfortable chairs reading books. As Sonia passed by, she heard them speaking Russian. Wow!

"Are you from Israel?" she asked.

"We are. And you?"

"I am going there to live with my mother."

Miriam and Haim Goldberg invited Sonia to join them for dinner. They were originally from Poland and had immigrated to Israel three years ago. They had just been on vacation, spending two weeks in Europe—mainly Italy. They were cultured and interesting to talk with. Sonia spent the rest of her time on the boat with them.

The Goldbergs had one son studying at Technion in Haifa.

"I believe you and Boris would be good friends. You have a lot of common. Boris is a very bright and kind young man." Miriam seemed eager to have Sonia and Boris meet as soon as possible.

Far away in Vilnius, the golden fall was fading, zealously grasping the last warm rays of the autumn sun, yet scarcely heating its bare, and by now, withered bones. Here, in the calm, blue Mediterranean Sea, the sun was enticingly kissing the sleepy and salty waters. The sky, fluffy with white clouds, gazed lazily into the velvet smoothness. Faint splashes on the ship's prow lulled Sonia into deep dreams.

A surprising enthusiastic noise woke Sonia up. For most of the passengers, the approaching view of Haifa with its golden Bahai Temple was a well-known site. Still, seeing it in real life was a truly emotional experience. Sonia thought of the Taj Mahal while looking at the temple's golden dome. Sonia didn't understand Rumanian, but she watched as passengers pushed each other to look at the majestic panorama of this ancient, magical port.

The ship anchored. A message calling for Sonia to disembark was broadcasted in Hebrew, English, Yiddish, and Rumanian, but Sonia didn't know any of these languages so she didn't relate to the message. Sonia allowed herself to be absorbed in the vibrating, emotional turmoil around her. She was in no hurry; she had finally arrived.

Someone approached Sonia and asked her to follow him down the stairs. The very moment Sonia touched the ground, she found herself looking into the same wide eyes like hers. The feeling was very similar as at the airport in Vilnius.

But at the same time much different now. Sonia was here, willing to be a daughter to Raisa. Raisa was not a stranger anymore. Sonia and

Raisa hugged, uninvited excitement tickle in her throat, and her tears came without permission. She was holding onto the person who gave her life, her heritage; she was the reason Sonia was where she was at this moment.

"Sonia?" Her mother's face was so close. "My prayers are answered."

Raisa quickly pulled Sonia away from a crowd that was busy with necessities for immigration. Sonia had no need for any of that. She followed Raisa to a taxi. It was a short ride through what looked like paradise. Never before had Sonia seen real palms. There was a lot of them; there were fascinating stone homes surrounded by lush trees and many colourful flowers. What a breathtaking ride. It was like a dream!

Raisa's apartment was on the ground floor of a three-story house. It was small, but cozy. An apartment had two rooms. The one you walked into from the street was very dramatic looking. It had big windows with heavy, wine-coloured drapes, a large, deep, red-coloured sofa, a mahogany, Victorian antique cabinet with porcelain figurines, and many photos on the walls. It didn't have much furniture, but it was very impressive.

"This is your father." Raisa stopped in front of a faded photo, obviously enlarged from a very small photograph.

A handsome, smiling face looked straight at Sonia. Wow! Sonia's heart jumped. Her father?

"How old is he in this photo?"

"Twenty-four. It was his passport picture. We needed a passport to go on our honeymoon. It kept me alive for three years. He knew where I was," Raisa said, starting to cry.

"Please, please don't cry." Sonia didn't know what to say or what to do. She sat next to Raisa on the red sofa, stroking her gently.

"Who do I look like more, like you or like him?"

"Like both of us. I am not sure, more like him, I think. I was very beautiful at your age."

Raisa couldn't stop talking about Sonia's father; she talked about how she met him, what a wonderful husband he was, and what an amazing father he made. It was a true love story. Sonia went to sleep hoping to see him in her dreams.

Bright Israeli sun seeped through the drapes and kissed her eyes. Sonia was in a daze. For a split second, she didn't remember where she was. She didn't recognize the room or the bed. Then she remembered. It was too early to get up.

"Sonechka, hurry. Hurry up. Don't pretend you are sleeping. I know you are awake. A young girl your age has to jump up early in the morning, ready to start a day. God forbid the neighbours find out that you like to sleep so late. It isn't a custom in our country."

"I am not ready. I still want to doze off." Sonia pulled the blanket over her head.

"No. Listen to your mother. I understand you were not taught to listen." With a big smile showing her perfect teeth, Raisa pulled off the bedcover. "Please do it quickly. Dress yourself, and join me in the kitchen."

"Let us have breakfast together. It is late, ten o'clock already. Please make yourself an omelet. I have fresh eggs from a farm," Raisa said when Sonia walked in the kitchen.

It wasn't really a room; it was just a corner with a stove, a small refrigerator, and a round table enough for two people.

"I don't like eggs," Sonia lied, shy to admit she had never made an omelet. Sonia never spent time in the kitchen back home. She always ate in the big dining room. Mama was the one in the kitchen preparing their meals.

"Sonechka, you really shouldn't be so picky. I bet in your poor Russia that you ate whatever was available."

Raisa had registered Sonia for Hebrew lessons at Ulpan in Bat Galim near the ocean. Every morning she gave Sonia one Israeli pound for her bus fare and lunch.

During the first few days, Sonia thought that she could never learn this strange language with its unbelievably complicated alphabet. Most of the people in her class were middle-aged Rumanians with adult children. They lived at Ulpan. Between themselves, they spoke in their own native language discussing money, jobs, and loans; they were impatient to learn a new language and yet eager to know just enough to start working as soon as possible. Being young, Sonia felt liked by the people around her, but she could not have much conversation with them.

Sonia was mesmerized by the colourful crowds on the streets wherever she happened to be. She saw a tall girl with green eyes and long, red hair; a short, bald man with a small nose; a person darker than any Negro Sonia ever saw in the movies or in pictures, and a pretty woman in a sari. They all astounded her by being Jewish.

In Vilnius, you could immediately recognize a Jewish person on the street. One of her main concerns was that people on the streets of Israel would be short and fat; that women would mostly have dark, curly hair like Malka. Not here. It was thrilling to be part of this exciting crowd, to be different yet like others at the same time. To be, to feel, Jewish.

"How do you like it here?" asked an elderly woman who worked as a secretary at Ulpan.

She still spoke excellent Russian after forty years in Palestine.

"I love it here. I feel good to be a Jew in Israel. This must be the only place on the planet where you don't think about it. You just are. In Vilnius, it was so different. One was immediately singled out as being or looking Jewish. Besides, you can travel from Haifa to Tel Aviv and stay there without being registered. You could not stay in somebody's house in Vilnius or in Moscow or in any place in the Soviet Union without special permission from the authorities. In Israel, it isn't like that. It's amazing. There's so much freedom!"

It was promising to be an exceptionally exciting day in Sonia's life. Dana Avidar, the stunning daughter of Jamima and Joseph Avidar, whom she met at the Israeli Consulate in Moscow, was coming to Haifa to meet Sonia and to take her on a small tour. Sonia understood very little Hebrew, but Dana did speak some Russian.

Dana was a *madricha*. In fact, Dana was taking Sonia along with a group of young girls, ages twelve to fifteen, that she was guiding. She would show them part of the country and teach them about Jewish traditions and history.

In her strong and alluring voice, Dana sang Israeli songs. Dana knew a lot of Israeli songs, and she knew how to tell interesting stories. Her boundless energy and her passionate love for the country was inspiring, contagious, and precious.

Dana's warm smile and laughter made everyone on the bus laugh with her stories. Sonia didn't understand a word. Dana spoke in English for students visiting from the United States, but the atmosphere, mood, and cheerful excitement floating in the air, along with the exhilarating touch of new freedom, stirred new and unknown emotions within Sonia.

Sonia could not believe how well these innocent American teenagers acted and how groomed they were. The girls seemed to be captivated by

Dana's energy, her spirit, and her beauty. Sonia was too. She could not take her eyes from Dana, wishing she could be like her.

As their bus rolled through the charming coastline of Haifa and up north toward Safed, Dana taught the teens Hebrew, told Bible stories, and talked about her beloved country, Israel. The American teenagers were so sweet, so refreshing and so kind. Sonia could not believe her eyes or ears. Dana got a kick out of Sonia's astonishment.

"Did you imagine American teenagers to be mean monsters?"- Dana teased her with her perfect smile.

"Kind of."- Sonia laughed at her question.

Sonia thought Dana was gorgeous. She was tall and strong, with green eyes, and a straight, Greek nose. A thick, reddish braid hung over her shoulder. Dana looked very much like her father, Joseph. Intimidated by Dana, Sonia nevertheless fell in love with her. If Sonia had a choice to be like anybody else on the entire planet, she would like to be Dana Avidar. She felt like a little ugly duckling next to her ravishing new friend.

Sonia stayed with them in Safed for three days. When Dana took her kids to Galil, Sonia went back to Haifa. It was hard to part. These had been the happiest days for Sonia in Israel so far. Dana invited Sonia to visit her in Jerusalem.

One afternoon, Boris Goldberg, the son of Miriam and Haim Goldberg whom Sonia had met on the boat, appeared in front of their door. Boris was elegantly dressed; he looked very different from other Israelis. He was tall and straight and wore a silk foulard around his tanned neck. There was an aristocratic aura around him. Miriam clearly put a lot of energy into bringing him up European. Raisa was surprised and impressed.

Boris did not ask any questions, and he let Sonia choose what to do. Apparently, Boris was a great dancer and liked modern music. But Sonia did not know modern dancing. In the end, they went to see the Israeli play *Fiddler on the Roof*. Sonia's Hebrew was pretty bad, but she did enjoy the play. Boris tried to explain to Sonia what was happening.

"Would you like to see an Opera this week?" Boris asked before leaning over and kissing her on her cheeks while saying good-bye.

He was intelligent, kind, and gentle, but Sonia was not attracted to him. She wanted an Israeli type, a *sabra*. They went out a few more times.

"How was your date? Boris seems an educated and promising young man," Raisa said one evening.

"I am confused. He is actually very different and intelligent, but somehow, I am not excited enough. I want to be in love."

"Sonia, you live in a fantasy world. Romances are in movies. A movie is two hours long. You need a serious and responsible man to build a family."

"Right. But it has to feel like the right man, a man I am attracted to. I want to be in love like you were."

"Be realistic. You are not very pretty. Nobody will fall in love with you from first sight. Have patience. Before you arrived, I was thinking about it. There is a young professor at Technion from Poland. Joshua Steg. I met him already. He is a little older than you and is very bright. I am working with his aunt, Sara. She is from Vilnius. He is very suitable for you. He is looking for a serious, smart wife."

"I don't want a matchmaker like in the *shtetl* before the war. I will find a man myself."

"You cannot be too choosy. You are fat and not very pretty, but you are clever."

Sonia could not believe what she heard. Mama would never, ever say that! Fat? Mama always insisted that Sonia eat well, gain some weight, and not be too skinny. It wasn't healthy to be just bones. Sonia wanted to say something mean, something sarcastic, but she swallowed, counted to seven, and said nothing.

She called her new friend Dana the next day to talk about Boris and about Raisa's comments.

"Sonia, don't take it so personally. Your mother wanted to be helpful. You are very young, very naïve; you are a beautiful and innocent soul. You don't have to look for a husband."

"Dana, how will I know when the right person comes along?"

"Your heart will know. The heart does not lie. We can easily fool others, but we cannot fool ourselves."

"I just want to be excited, to be in love."

"I know, I understand. Me too. We all do."

Sonia could sleep in on Saturdays. There was no Ulpan.

"I am perplexed by how much sleep you need. At your age, I jumped out of bed with the sun." Sonia heard Raisa's voice before she opened her eyes after a deep sleep with interesting dreams. It was annoying to hear this comment again, but Sonia bit her lip. She wanted to stay in bed with her eyes closed and recapture her dreams.

"Sonechka, I heard that you were lazy. In Russia, it is a cultural thing. Everyone is lazy. Nobody pays, nobody works. But here, in Israel, laziness is the biggest shame. God forbid someone should find out."

Who could complain to Raisa that she was lazy?

"What is for breakfast?" Sonia asked, walking into Raisa's spotless kitchen.

"Open the fridge and take whatever you want. You don't expect me to serve you, do you?" Raisa's perpetual smile was starting to irritate Sonia. But Raisa was one hundred percent right. Sonia expected to be served. This was what Mama had done. Mama served her breakfast, lunch, and dinner; every single meal. Mama was always in the kitchen ready to serve.

"Don't stand there like an invalid. Take a healthy yogurt for breakfast," Raisa suggested.

"I don't like yogurt."

"Don't play princess with me. I know exactly what life was like in Vilna for you. You may fool others, tell them stories, but not me. What did you have there? I have seen it with my own eyes. Two small, dark rooms and an old, sick woman. You were obeying her like a little doggie." Anger rose from a very small spot in Sonia's stomach, reached her throat and choked her. She left the kitchen and walked out to the fresh air to be outside. Sonia briskly walked dawn, almost running, all the way to the blue ocean.

What was Mama doing by now? Would she ever forgive Sonia for leaving? How were Irina and Dadia Kolia? Do they despise her? Did they think about her at all? Maybe they decided to forget about her. She hadn't gotten any letters yet. Maybe Mama had written her a letter but Raisa decided not to give it to her?

Sonia passed what was most probably a synagogue. She could tell by the way people who walked into the building were dressed. Sonia had never been in a synagogue. She was tempted to go in, but she wasn't dressed appropriately.

The cool air calmed her down. The pain in her stomach went away. She should talk to Raisa about Mama; she should open her eyes to what a wonderful, kind, and noble person her Mama always was and is. Sonia knew that after the war, Mama let Raisa stay in the salon for a full year, helped Raisa escape from Vilnius, and protected her from the Soviets. Why did Raisa talk so ugly about Mama now?

13

(Voice of Israel)

Me and my daughter?
When Sonia is really lonely and miserable, she tries to talk to me. She begs me to help her. She knows I will protect her. Really, she is a good girl. She has no fear. Sonia is a social animal like I was, much more like me than like her mother, my sweet, dear Raisa. I worry about her. There are two different yet precious women in my soul. I spend a lot of time thinking about them and talking to Hashem.

Raisa was always so pedantic. Everything had to be in its place. I remember when we were just married, I loved to read the Yiddish newspaper. She would fold it carefully, like new, before throwing it out.

I sensed there would be trouble when Sonia arrived at age twenty to live with Raisa. Subtle trouble. Different approaches, very different temperaments. It was never easy for Raisa to take another person's side. She had to have her way, to explain again and again what the right thing to do was under all circumstances. But Raisa was so young and so beautiful. I could never get upset with her. I melted under her charms, her coquettish seductiveness. Most of all, I appreciated her love and endless devotion for me.

When Sonia was born, Raisa adored our baby. She would look at her for hours. She talked to her as if she were a grown-up person. The baby was only two months old when Raisa sang her Yiddish songs and told her Yiddish stories. Her Yiddish was so rich. She wrote poetry in Yiddish, mostly love poems for me. Then she wrote funny little poems for our baby.

Raisa is a different person today. Sonia doesn't know her the way I know her. For my daughter, Sonechka, Raisa is not cute and charming.

Sonia had a loving mother in Vilnius, a mother for whom she could do no wrong. Sonia knows what a mother's love means. Raisa cannot compete with Elena Stepanovna. Her preaching and well-intentioned teaching falls on deaf ears. It annoys Sonia. She is bored, tired of Raisa's talking. She does not want to be treated as a child. At twenty, Sonia feels herself to be a confident, attractive, and intelligent woman. She does not want to be told what to do. She doesn't need another mother. Sonia wants Raisa to be her friend, but not at the expense of disloyalty to Elena Stepanovna. Guilt of leaving Elena Stepanovna is hurting her. For long time now, Sonia has had dreams about going back to visit her but then not being able to leave Vilnius again.

Raisa lives in the past. She is deeply depressed. Raisa has nightmares. She takes a lot of tranquilizers and doesn't want to talk to other people. She is not very present in her everyday life, but she did put all her energy into getting Sonia out of Vilnius. She wants Sonia to appreciate it, to not take it for granted. Coming from very traditional and religious home, Raisa is angry with Hashem; she no longer lets Him into her heart. If God did exist, He is too cruel for her to communicate. She lost everything. She is not able to forgive. My Raisa is no more. She changed; she wilted like a flower. From a happy, dancing butterfly, my Raisa turned into a sour turtle with stooped shoulders and a whispery, hoarse voice.

For all these years, Raisa had dreamed her life would change when Sonia came to live with her.

Raisa goes to the office on time, but she is never totally there. Her body is there, but her mind, her thoughts, are far away. She finds it much easier to talk to her dead mother, to her father, to her sister Leah and to me than to strangers who seem to live their lives as if the horrible war didn't happen. Her dead family is more alive to her than her neighbours who find her aloof, stiff, and unfriendly. Raisa has no patience for small talk. She feels that if she did choose to talk to them and to share her story, they would never understand. Maybe staying hidden in a hole underground for three years gives her right to keep silent and to try to appear sane.

Our Sonia knew nothing about the war. In Soviet Russia, they didn't tell them what happened to our people. Since arriving in Israel, Raisa decided that her mission in life, her reason for living, was to save Sonia from Soviet occupation and to give Sonia the chance of a good life in Israel. In her eyes, Sonia should be grateful.

In the beginning, Sonia was excited to have a young mother of thirty-nine after all these years of having a mother who seemed an old person to everyone else. Raisa wrote to her again and again saying that she, Raisa, was young, pretty, and had very sophisticated taste. When they met, they would be best friends. They would go shopping together. She, Raisa, would teach Sonia everything that the old Russian lady couldn't teach her. Sonia was very curious about what that could be. There seemed to be nothing that her Mama didn't know or that her Mama didn't understand. Sonia could share everything with Elena Stepanovna.

I never understood why my sweet girl had such little self-confidence as a child. Sometimes I think that the fact that Raisa left for Poland without her affected Sonia subconsciously. She may not be aware of it, but there is a complicated sense of abandonment deep down that manifests in many unpredictable ways. Raisa was very young and very damaged emotionally; she could not function as a normal person after spending three years in a dark hole. Raisa had nightmares about seeing the dead bodies of her family covered in blood on the fresh snow. Who could ever get over that? At first, she thought that I was killed in Ponary the night they took us from the Orlovich barn. There were many nights she wanted to die!

Then she found out that I had managed to send a message to my mother in the ghetto that I was alive and well, playing in the orchestra. Raisa hoped I would survive. Her body had survived, but her soul was shattered.

I watch over her and pray for her. She talks to me every night. She asks me what to do with Sonia. I answer her in her dreams, but she hardly sleeps and usually wakes with a headache. Somehow it is this Raisa, not my beautiful bride, who entered Sonia's consciousness. To be rejected by her seemed like trivial information for Sonia, but was it really trivial?

Sonia did not love herself enough. In her heart, Sonia felt rejected by her classmates as a teenager, not feeling as smart or as pretty as the other girls in her class. But this was not true. She was clever, energetic, and quick, and had a phenomenal memory. All the teachers liked her, and they often asked her to perform in front of her class. It was easy for her. She did not think much of it. Sonia was first to finish any assignment, in math or in literature. Others were impressed, but Sonia did not notice. Larisa liked her, but Sonia somehow felt surprised and privileged that Larisa wanted to be her friend. Sonia could not imagine that her tall and beautiful friend Larisa was jealous of her spontaneity, her ability to talk to strangers, and her boundless energy.

Many years later, Larisa would tell Sonia how much she valued and admired her. But as a teenager, Sonia felt unattractive. Whenever they went skating, the boys asked other girls to skate with them. She was never asked. She was simply younger than the other girls and not yet at the age that boys noticed.

"Nobody will ever fall in love with you at first sight, but once they get to know you, they will love you," Larisa had told her. Sonia had never forgotten this comment. It was painful to hear at twelve. For her, it meant she was ugly. Sonia had read enough books about a young, handsome man seeing a girl for the first time and immediately falling in love with her. It definitely was her dream. Brought up on heavily exaggerated romance novels, Sonia dreamed about being swept away and happy forever.

Now they are in conflict, my Raisa and my precious child. When in distress, they both talk to me. They complain about each other. I am watching over them, trying to figure out how to help!

Raisa wanted her daughter next to her heart and to be able to teach her the way her mother taught her. In Raisa's mind, Elena Stepanovna must be a good person, but she had her own two daughters. She was a stranger, after all. Who knows why she kept Sonia all those years? Raisa believed that Elena Stepanovna expected Sonia to take care of her in old age. Now they were really poor, not like before the war. Raisa did imagine Sonechka not having enough to eat, but who knows?

At Ulpan, Sonia was popular and made many friends. Boris occasionally came to pick her up on his motorcycle. She rarely invited him to the house. Once they stayed in the doorway talking and laughing until midnight.

The next morning, just before Sonia was to leave for Ulpan, Raisa approached her with a smile and gently touched her left shoulder.

"Darling, I have to tell you something. You see, my dear daughter, I may look very young, but I am as smart as if I were one hundred years old. I have more brains in my finger than you will ever have in your head. I believe you know it already."

"What do you want to say? I don't want to be late for my classes." Sonia was visible annoyed with Raisa's smile, with her sugary voice.

"Wait, don't be in such a hurry. A mother's advice is a rare privilege that you never had, so you don't appreciate it. I would gladly give ten years of my life to have my mother next to me, to hear her advice."

"What do you want to tell me?"

"Don't be so nervous, so impatient. I have read many books in my life. I am especially strong in psychology. I can see through you, understand you better than you understand yourself. All your thinking is as clear to me as if it was laid in the palm of my hand."

"What is it? Say it already!"

"Don't raise your voice. Listen quietly. Last night you thought I was sleeping. The truth is that a mother cannot sleep if a daughter your age is out. You can do whatever you want, but not in front of our house. We live in a very respectable area. A girl's reputation is all that she has. God forbid if one wrong word is spoken. Nobody will ever want to marry you. It is like spoiled fruit."

"What are you talking about?"

"I understand that a girl your age needs a man. This is how girls are brought up in Russia. Soon you are going to Technion. There are hundreds of boys. You can pick anyone you want, nobody will know, but be careful bringing someone here."

"I don't get it."

"Sonechka, I have something important to suggest. Already when you were in Vilno, I was planning your future. There is a very suitable man I would like you to meet. I told you about him before, but you rejected my clever offer. His parents were Polish citizens, perished. He arrived in Israel a few years ago from Vilna. He is a professor at Technion. He is very respected and very suitable for you."

"Ima, I heard it before. I am not interested in matchmaking."

"If there is someone who fits the bill, don't miss the opportunity. In life, sometimes we are deaf when the right opportunity knocks on the door."

"I am not thinking about marriage."

"You are right. You can wait, but why miss a good chance? I know his aunt. I spoke to her already. We can go there for the Sabbath meal. Should I call her to make arrangements?"

"Absolutely not. I don't believe in matchmakers. I will find my own man. Just forget about it." Angry, Sonia slammed the door and ran out.

Sonia felt good at Ulpan and hated to go home after classes. Usually, she took a bus. On this day, the late afternoon sun, with its shimmering rays, gently stroked treetops and roofs of appealing private homes, while slowly disappearing on the horizon. It was getting dark early this time of the year. The banana-shaped moon chased the light away as the palm's contours majestically drew a skyline.

Sonia walked home from her bus stop at Marcaz Carmel, watching how people flocked to the streets, cracked sunflower seeds, bought falafel, and ate freshly cooked corn. There were flowers sprouting regally in a little park. They had flaming orange spikes pierced with blue, proudly stretching out of a cocoon-like, green bed. They radiated, claiming royalty and privileged rights in the kingdom of flowers. Their delicate beauty filled her heart with peace and appreciation. They took her breath away. Sonia had never seen something so sublime.

The moment Sonia stepped into the apartment, she felt a drastic change; there was unpleasant tension inside her stomach. Raisa noticed her angry mood.

"Sonia, you are very stupid and ungrateful. Before, you had two mothers. But the way you are behaving, you may end up with none," she warned her daughter. "Remember, there are no bad mothers, only bad daughters. If I wanted, I could send you back to Russia."

Sonia had arrived in Israel in a yellow, light summer dress, but her shoes were too hot to wear. She wanted to get sandals like everyone else. Following Raisa's instructions in her last letter, Sonia had brought nothing but herself to Israel. Her small, brown suitcase just had some underwear, two brassieres, a few photographs and books.

"What should I wear tomorrow to Ulpan? I have only this yellow dress," Sonia asked Raisa.

"Wear a blouse with a skirt."

"I don't have a skirt," Sonia snapped.

"What do you mean? What about the green one you got from our neighbour upstairs?"

"It is torn."

"You can sew it. I have green thread." Raisa went to look for it.

Sonia didn't know how to sew. She never did. Raisa went to her cupboard to look for one of her own dresses to give to Sonia to wear.

"Look here, it may fit you. But you are bigger than I am. You have to lose a few kilos. A young girl with a big stomach is not attractive." Raisa turned around in front of a large mirror on the cupboard door. "See how flat my stomach is? Look at yours. It's protruding like old woman's. Look, here is a nice dress with flowers."

Sonia did not like the dress. It had an old smell. Everything in Raisa's cupboard looked old and smelled of naphthalene, of moth balls. There was too much stuff. There were old silk blouses and old sweaters. They were most probably the ones she brought to Israel from Germany thirteen years ago. Raisa hoarded everything. She would not part with old bags, old shoes, or old plastics. She was exceedingly frugal, counting small change every day.

Raisa left one pound of the counter every day for Sonia to take the bus to Ulpan. Then one day, Sonia didn't see it.

"Why are you surprised?" asked Raisa. "You thought I did not know that my friend Gita gave you twenty pounds?"

"I didn't mean to hide it. She gave it to me as a present."

"Sonechka, life is very expensive in Israel. Now you can use your own money for the bus. I have to be careful with every penny. Don't look so disappointed."

Sonia decided never to ask Raisa for money.

During the Succoth holiday, Fania was supposed to come to meet Sonia together with her daughter, Esther. Did Esther ever know or guess how jealous Sonia had been of her when they were little?

Sonia saw a sexy and gorgeous young woman walking up the hill on their beautiful street. The first thing Sonia noticed was her long, wavy, reddish hair. Her tall figure was straight as an arrow. She wore a red, flowing, silky skirt with flowery, sleeveless, batik T-shirt. She was holding hands with an older, unattractive woman about forty-five years old. Esther? It could not be.

She looked like Venus coming out of the clouds and floating above the ground. *My God, she is gorgeous*, thought Sonia, her heart jumping inside her chest. A wave of unfamiliar warmth and admiration swept over Sonia, covering her from head to toe.

"Oy, I don't believe it is true! Finally!" Esther squeezed Sonia with her strong arms. "Sonia, I dreamed of meeting you so many times."

Raisa had already set up the table with herring, sandwiches, and vodka.

"I had no idea you speak Russian," Sonia said to Fania.

"Sonechka, we had no choice. Esther refused to learn Yiddish. She was heartbroken for a long time. She cried every night and prayed like she was taught to by Elena Stepanovna. Esther begged to go back."

"Is it true?"

"It is. I remember how much I missed Irina and our Mama. I wanted to run away."

"But you were so little."

"Not so little. I remember crying, hating to be with my mother and her new husband."

"How long did it take?"

"Long, it felt long for me."

"Esther is right. She did not calm down till we got to Germany, maybe two years later." Fania was willing to tell their story from very beginning. "I am so grateful to Raisa who actually saved my Esther together with you. Raisa is my angel. Sonechka, you cannot imagine how much Raisa suffered to get you here."

"Esther, did you ever know that I was jealous of you and hated you passionately?"

"How would I know? No, I never did."

"Did you remember me?"

"Not much. I remember that we were supposed to be twins. I remember that we slept in a big, high bed with Elena Stepanovna in between us telling us fairy tales. I remember praying every night on our knees."

"I don't. When I grew up, Mama did not ask me to pray," Sonia said, surprised.

"Maybe because when the Communists took Vilnius under their control, being religious was discouraged."

"And how!"

Fania and Esther seemed to have a very close relationship, almost like sisters.

"My mother is very clever. Look, she studied psychology here in Israel, learned Hebrew, and worked with kids all her life."

"I am impressed."

"Esther exaggerates," Fania said, smiling almost shyly with her full lips.

"I don't. I remember when I complained and wanted to run away and made their life miserable, she let me. She spoke to me in Russian. My mother let me pray the way we did then. She listened to me talk about Irina and Elena Stepanovna. She promised to take me back if I really wanted to go so much. She said I just had to wait till I was allowed to go back. She claimed the border was closed and nobody could cross it. I believed that the moment the border opened, they would take me back."

Raisa didn't say a word during this conversation. When they left, Raisa and Sonia sat in silence.

Sonia did not have the nerve to ask why Raisa left her in Vilna when Fania immediately took her daughter with her. But they both had it on their minds, in their hearts. Words did not dare come out.

On this particular night Sonia, too, wanted to go back, to be next to her Mama. She felt lonely. She could not see Raisa as her mother. Sonia knew she did not like Raisa. Sonia did not even consider her a pretty woman even though everybody claimed she was still very attractive looking like Ingrid Bergman.

Raisa was slim, but her behind was flat. Sonia did not like her voice. She was irritated by her smile. She definitely did not want to hear Raisa's opinion or advice, which was offered constantly. Raisa talked without any intermission. Sonia wished to scream "Shut up!"

But she did not have a courage and tried to keep cool. Raisa was just a young woman who gave birth twenty years ago to a little baby named Sonia. Mama was far away. Sonia finally fell asleep, wishing to tell Mama how she loved her and missed her, and missed her cooking.

Raisa did not know to cook. After eating two small cutlets for dinner, Sonia was still hungry and asked if there was more.

"Sonechka, it is about time to change your eating habits. In Russia, people are very poor. There is not enough to eat. They stuff themselves with soups and porridge. Russians jump on food like starved dogs." Raisa could preach for hours. "Don't think that I pick on you. You lived all your life like a little kitten with its eyes closed. Nobody taught you anything. It is my duty to open your eyes, to teach you."

The tone of her voice and her unfading smile regardless of what she chose to talk about rubbed Sonia the wrong way.

"You think that you live here like in a hotel. I can read your mind. You are angry, moody, and unappreciative. You have no concept of what a normal, healthy, and loving relationship between a mother and daughter should be. I cannot blame you. You did not have an example. All my friends know how clever I am, how deeply I can evaluate complicated situations and see through people. You don't seem to appreciate it. Your mind is still in Vilnius with that old woman, waiting for her letters. Do you know what a good relationship I had with her when I lived with her after the war? She can be very good as long as you are close to her. But once parted, she does not want to know you. Her heart is made of stone. She must have forgotten about you already. She needed you to take care of her in her old age. It was easy to exploit someone as naïve and stupid as you."

"Stop talking. Stop it immediately. Do you hear me?" Sonia was ready to hit Raisa.

"You dare to raise your little voice at your own mother because she wants to teach you, to open your eyes, to put some light into your silly, confused head?"

"Never again dare to talk badly about my Mama. Whatever you say, I will always love her."

"It is because you are stupid. You don't know the value of what you've got here. Forget everything that was there in Vilna. Be grateful that I managed to get you out of that slum. If not for me, you would stay rotting there. Now you have a young, clever, modern mother. Appreciate me. There is nothing more precious than a Yiddish mama. When you get married, who will you ask to babysit your *kindalech*, to whom will you run for advice? Only to me. You behave like a stranger while still thinking about this old woman. She may die soon. What would you be left with? Alone as a finger."

"Stop it, it is enough. I don't want to hear more."

"You wait for her letters. She must have forgotten about you already. She needed you to feed her in her old age. It was easy to exploit someone as naïve and stupid as you," Raisa continued with the same pasted smile on her face.

"Shut up, I told you!" Sonia screamed.

Sonia couldn't help comparing Raisa to Mama, how little Mama talked, how many things Mama had done for her, never her asking to be grateful or appreciative. When Sonia had difficulty with math problems, Mama found a student from the university to solve every problem in her school book so that Mama knew all the answers to help Sonia do her homework. Sonia didn't know about that for a long time and had always wondered how Mama knew so much about math. Years later she met this young man. Sonia would never find out, but this man was now a teacher at Vilnius University and had a serious crush on one of Sonia's classmates, Alla Kleimenova.

He had been their neighbour. He came to her graduation and asked for Sonia, wanting to know if his work was helpful. His name was Igor

Orlov. He said Mama was very generous to pay him for working out all the problems, particularly the word problems in math.

Mama had also hired a very capable Russian musician to teach Sonia to play piano, but Sonia hated the lessons.

"Elena Stepanovna, you are throwing away your money. Sonia has difficulty distinguishing melodies. Playing the piano is not for her," the teacher had said.

Mama persisted claiming that it was classy for a young girl to play piano and eventually Sonia learned to play quite well. She could not play by ear but she could follow the music notes. Mama was proud of her.

Sonia felt that Mama lived for her. From the morning until Sonia went to bed, Mama did everything to make her happy. Did she ever asked to be appreciated?

It was true Sonia had grown up without a father, without aunts or uncles, but she never felt like an orphan. Her Mama was everything for Sonia.

Sonia promised herself not to discuss the past with Raisa who had actually left her behind while escaping Vilnius. Sonia could not allow Raisa to insult her kind, noble, and patient Mama who took Raisa to her house when she had no place to go after the war and who never said a bad word about Raisa to Sonia.

"Look at me, look at my figure. You are a young girl with a stomach like a pregnant woman. The old woman didn't care how you looked," Raisa said many times, proud of her flat stomach and flat behind.

Sonia noticed that Raisa's legs were thick and hairy. She had no waist, no hips. In Sonia's eyes, Raisa's body was less attractive than the big and well-proportioned body of Mama with her beautiful, silky skin.

"You have to know who your parents and grandparents were. My father was a very well-known and respected businessman in Vilna. People came to him for advice. He gave a lot of money to charity. Your grandfather sent my brother, Sema, to Palestine to buy some land, but Sema didn't like Palestine. He came back to the hell of Hitler."

Sonia was sincerely interested in her family's past. Poor Raisa had lost everyone. Sonia was willing to forget their differences. But she could not call her mother.

Raisa's house was not like home back there with Mama.

Raisa had no relatives besides Fania and Esther, but she did keep in touch with some survivors from Vilnius. One of them lived in a kibbutz, another in Haifa.

They had heard many sad things about Sonia's life in Vilnius over the years. Now they rejoiced to see Raisa and Sonia reunited.

"You look like sisters," said Raisa's best friend, Gita, visiting from the kibbutz. "I am excited for both of you. Thank God you are finally with your mother and not with a strange goya." Gita had tears in her eyes, tears of joy.

Strange Goya? There was never a strange Goya in Sonia's life. It was her dear Mama. Her caring, loving, old Mama with her gentle hands, her small grey eyes, and her straight posture. Tall, big, and warm.

"Was she mean to you?" Gita's soft voice trembled with empathy.

"Who are you talking about?" Sonia pretended not to understand.

"This Goya who made all the troubles and did not let you come here for so many years."

"There wasn't a Goya in my life. It was and is my Mama, the most remarkable person on the planet."

"Gita, you have to understand. She brought her up. Sonia got used to her." Raisa tried to justify Sonia's reply to Gita.

When Gita left, Raisa gave Sonia a different speech.

"My dear Sonechka, you humiliated me again today in front of my best friend. Every child knows who his mother is. There is only one mother in a person's life. You are like a stubborn donkey calling an old, senile woman "mother" in front of my friend. Gita knows how much I suffered to get you out of Vilnius, how I cried, how much money it cost me. And here you call this old woman your mother. I am really ashamed for both of us. People will think you are stupid girl."

Sonia hoped to find an appropriate time to explain to Raisa how good Mama was. For now, she wanted Raisa to write a nice letter to Mama, to make friends with her.

"You are actually asking me to write her a letter? It will calm you down? Okay. You dictate, and I will write," Raisa agreed. "I have no desire to write to her, but if you insist, fine. As you know by now, I am a very honest and practical person. I always keep my word. Tell me exactly what I should write."

"Not like that. If you can, I hope you would compose a kind letter on your own. You can write that before I arrived in Israel you had no idea what a wonderful person she was, but now that you know from me how Mama took care of me, you are sorry for the many ugly things you wrote to other people in Vilnius about her."

"What are you talking about? She fooled you and brainwashed you for twenty years. But it does not matter. I will write to make you happy."

"Let's go shopping," Sonia suggested one hot day. She hoped to get sandals.

"Sonechka, don't be in such a hurry. This week we will have visitors from Tel Aviv. I have invited the relatives from your father's side. They will bring you lots of presents, more than you need. Trust your mother, be patient."

"Do I have many relatives?"

"Look, unfortunately, we don't have anyone from my family, but your father had aunts and uncles who left for Palestine and America before Hitler."

The next week Raisa took Sonia to a hairdresser. Sonia had never been to a beauty salon, had never seen the huge, metal turbans under which women with big rollers dried their hair. After Sonia's hair was washed, cut, dried, and set, Raisa looked at her very satisfied.

"Imagine what a new hairdo can do for a person. Now you don't look like you came from Russia."

Sonia glanced in the mirror. She did not like what she saw, sorry to have lost her braids and hating her new, short haircut.

"You have no taste. It is not your fault. People in Russia just don't have a good taste. Born *mujik*, stays *mujik*," said Raisa, trying to console her.

The days were still very hot. After opening the many presents Sonia received from different relatives, she still wished to have sandals like everybody else wore. Raisa tried to assure her that the warm days were almost over and that winter was coming with lots of rain. It would be a waste of money to buy sandals in October. To Raisa's dismay, however, the hot weather stubbornly persisted. Sonia's feet, locked in heavy shoes, continued to sweat.

"We are going to buy sandals today," Raisa grudgingly conceded.

They went all the way from Carmel down to the port and, after trying on similar pairs of sandals in five different stores, Raisa finally bought her a pair.

"Why did we have to go so far and to so many places?"

"Because practical *balabustas* know where to find things cheaper."

"Thank you. Let's go home. I am tired of this shopping. It is not fun."
"We also need to get you a new dress."
"Can we buy a dress next time?"
"Why? Why waste another day? We are here in the shopping area."

Raisa chose Sonia a dress with apples and green leaves. Sonia hated the dress.

"I would rather choose one with stripes."

"Sonechka, how can you know what is good for you? You don't have a refined taste yet. Did you ever go shopping for beautiful things? I understand there was nothing to buy in stores in the Soviet Union."

Raisa was right, Sonia never went shopping. Mama bought everything she needed, or Jadviga made dresses at home.

That evening Sonia sat in the only comfortable fauteuil near the bookcase looking at the same page in her book for a half an hour. Raisa was busy cleaning the kitchen. Maybe she should get up and help. Sonia wondered if Raisa was as happy with her as her smile claimed.

In her letters to Vilnius, Raisa had written that Sonia could not understand the meaning of the word "mother." She would only discover what it meant when she came to live with her in Israel. They spoke Russian. She couldn't call her "mama," and she was not used to calling her "Ima." Sonia had chosen not to use her name, hoping eventually to adopt "Ima" as the most appropriate.

"Sonechka, I would like to talk to you before you go to sleep." Raisa took her away from her thoughts.

"I have to tell you something important, my dear daughter." Raisa literally pulled Sonia from her comfortable armchair and brought her in front of the full-length mirror on the cupboard door.

"You have to do something about your appetite. Look at yourself carefully. Look at me. Look at your figure, look at my figure. Examine them. You have to lose weight. It is not a body of a twenty-year-old girl. You are too fat."

Sonia didn't think she was too fat. As a matter of fact, she would have gone to the student cafeteria in Kaunas to eat soup with bread to gain some weight to not look so skinny. But there was no point in arguing with Raisa. Mama never said Sonia was fat. Mama said she was pretty. Sonia recognized that Raisa meant the best for her, but it was painful. Maybe Raisa was thinner than her but Raisa wasn't very attractive with her flat behind and no waistline

"My dear precious, amazing, wonderful Mamochka; my lovely inspiration, the only one who always knew everything.

I never ever had to ask any questions. You knew everything before I could ask.

There is no day I don't miss you, Irina, and even Dadia Kolia.

I often imagine you are next to me. And I tell you everything that happened in my day like I did back home all my life.

I want you to be here, close to me, hold your big warm body, knowing that you love me and will take care of me.

I am anxious, nervous, restless, confused. But I don't need anyone, just you.

Mamochka, you always were and always will be the only one who understands me right even if I say it wrong, the only one that can heal pain of mine just by the way you look at me lovingly, by your soft voice, by your gentle smile

Mamochka, my love, you never told me you loved me but I always knew you did. You didn't say much. I talked for both of us.

Do you remember how often we chatted about living together? For many years, I said that when I get married my future husband will love you and we will all live together happily.

Do you remember these conversations?

Here, in Israel is very, very different. Young girls cannot wait to get away from their home, to be free.

I dream of you coming here, to Israel be with me. I am going to be an architect, will build us a modern beautiful house. Just for us, no strangers to share, no aggravations.

You will have your own big bathroom with white tub, warm floors and all in marble, bright modern kitchen with big windows and large sink.

But it is useless dream. You will not come to me to Israel.

You will never leave Irina and Dadia Kolia; you will be afraid to take a plane to Israel. You will claim it is too far. You never flew by plane yet. You will say you are too old to travel. I know that you will not come. I know for sure.

I can beg and cry for long time. Maybe you already forgot about me, maybe you are very angry with me, angry that I left, angry that I didn't tell you how I tried to get my papers to leave.

But mamochka, I never believed they will let me go. So I didn't want to upset you for nothing.

Now I cry and write. Why don't you write me how are things at home?

I know nothing about your life at this moment. Nothing. I have to guess.

It is late. I am going to bed, very tired.

Big hug, kisses, miss you terribly…

Always yours, Sonia."

Sonia longed to be again a little girl when life was so simple with Mama, when even the horrid war could be perceived as if through coloured kaleidoscope. She tried to close her eyes to bring her first memories.

Sonia felt truly fortunate not to have any memories of the war.

The very first thing Sonia seemed to remember was an intrinsically beautiful orange-red carpet. Sprinkled with black, glowing before her eyes. Covering the sky with generous splashes. In the background was overwhelmingly loud powerful music. Standing on the balcony watching the sky Sonia didn't want Irina or Mama to get her away, she wanted them to be with her on the balcony and share her excitement.

Was it her real memory or was it something Irina and Mama told her after?

She just couldn't sleep. After finishing her letter Sonia laid down for a long time listening to the rhythmical banging in her ears.

These piercing staccato noises gripped her whenever she felt tense.

Would be so good to talk about it with Mama. Sonia wrote letter but never thought about calling by phone. The idea to call Mama didn't enter her mind yet. Mainly because they didn't have a phone at home.

Mama would have to go to Central Station.

What if she didn't get a message for the telephone invitation?

The night was gone, one could hear birds chirping cheerfully, car engines starting below her window.

Zing…zing… Sonia was startled, fast clutched warm, red receiver.

"Hello, hello! I am here," she actually screamed.

"Your call to Vilnius is connected. Please go ahead."

"Sonia? It is you? Speak louder. I. Cannot hear you."

"Ira, I. Don't believe it. We are connected. Where is Mama?"

"Mama couldn't come Her legs are very weak. She doesn't leave the house anymore."

"No, Ira. I cannot believe it."

"What is new with you, Sonia? Here nothing much has happened. Our old dressmaker Jadviga passed away a few weeks ago.

Do you remember Helga? She died too.

"No, it is so sad! Ira, how are you and how is Mama?"

"I am on my feet all day. Then run shopping, carry heavy parcels. I am not getting younger, you know."

"Did you get my pictures?"

"Sonia, you look bad and too skinny on the pictures. Eat better, sleep better, don't work so hard. Mama is very worried about you."

"Ira, Irechka..." Tears stubbornly blocked her words.

"Look, Sonechka, it must be very expensive to call from Israel. You should not have called. Just write letter. It is enough. It is hard Roget away from my job to get to the Central to talk to you.

You forgot how late we work here."

The line went silent. Did Ira put it down?

Grown young woman, Sonia sat on her bed weeping like a child. If there was any wish good fairy could grant, it would be to have Mama next to her, to hide all her concerns and thoughts on Mama's big chest.

Her Mama is like no there one on the entire planet. Her Mama is like a generous flowing loving river but very far away, in a small medieval town called Vilnius!

Raisa had been sleeping in the living room on the sofa since she gave Sonia her bed. The tiny room with a single bed looked poor compared to the living room that Raisa furnished to make a rich impression. For the last thirteen years, Raisa had lived alone in this small flat on the ground floor. It really was a beautiful neighbourhood in Mount Carmel. Raisa decorated her living room with heavy, burgundy-coloured, velvet drapes and nicely framed family portraits on the walls. But her bedroom had no furniture, just a narrow bed with a round wooden night table. Gita's cousin had built her a wall-to-wall cupboard that was bursting with everything Raisa piled into it over the past years. She even had boxes of stale food that she could not bring herself to discard.

Sonia ventured out to visit Raisa's friend Gita, who had moved recently from a kibbutz to a new apartment house near Rishon Le Zion. Looking through the blurry window of an old bus, Sonia imagined the cramped quarters of poor people living in tiny huts made from what appeared to be a combination of metal sheets and wood stuck together. She figured out that newcomers, Sephardic Jews from Arab countries, were given these as temporary homes.

The bus, half asleep, lazily climbed the hills. Two little girls in front of her hugged their mother's neck with their plump hands. The driver's head swung with the rhythm of music on his radio. Sonia drifted off to sleep.

"Wake up. We arrived," the driver said, tapping Sonia on the shoulder.

Gita was there to meet her.

"Sonechka, are you impressed with our little country, Israel? After Russia, everything must look amazing, no? Look around you. Look at our buildings. When they were originally built, it was only to show academics and American immigrants an example of modern living. But then the government decided to clear some slums in the area and moved people here—poor Jews from Iraq, Libya, Tunisia, and Morocco.

We used to have grass, gardens, and nice landscaping. But once you move a family with eight, nine, sometimes as many as eighteen children, things get out of control. These kids were always outside yelling, screaming, fighting, breaking things, and pissing on the grass. It got unbearable noisy. We could not keep the windows open. There is a lot of tension between Ashkenazi and Sephardim Jews. On many levels."

"Now you teach me about domestic problems. Thank you. I have to know. Gita, were you always a Zionist?"

"All my family was. We came here just before the war."

"How lucky that you stayed."

"Unfortunately, most of our family stayed in Vilna. But enough about me. Let us talk about you. How are things at home?"

"Fine, really good."

"I could sense that things are not easy for you. Raisa is your mother. Be smart, try to understand her, ignore little things. If I had not known her before the war, I would have never believed that a person could change so much. Remember that the horrible war destroyed people.

I never figured out why Raisa left Vilna without you. Sometimes I thought she was mad, really crazy. She was so much in love with Izia. You were his gift to her. But to her credit, once Raisa arrived in Israel, she became obsessed about bringing you here. I helped her write hundreds of letters. Raisa is stubborn; she wants to teach you, to help you. Don't argue with her and try to ignore what you don't like to hear. Raisa wants your relationship to be close like mother and daughter, like she had with her mother."

Sonia made an impression on people of being an independent person. This was pretty easy for the first twenty years. Mama always took care of everything. Sonia had never been to the store. She had no idea what it meant to buy a bra, a dress, to buy anything at all. Whatever she needed, Mama got it for her. Actually, Sonia thought that Mama got her much more than she needed. She never thought she needed a thing. But Sonia needed friends. Sonia wanted other kids to like her. She did not know to like herself. She felt skinny, tiny, uncoordinated, clumsy, and not very capable. There was not much to like about herself, but her Mama liked her. Sonia never doubted that. She trusted Mama's love one hundred percent. Sonia did not feel stupid, but she felt physically weak and much inferior to others in her class. There was only one person that her world turned around—Mama. Life was easy. It was easy to appear independent when everything was taken care of by Mama.

Many years later, Sonia realized how totally dependent on her Mama she had been, and happily so. It was her choice. It was a privilege to be brought up by her, to be loved by her. Sonia figured out that what she understood love to be she learned from Mama.

Sonia expected Esther to visit them soon. Esther promised to show her Haifa and to take her to Beit Rothschild. Sonia wanted to be friends with her and to ask for her forgiveness for being so insanely jealous when they were little.

Beit Rothschild was a cultural centre with a lot of activities for young people. On Saturday nights, it was mostly dancing. Sonia was not a good dancer. She could move to slow tango music or even the waltz, but not to quick modern dances like the Foxtrot or Paso Double.

Young Israeli men, local sabras, invited Sonia to dance. They talked fast, and she could not figure out their Hebrew. There was no conversation, and Sonia found it boring. Sonia could move to the music, more correctly to the songs in freestyle. Everybody did what came to their mind. Somehow everyone tried to outdo each other, to be very sexy.

Sonia was embarrassed to move her body in any provocative way. She felt awkward and unfeminine on the dance floor and did not enjoy it at all. But Esther had a great time. She knew how to be sexy, how to attract everyone's attention. It was so natural with her, the way she moved her body and worked the room.

"Sonechka, don't be discouraged. You are not used to it. It will come with practice. Don't worry about anything. Just follow the music and invent your own moves. Let your body direct you. Love your body. Don't be shy."

"I am just too clumsy. I am not shy. I don't know to dance."

One of the young men who invited Sonia to dance offered to walk them home. He was handsome and very talkative, but Sonia did not understand a word he was saying in his fast, natural Hebrew. Sonia was surprised that he paid so much attention to her and not to Esther. Maybe he was intimidated by her beauty.

Esther stayed with them for the night. She left early the next morning to teach at eight thirty in the morning.

It was a sunny and crisp morning. Sonia walked slowly toward the centre of Carmel, this beautiful neighbourhood on the top of the mountain. Sonia had decided instead of going to Ulpan, that she would take a bus to Technion.

She approached a middle-aged man near the main entrance and asked him where the administration building was so she could enquire about how to register as a student in the program. Once Sonia found the right office, there was a short man with a double chin and red, tired eyes behind a huge desk, messy with papers.

"How can I help you, young lady?"

Sonia explained that she had finished three years of Electrical Engineering in Kaunas and would like to continue her learning here at Technion.

"I have all my marks for the courses I took. My marks are very good."

"Congratulations on your good marks, but my advice would be to finish Ulpan; learn to read and speak Hebrew properly first. Then start the academic year in September, not in the middle of semester."

Since Sonia wanted to continue her studies as soon as possible, he gave her permission to go to some lectures and to find out how much she could understand at this point after such a short time in the new country.

"I understand you are good at math, so go and listen to some classes in a familiar subject. Then come back and let me know how it goes."

Sonia received a personal invitation from Golda Meir to visit her in Jerusalem. She did not know much about Golda Meir. They were never taught about other countries in Russia. Nothing about Israel was ever mentioned in school. Jewish kids did not know about Jewish culture or Jewish holidays. Some had only learned about Passover or Rosh Hashanah from their grandparents.

Golda Meir was the first Israeli Ambassador to the USSR after the establishment of Israel. She was a big success in Moscow. Jews were elated to meet her. But at the time, nobody had heard about it in Vilnius.

Here in Israel, Golda Meir was an icon. It was an enormous honour to be invited to her house. She was not just a famous respected politician; Golda Meir was the Foreign Minister of Israel!

When Sonia arrived at Golda Meir's house, she was met by the guard who sat in an enclosed structure built by the gate close to the sidewalk. Sonia introduced herself, waited a few minutes, and was let in. The place seemed surprisingly modest for a Foreign Minister's residence.

Golda warmly invited her to the kitchen and asked a lot of questions about her relationship with Raisa.

"I don't know what to say. She talks ugly about Mama. I cannot bear to hear it. It is not right, not fair. Mama was good to me. I love and miss her. Ima gets upset by how ungrateful I am and that I don't behave as normal daughters do. I don't get what I am supposed to be grateful for."

Golda listened, looked at Sonia with her clever, intense eyes.

"Would you like to come and live in my house and study in Jerusalem?"

A few weeks later, Sonia was invited again. This time Golda took her to Tel Aviv to look for kitchen curtains. They were for her daughter, Sarah, who lived in a kibbutz. Sonia was amazed that such an important person, the Minister of Foreign Affairs, took her precious time to shop for her daughter's kitchen curtains.

That evening they went to Hebrew University for a concert. Golda's son, Menachem, played the cello and gave a solo performance. There were very few people in the audience. Sonia felt bad for Golda watching her son play to such a small gathering.

"Would you like to move to Jerusalem and live with me?" Golda asked her again. "We have an excellent Department of Physics and Mathematics. It should be easy to transfer from Technion."

It was tempting and flattering to be invited by Golda. But somewhere in her heart, Sonia didn't feel satisfied with her choice of studies. She did not like physics; she liked math even less. If she had to study a science, it would be Architecture. She hoped to transfer if they accept her.

There was no Architecture in Jerusalem. What should she do? Leaving the gate and the guard behind, Sonia wondered how interesting it would be to stay at Golda's house.

Had she planned on staying in Vilnius for the rest of her life, Sonia would have studied Russian Literature or poetry, but these subjects would be useless in Israel. So instead, she studied Engineering so as to not be dependent on language in her profession.

Sonia had always liked literature and art. Sonia had never learned to paint, and most probably did not have a special talent for it. She just liked it. Architecture had lots of art in it, and one could be creative. It wasn't as boring as engineering. If it worked, if Technion accepted some of her credits to switch her to the Faculty of Architecture, Sonia would have to stay in Haifa, as tempting as it was to move to Jerusalem.

Sonia attended many lectures in the mathematics department during the week. There were eight other students in her class, all boys. They looked much older. Later she found out that these eight students started Technion after their army service.

In the beginning, Sonia hardly understood what the professor was saying or what was written on the blackboard. One afternoon, while really discouraged after class, Sonia walked over to the library on the second floor. It was a nicely paneled room, mainly used by professors and graduate students. There was no librarian, and very few people.

Sonia found a comfortable armchair behind a magazine display and pretended to read. Overwhelmed by a sense of privacy and lulled by soothing silence, Sonia allowed her tense nerves to relax. Suddenly she heard the clock strike six o'clock.

"You have a key, don't you?" the last person leaving the library asked her, apparently expecting her to close the door when she left.

"I don't." Tears blocked her vision.

"I don't believe we have met before. Are you a graduate student?" There was kind and concerned look on his face. He walked over to her. "Please come with me."

Sonia followed this strange professor, grateful that he asked no questions. He actually spoke Russian and lived with his wife and son in a beautiful old house with a fireplace and fancy European furniture, ten-minute walk from the campus.

His wife, Bella, asked Sonia to join them for dinner. It was delicious. Sonia ate quietly, expecting them to ask her personal questions. How was she going to say that she had no intention of going back to Raisa? But nobody asked any questions.

After supper, Sonia clumsily tried to help in the kitchen. She was afraid to say that it was the first time in her life she had washed dishes. Bella invited Sonia to stay overnight. Sonia did.

The next morning, she walked with Professor Evans back to campus to sit in on other classes. In the afternoon, Professor Evans came to meet her. He gave her a letter to be given to the person in charge of the student dormitory. Thanks to him, she got a nice room on campus.

Sonia was surprised to receive another letter from Boris who was living in Tel Aviv.

"Dearest Sonechka," he wrote. "Maybe, sure, this is the last letter I will send to you. The very last one. I am genuinely sorry. No, I am not sorry, but sorrowed, and I know that I have to learn to move forward. Thanks for having existed."

Sonia had sweet memory how Boris took her to Tel Aviv on his motorcycle. Scared, she had held onto his back with both hands, trembling from the strong wind. He seemed to be very pleased with her and her company. He made her laugh.

But in the evening when Boris wanted to kiss her on her cheeks, Sonia pulled her face away. She was not attracted to him. She did not like his mouth or his big, Jewish nose. It was okay to be friends, but Boris wanted romance. Too bad. It was a bit sad for they did have good times together.

Sonia's new life in Technion was very simple. For Sonia, Israel was a very easy place to adjust to after arriving from the Soviet Union. Over there, where she grew up and lived for twenty years, there was lots of talk about Communism, brotherhood, and world peace.

Here, in Israel, there was a real pioneer spirit. Proud Israelis were building a new country with their own hands and were praying every day for peace with the Arabs. The society around Sonia seemed to be changing constantly, and it was united by a common faith in the future with deep pride in how much had been achieved in such a short time. It had not yet been thirteen years, not even a Bar Mitzvah! Most people wanted a good life for themselves and their children, and they knew how to wait patiently and sacrifice silently.

Stubbornly aloof sabras did not look for anybody's friendship; they kept tightly to each other. They seemed suspicious of and indifferent to foreigners. It was difficult to penetrate their inner circle, to get to know them and to befriend them. Foreign students, astonished by the sabras' rudeness, felt left out. Removed from their familiar environments in different parts of the world, foreign students desperately searched for friends with whom they could share their problems and identify with.

There were numerous groups in Technion that did not connect with each other: Sabras, North Americans, students from South America, and new immigrants from Rumania. Each group kept tight to their own circle and spoke their own language. All languages were spoken except Russian.

Israeli students did not have to find themselves. Physically and emotionally, they matured much too early for their age, knowing exactly what they wanted from life. Early on in life, Israelis learned to rely on themselves, to earn a living, to be independent, and to fight for their rights, even at Technion. Studies were treated seriously. Each student meant to get the most for his money.

Not knowing English, Spanish, or Rumanian, Sonia did not belong to any group. She stuck close to her classmates. Maybe because she was a girl, the only girl in her year, Sonia was accepted by her sabra colleagues. They gladly helped her with lab reports and with difficult homework assignments. Sonia received lots of compliments being the only girl in her class with eight Israeli young men. She was admired for her ability and her desire to study scientific subjects. It was hard to admit that she did not like any of the classes.

Sonia studied with her classmates for exams. They were willing to explain anything she could not get on her own. Sonia respected their self-assurance, shimmered through every word, and reflected in the tone of voice they spoke with, between themselves and to others. This precious feeling of freedom and pride carried a generous tinge of arrogance. Full of ideas and prepared for serious sacrifices, Israelis did not hide their ferocious interest in money and material goods. Having set their own standards, they could not tolerate to be criticized. Feeling Israeli first and Jewish second, the native youth did not feel a strong bond with international Jewry the way the older generation did. Young Israelis were indifferent to Diaspora Jews and basically ignored them. Sonia was attracted to these proud and independent people; she wanted to be a part of them, to be accepted by them, and to participate in building the young country.

After three months of sitting in on different classes, Sonia could understand most of what was said. She registered for three different courses. The boys in the class were exceptionally friendly to her. They laughed a lot and tried to translate some jokes for her.

Sonia still did not know to write in Hebrew.

Many times, she was invited to Professor Evan's house for Friday dinners. Despite their age difference, Bella Evans became a very good and sensitive friend to Sonia.

Bella was brought up in Russia by her grandparents. She was only three months old when her father and her uncle went to the forest to chop some wood. Ukrainian bandits attacked them, cut them into pieces, and left the cut body parts on the doorstep of the house where they lived. Her mother died soon after. Bella's grandmother took care of Bella and her two older brothers for two years. Then, in 1921, they managed to leave for Palestine. Bella grew up in the country on a kibbutz near Tiberius and was proud of every inch of the unique and ancient land. Her two older brothers, Misha and Daniel, were attacked and killed by Arabs in 1928.

Bella knew how to manage a hospitable household, how to be generous, and how to count every penny at the same time. They had one son, Roni, whom Bella adored. Roni was exceptionally handsome, and an amazing athlete with dark, smooth skin. He was a spitting image of his distinguished father. Sonia found him very attractive, but Roni hardly said a word to her when she was visiting.

Sonia could talk to Bella about anything—Mama, Irina, her friends in Vilnius, love, and marriage. Bella had an amazingly young spirit; she wanted to make life for Sonia and her adjustment to the new country as smooth as possible. She offered Sonia advice on everything, except Sonia's complicated relationship with Raisa. On this topic, Bella was reluctant to give any advice.

Drip, drop.

Sonia was pleased it was raining. She was happy to be here in Israel. For no reason at all, she remembered her old friend, a Russian poet named Sasha who had written for her a beautiful poem about what a precious gift it is to be nineteen, free, and to belong to no one. Now she was twenty-two, free, and in love with life and love. Every day was filled with hope. The most exciting part of it all was that one never knew what may happen. Someone, a total stranger, could appear in front of her and Sonia would stand there overwhelmed with joy.

She dreamed about meeting her Prince Charming and experiencing the magic of true love. Without love, life would be an empty existence. Just anticipating love was exciting. Sonia felt the smiling, ticklish, hugging effect of expectation touching her heart, warming her cheeks, whispering into her ears, and touching her burning lips.

14

Sonia received numerous warm letters from Jamima and Joseph Avidar who were in Argentina. Joseph had been sent to Buenos Aires as an Israeli Ambassador after serving in Moscow. They were thrilled about Sonia's arrival in Israel. Joseph was coming to Israel to check on a project that was building a new city in the Negev. Arad was going to be the first pre-planned city in Israel.

Joseph was an Israeli General. He planned to come to Haifa to pick up Sonia before going south to inspect how the construction of the new city, Arad, was progressing. He had with him a short and fat soldier to drive.

Driving out of Haifa, they stopped in a small restaurant for falafels and Israeli salads. Joseph Avidar invited his driver to join them.

"Would it happen in the Soviet Union?" he asked a startled Sonia.

"Never."

In the Soviet Union, an officer—never mind a general—would not sit at the same table with a simple soldier. Sonia remembered when the colonel moved upstairs from Mama's flat; he just sat on the balcony ordering soldiers to move the furniture.

Joseph Avidar was proud how authentically his country, Israel, lived in a real democracy. The Soviet Union, which preached equality, kept a clear separation between the ranks.

Joseph's driver was new and did not have exact directions. He almost crossed the border into Jordan by mistake. Joseph realized it before the driver did, how close they were to Jordanian soldiers.

"Turn back." Joseph Avidar was upset.

They went back to Tel Aviv to get another driver. This time they drove straight to an area where new roads were built.

"In the Soviet Union, they build villages and towns with unpaved roads," Joseph explained. "We start with building roads for people. Only then will they come to settle. First, we will bring local Israeli families. After that, many others will come. One day, in twenty years, there will be thousands of people living here. We will build a beautiful green city in the desert. It will bloom!"

Sonia believed that Joseph Avidar was right. She felt proud and privileged to accompany him on this important mission.

Soon both he and Jamima would be coming back home to Jerusalem after serving in Argentina. Sonia had not written to Jamima about her difficult relationship with Raisa. Jamima was a writer, very intelligent, and very sensitive. She would understand once Sonia told her.

Sonia waited patiently for them to return. The first week after their arrival, Jamima invited Sonia to visit them in Jerusalem.

Their chic, sophisticated apartment was the most beautiful place she had seen in Israel. Sonia was mesmerized by the artwork from Russia and the numerous other countries they visited.

Jamima and Joseph had been all over the world. They collected the most beautiful items, including sculptures, paintings, and handicrafts. Sonia admired their exquisite carpets the most. They were humongous, at least twenty-five feet long, and made of turquoise silk with delicate birds and tiny roses sprinkled all over.

Jamima found it amusing that Sonia knew so little about Jews and Judaism. Sonia had never heard of Hatikvah.

Jamima loved Sonia's exciting, restless, and curious mind. Sonia admired Jamima's elegant, magnificent house, it's inviting and warm ambiance, Jamima's young spirit, and her compassionate and cultured soul.

She wandered in her lush garden, full of huge, healthy plants and flowers. It had a little, flowing brook and an iron bench they had brought from New Orleans.

Jamima often had her family over for dinner. She liked Sonia to join in, and to share with them her experience of growing up in the Soviet Union. Most of the time, Jamima preferred Sonia to speak to them in Russian.

Many of Jamima's friends and family had arrived in Israel from Russia or the Ukraine just after the revolution. They spoke Russian and Hebrew, listened to Russian music, and read Chekhov, Turgenev, and Dostoevsky.

Sonia's Russian was very pure, apparently. It sounded like poetry or music to their ears. It was really flattering for Sonia to be so wanted and so welcome.

Jamima's guests were surprised, however, by how little Sonia knew about French, British, and European history. She really did not know anything about it. It was not taught in her school. Back home, in Vilnius, in their school books, everything was discovered by Russian scientists.

On May 9, 1962, it was the fourteenth anniversary of the Israeli Day of Independence. Joseph and Jamima had Sonia sit with them on stage during the celebration. She could see President Yitzhak Ben Zvi a few rows away. The air was filled with exhilaration. A lot of important people attended. Sonia felt goosebumps on her arms and her spine.

When Israeli tanks passed in front of them, her heart almost jumped out of her chest with pride. Tears came to her eyes. It was such a magic moment. She was sitting on main stage "B" next to Joseph and Jamima Avidar, the nicest, smartest people she had met in her entire life. She was in Tel Aviv watching the parade.

Sonia felt so much love for Jamima, for Joseph, for Israel, and for the young boys and girls serving in the Israeli Defence Forces. They walked in straight rows and were proud to defend their young country and to build a better society. Life seemed to be so good. There must be an angel high above who helped her to get here and to finally be proud of being Jewish. It must be the soul of her father who was now here next to her. And Jamima was another angel with a heart as big as Siberia.

One day Jamima arranged for Raisa and Sonia to get an invitation from Golda Meir to visit her in Jerusalem.

At this point, their relationship was really tense. Sonia lived in student dormitory; Raisa was obviously disappointed in her daughter. She did not like Sonia as a person. Raisa did not like Sonia's looks or her stubbornness.

Raisa was enthusiastic about their trip, proud to be invited. She had admired Golda Meir for years, and she had written her numerous letters seeking her help in reaching Sonia.

It did not register with Sonia yet that her arrival in Israel from the Soviet Union in 1961 when no Jews were allowed to leave was an exceptional event and had involved a lot of effort, mostly on Raisa's part.

Raisa expected Sonia to appreciate that she literally saved her from the abyss of rot in the evil country; she wanted Sonia to forget what was before and to be grateful to her for what she got in Israel instead.

But Sonia missed her Russian mother. She missed her small loving eyes; she missed her preparing her breakfast, missed kissing her beautiful, soft hands and sharing with her what was happening in her everyday life.

So off they went to visit Golda Meir who was eager to how Sonia was adjusting to her new country....

At this meeting Sonia was not supposed to talk about Mama. But Sonia could not control herself. She talked a lot about her life in Vilnius, about Elena Stepanovna. She could not stop knowing that it hurt Raisa a lot.

Sonia could not find one word to praise Raisa. More than that, Sonia somehow communicated her disappointment with Raisa, her lack of understanding her, and her annoyance over Raisa's harsh criticism of Elena Stepanovna.

It came across to Sonia that Golda actually understood her frustrations. Golda Meir, being an extraordinarily wise person, did not hold these thoughts against her. She seemed to take her side on some level, which gave Sonia comfort and the confidence to show even more negativity.

Raisa and Sonia did not come across like a loving mother and daughter. They already arrived tense and anxious. They left Golda's home with even more anxiety.

Sonia had to change her prescription for her glasses. They put drops in her eyes and she was not able to read or study. Dana was abroad, and Sonia was restless. She decided to go see Jamima in Jerusalem. Obviously, Jamima wanted to know what was happening between her and Raisa.

"Jamima, I feel sad bringing so much pain into her life. I often think about our visit to see Golda Meir in Jerusalem together. Raisa was so excited to go. It was a moment, an opportunity to make her happy. Instead, I was in a bad mood. I was irritated and was mean to her. I blew it! Will she ever forgive me for that?"

"She has, Sonia."

"How can you sound so sure?"

"Because she is your mother. That is what mothers do. They always forgive. True, on the other hand, there are a very few mothers who abandon their children. Her tragic journey during the war is not an excuse for what happened afterward between the two of you. You were a kid; you could not understand it then. You also were not supposed to understand it when the two of you met."

"I was cruel and resentful. I lacked compassion."

"Sonia, you were lucky to have an amazing mother who brought you up with love. You cannot help but compare them. It was meant to be this way."

"Maybe you are right. My negative memories of her slapping my hand for touching ivory elephants on *our* mantel piece, or pulling the carpet from piano, her angry voice, and her chasing me out of the room that I considered to be MY room, stayed in my little head. I remember not liking her. I also remember Raisa not liking me. Maybe she did like me but pretended not to. Maybe she thought it was the right strategy for distancing herself from me. God created us to keep our thoughts sealed; nobody can read them. They can only guess. It was clear that Raisa was ready to leave me behind, never to see me again. Once I knew it, I could not forget."

"Dear Sonia, time heals all wounds. Don't blame yourself. Now you are finally here, in Israel. What do you think about our life here?"

"Jamima, I love it. I love Israel."

"This is what counts the most. You are home and you have to plan your life. Tonight, you are staying with us. I invited my brother for dinner. I want you to meet him. When you left Vilnius, my brother was an Ambassador to France. I had hoped you would go visit him. We had planned to arrange it for you. We expected you to arrive in Moscow after leaving Vilnius."

"Sorry, I did not come. The moment I received my passport to leave, I was scared to go east in case something went wrong. I ran west to the nearest border."

"You did right thing. Joseph and I were overjoyed knowing that you were getting your documents. You have no idea how many people were involved. And your mother was relentless. I have to tell you that. I think she wrote hundreds of letters to every person she could think off. She is very intelligent and beautiful too. You look very much like her."

"I am not beautiful. I look more like my father."

Jamima told Sonia how she met her husband, Joseph, showed her family albums, and talked about the difficulties they faced in the beginning when they first arrived from Chernowitz.

Sonia wanted to know how Dana was doing. Dana was in the United States and was supposed to be back in Israel in the summer.

"I am proud of you. Your Hebrew is pretty good. I understand you are doing well in your courses."

"They are difficult. In science subjects, particularly math, language is not so important. I understand most of the lectures. It is still hard for me to write and read in Hebrew, though."

"It will come with time. Now, I think, would be the right time to learn some English."

"Why?" Sonia was perplexed.

"Sonia, most of the books are in English, aren't they? Educated people all over the world learn English."

A week later in Technion, just when Sonia was ready to leave her desk in the library, a young man approached her.

"I am here to teach you English. Let us look at your schedule to find a time."

Sonia understood that he was sent by Jamima. She was deeply touched.

Sonia found Roni, Bella's son, very charming, but she was not his type. As much as she tried to get his attention, it never occurred to Roni to ask out Sonia despite the fact that Bella loved her to pieces. It was not that men didn't find Sonia attractive. The ones who found her attractive she didn't like, and the ones Sonia wanted looked through her, never at her.

Professor Joshua Steg was a completely different story. It was all a bit upsetting. More than that, Sonia was amazed how Raisa had a sense to find out exactly the kind of man Sonia was fantasizing about. Sonia had never allowed Raisa to introduce her to Professor Steg, to meet him through his aunt, as Raisa had carefully planned before Sonia's arrival in Israel. What a big, HUGE mistake!

Later, Sonia often regretted how hostile she had been toward Raisa's suggestion to meet the unusual, brilliant man in his own house through his aunt, the aunt who knew Raisa from their youth in Vilna, who knew her family. Perhaps Professor Steg would have related differently to Sonia than he did now when they met completely by chance in the library where she worked as a librarian.

Proteczia was as natural and necessary in Israel as it was in Vilnius. Who do you know, and who can help you by introducing you to the right people in your life? This determines your chances of success in life.

When Sonia left Raisa's house she was helped by Bella and her husband, Professor Evans. to get a room in a student dormitory.

Soon after Sonia got a job as a librarian. It was almost inconceivable to be the librarian in a library where all the books were in Hebrew or English for someone like Sonia who knew little Hebrew but didn't know English. Apparently, it was Golda Meir who recommended her for this position after Sonia's visit to Jerusalem. That what knowing right people does, that is what you call *proteczia*. Very convenient.

The small research library was not open to everybody, only to professors and graduate students. It was the same library where Sonia had met Professor Evans for the first time.

In her job Sonia basically babysat the precious books. Professors and graduate students knew exactly what they needed. They walked in, picked up their books, signed them out, and left, all while Sonia continued doing her homework and reviewing her lectures.

One day, she looked up to see a tall, slim, gorgeous man about thirty to thirty-five years old.

"My name is Joshua Steg. I don't want to disturb you. Continue your studies," he said while signing his name and the name of the book he was taking.

He had dark, piercing eyes with long eyelashes, wavy hair, a sculpted face, and long, elegant fingers. He was exactly the type Sonia was always attracted to. Professor Joshua Steg? The one Raisa was always talking about introducing her to? Wow!

"You are not disturbing me. The books are my responsibility."

"You must be a new graduate student?"

"I am not a graduate student. I am a new librarian here." Sonia wished her Hebrew was better.

"I hear a clear, Russian accent. Rather unusual."

"I am from Vilnius," Sonia said, blushing.

"Vilnius? I am from Vilnius too." He gave her the most charming smile.

Professor Steg didn't ask more questions. He just took his book and sat in a comfortable armchair reading it.

As were many others, Sonia was mesmerized by his looks, by his reputation, by the way he spoke beautiful Hebrew after such a short time in Israel, and by the way students worshiped him. He was ten years older than Sonia and one hundred times smarter than she or anybody else she knew. Professor Steg was plain brilliant. He had arrived in Israel as a Polish citizen in 1955. Sonia did not know how to get his attention.

Professor Steg often came to the library and was very sweet, but he did not seem to see her as an attractive, young woman. He was obviously single, unattached as he worked late most evenings.

Sonia tried to ask him many questions to engage him in conversation. He was exceptionally polite and took his time answering them. He brought her books in Russian to prepare for her classes, but never asked her any personal questions. Did Sonia feel rejected? It was painful to have a crush on someone without the hope of having it reciprocated. She pined for him in vain.

It was heartbreaking for Sonia to think about how carefully Raisa had planned this match before Sonia arrived. In her ignorance and silly stubbornness, Sonia never gave Raisa or herself a fair chance.

Now Sonia wished she had trusted Raisa to introduce her to Professor Joshua Steg soon after her arrival in Israel. She deeply regretted her flat refusal to go for dinner at his aunt's, not trusting Raisa's choice. There was no way to turn the clock back. Try as she did, Joshua Steg did not pay any attention to her besides being kind and helpful by offering her good books.

Fantasizing about him for a long time, Sonia wrote a poem:

MY MOUTH IS OPEN, THIRSTY FOR THE MAGIC

For years I cherished my jewel box
That kept my secrets in.
They blossomed into flowers
Stayed cozy in my purse.
In vain I hoped for magic to sprout
Dreaming to be caressed...
Sorry, the wrong address
I ended with the box intact
To open it alone in the dark.
Most blossoms wilted.
Some others dried.
Let us remain hoping
That in search of meaning
The real world will always stay
One step ahead of logic.
Joy and laughter may mask the sorrow.

> Behind sorrow there is lots of longing.
> And if it wasn't there
> I wouldn't dare to dream.

Enthusiastically, Sonia shared her infatuation with Esther and begged her to come for a visit. Esther could stay with her in the dormitory.

Esther arrived one afternoon driving her new Vespa. Sonia was preparing for her midterm exam when Esther walked into the library. Tall, tanned and slim, she looked like a model. There was only Professor Steg working on his research papers by the window.

"Be patient. In about half an hour, we can leave," Sonia whispered to Esther, not wanting to disturb him. When the time came to close the library, Professor Steg got up.

"You can stay. We are leaving, but you can close the library later," Sonia suggested.

"It is okay. I am ready to go."

"Professor Steg, this is Esther, my only cousin. She is from Vilnius too." Sonia was proud to introduce her.

There was an unfamiliar look of fascination on his face when he looked at Esther.

He never looked at me like that, thought Sonia, envious.

Sonia was devastated when Esther came to Technion again two weeks later, but not to visit her. She had a date with Professor Steg. Sonia felt totally betrayed. It was a bitter pill to swallow.

There was another young man in the picture. He was a graduate student with green eyes who Sonia tried to flirt with every time she met him in the student cafeteria. He, too, was friendly, but not more than that. His name was Ariel. Ariel also seemed to spend many hours in the library where Sonia worked. She was clearly intimidated in his presence. It was as if she were from another planet. To Ariel, Sonia wasn't Jewish. Sonia arrived from the Soviet Union knowing nothing about Judaism. Sonia could never be one of his friends. They belonged to different communities and different worlds and had very little in common. Ariel was the only one Sonia met in Technion who always wore a *kippah*.

"Learning the Torah is what keeps the world going. If everyone stopped learning the Torah, the world would cease to exist," Sonia heard him say once.

Hard stuff. She did not understand what it meant!

After a few months of seeing Ariel almost every afternoon, Sonia asked him to help her with her lab reports. He was very sweet and helpful about it.

Ariel lived with his mother and younger brother not far from campus in a small, modest apartment. He worked for three years after being in the army, before deciding to study Architecture at Technion. His father had been an artist. He died on a Sunday at age forty-seven, one day after Ariel's Bar Mitzvah.

Ariel didn't say much, but he was an excellent listener. Sonia talked for both of them and answered all of his questions. Sonia was amazed by how interested Ariel was in her life in Vilnius, her impressions about Israel, and her adjustment to a completely new life. Ariel liked Russian music, classical music, and playing the piano. His mother was a piano teacher. His grandparents were from Odessa.

Ariel also introduced her to classical music and to Opera. Sonia's Israeli classmates had little interest in classical music or European literature. They loved nature and preferred spending most of their leisure time exploring every hidden trail of their tiny country.

Somehow in her heart, Sonia believed that even if she said something wrong, Ariel would understand her. It was not as important to her how rational or how detail-oriented his mind was. It wasn't important how phenomenal his memory was or how much of the Torah he knew. What amazed Sonia was how he understood other people, people who were completely different from him. She admired how much empathy and patience he had, how much respect and love Ariel had for humanity. Did it all came from the Torah, from Jewish teachings?

Sonia wished to have a fraction of his faith in *Hashem*, his commitment to Judaism. For now, Sonia was grateful for his friendship, for his willingness to teach her. Actually, if she were being honest, for his patience in teaching her.

There was nobody in all the country besides Jamima with whom Sonia could discuss her complicated relationship with Raisa, to share her guilt. Nobody. Also, she did not want people to know how it worked out so differently than they anticipated. Sonia was ashamed by how poorly she had handled their interactions.

"Ariel, do I bore you with my problems? Do I talk too much?"

"Sonia, you are not talking too much. I am your friend. I am here to listen. This is what real friends are for."

"How come you have so much patience?"

"*Hashem* made me this way. *Hashem* wanted me to be your friend. I want you to talk to me whenever you want to talk. *Hashem* will guide me to be helpful."

Why was it so easy to talk to Ariel? It was therapeutic to tell Ariel about Mama, about how Sonia missed her and how she felt guilty about leaving her so abruptly,

"I felt so safe next to her. Did I get it, standing on the grey platform of the Vilnius train station, that my train would cross the border never to return? I did not. She did. I was excited to leave. It was cruel and selfish! Mama was sad that I was going far away, never to return. Does it bore you to hear me talking so much about myself?"

"Not at all. I appreciate that you trust me enough to talk about something so painful."

"Ariel, it is not painful. It is just constantly on my mind."

More and more often, before going to sleep, Sonia caught herself going over his remarks. Maybe Ariel understood her better than she understood herself. Was it possible? Would he remain her friend for a long time? What would happen if Ariel met someone, fell in love, and got married? His future wife would not let them be friends. She would be too jealous. It is normal.

Surprisingly, the first thing Sonia started doing after wakening up was *natiat jadaim*, then she slowly recited the Jewish prayer *Modeh Ani*, thanking *Hashem* for returning her soul to her in compassion, for her health, for her good fortune, and for having Ariel as a friend. It was a very soothing way to start the new day.

Raisa knew how to annoy Sonia. Sonia thought her to be crazy, irrational, unreasonable, and demanding. Raisa expected Sonia tell her every little thing that was happening in her life, whom she was meeting, dating, and going out with.

Sonia had a new friend, American student who fell in love with an Israeli named Zevik. It looked like a promising romance for a few months. Then, without much explanation, Zevik broke off the relationship. Her friend Evelyn was crushed. She could not sleep, eat, or go out.

"Can I come stay with you for a Sabbath?" Evelyn asked Sonia.

"No problem. Come and stay with me. I am alone in the dorm for now."

The same day that Evelyn was coming, Raisa called to find out what was happening.

"Evelyn is coming to visit me for Sabbath. She wants to be with me alone."

Evelyn arrived that evening. They bought ready-made food and sat down to relax and chat. In the middle of their dinner, the door opened and Raisa walked in. Evelyn was surprised, and Sonia was absolutely furious.

"Ima, why did you come? I specifically told you that we wanted to be alone."

"I did not want to be home alone. I wanted to be with you."

Sonia was choking with fury but was unable to ask Raisa to leave. The evening was ruined. A few days later, Sonia received a letter in her mailbox about how disappointed Raisa was in her as a daughter. She, Sonia, was never taught to love, to respect her mother. She was not capable of a normal relationship between mother and daughter.

It was not the first time Raisa accused Sonia of being selfish, ungrateful, and cruel. At times Sonia thought she could not handle it. But she promised herself that she would ignore Raisa, never go to see her, and to try to forget about her.

"My Ima is so needy. It is so difficult to be with her," Sonia would share with Ariel, hoping for his understanding.

"How can you judge anybody, never mind your complicated mother? We have no idea what she went through in the hell of Europe. You may believe she told you everything. But what she didn't tell you may be more relevant. In everybody, there is divine sparkle, a heavenly soul. It cannot be ignored. When all physical layers are removed, our pure, naked soul is left exposed. We are not allowed to be angry or upset because our soul is always pure. We can only try to understand."

"Ariel, you are not helping me. You make me feel wicked."

"Sonia, not wicked, but not very kind either."

Each time after talking to Ariel, Sonia felt guilty, insensitive, lacking in compassion, and ready to run to Raisa to ask forgiveness.

Instead, she silently pleaded with Mama and with her father, Israel.

Mama, Papochka, I need you now. I need you very much. I am not going to cry over yesterday, over all the mistakes I made. Maybe there were no mistakes, maybe those were little destinies. So much time has been wasted in endless fantasies about romantic love, true understanding, and finding a real soulmate. How long does it take to figure out that the reality of life is comprehension? One should not expect someone else to make them happy. One has to learn to do what makes them happy, to learn to understand oneself first, to know limitations, to have knowledge. Knowledge provides power, security, and a right direction.

Where and how to learn? Too bad there are no shortcuts. There is sort of a shortcut if one is lucky enough to find a mentor, to follow their path, their wise counsel…maybe be truly religious…

Some people have more than one mentor. I have none. Too bad. I have wasted a lot of time trying to figure out life on my own. But maybe I should not complain because I always, really always, even when I did not know it, had my angels, the two of you. Every disaster over my head was lifted gently. You transported me into a warm, comfortable place before I could even grasp the actual scope and meaning of it.

Mama, do you remember buying me matzos every spring? I had no idea what it meant, but our neighbours Malka and Fedia were Jewish. Even if I did not like them or their looks or the way they talked about you, I did like their matzos. Dadia Kolia used to say that no matter where the wolf is, he is always looking to escape into the forest. It took twenty years to register that he was wise and had more laissez faire than anyone I had ever met. But Dadia Kolia did not particularly like me. It was traumatic to know that he considered me ugly. He often wondered if anyone would ever marry me. He made me wonder too. I think that right then, at the age of eleven, I decided that the first man who fell in love with me, if I ever met such a man, I would marry immediately and be a grateful and wonderful wife like Irina.

Irina and Dadia Kolia are a beautiful couple. I miss them. The way they looked at each other, it was clear that they were in love. For all the years that I knew them, they were not apart for a single day. When they came to visit us from the country, they always came together. Mamochka, Irina missed you a lot. Dadia Kolia too. He seldom went to visit his parents.

He just stayed in our house, read books, and let Irina be near you. It usually was a one-way conversation because you talked very little. You listened and smiled. I loved your smile. Sometimes you just nodded your head. I miss you so much. I was a bad daughter. I left, yet Irina stayed next to you. She, too, did not like me very much. I believe she was jealous of me, of our closeness. She had Dadia Kolia, I had you. It was enough for me. I liked both of them and wanted Irina to love me like her sister, but she could not.

I remember trying to engage Dadia Kolia in a conversation. I asked him about a million things that made me curious about him. Like why did he want to be a Batushka? Why he did not continue to study medicine? How come his mother did not like America and wanted to come back to Ukraine? Were they really robbed on the way? Why did they settle in Vilna? But the most important thing I wanted to know was how he fell in love with Irina. What exactly did he like the most about her? Was she stunning? I knew she was, but I wanted to hear it from him.

There was a photo on the piano of two of them just after their marriage. Dadia Kolia looked like a movie star. I loved to look at that photo. He had such a nice, calm expression; his face looked so happy. Seldom did he look like that in real life.

Mama, mamochka, do you remember me? Do you ever think about me? Do you still love me? Do you miss me the way I miss you? Do you believe we have a soul? Do you believe in the afterlife? Is my father's soul somewhere looking over me?

In the student dorm, Sonia shared her room with a Rumanian girl named Rina. It was not easy to understand Rina's begrudging disappointment with Israel. The standard at Technion was very high. In Rumania, Rina would already be an engineer making money. Here in Israel, she was struggling to pass her second year of studies. You definitely had to be exceptionally intelligent to do well in Technion. In Kaunas, Sonia hardly went to classes, never missed a movie, and studied only few days before finals. Everything depended on your memory. Sonia, who was top student in her engineering class in Kaunas, soon realized that in Israel she had to work very hard just to pass the courses. The academic standard in Technion was very high. At Kaunas, she simply memorized the material. There was never a question asked on the exam that was not covered in the lectures. One didn't have to be brilliant to get top marks. At Technion, however, the exam questions were original. All your books and your notes could be consulted. You were supposed to solve the problems using your knowledge of the material. The actual problems had not been covered in the class. It was tough.

After two years of struggling, she finally made the decision to quit Engineering and to transfer to the Faculty of Architecture.

Sonia loved to walk the streets admiring buildings, modern and old. Architecture smiled at her and lifted her spirits.

Rina had been a top student in Rumania, and, like Sonia, resented the exam system at Technion which was such a struggle to pass.

Everything was strange for Rina in Israel: the air, the trees, the climate. In her head, she knew that Israel was a Jewish country. She expected to have a special feeling for it, but feeling was just not there. Rina found religious Jews with long sideburns and dark stockings disgusting. Young Israelis struck her as narrow minded. The emotional distrust between Ashkenazi and Sfardim was intolerable.

"Have patience. We are a very young country. Don't let it bother you. With time, everything will be ironed out," Sonia tried to convince Rina. "Our young country is going through the pains of maturity; it is a difficult adolescence."

"Israelis talk mostly about the money, about refrigerators, washing machines, and the cost of German cars. It is boring for me. I need more culture in my life."

Rina invited Sonia for a vernissage of new, young, Israeli painters. It was incredibly exciting to look at the vibrant, original creations of so many young artists in one room. Sonia could not sleep that night. That same week she registered for a painting class given by one of the artists.

There was a nude model at her first class. Sonia was embarrassed to paint the naked girl, but she concentrated and tried her best.

"You should paint. You definitely have talent," one of the women in the class said while looking at Sonia's pink nude.

"You really think so?"

Sonia continued her painting classes and enjoyed them a lot. It was so much fun to paint no matter what the topic: nudes in her class, fruit in her kitchen, buildings outside her windows. It was good for her soul.

She became good friends with one of older people in her class. Olga had arrived from Belorussia in 1957 and was exceptionally happy in Israel.

"We knew very little about this country. I didn't want to leave Minsk but my mother did."

"Are you pleased that you left Belorussia?"

"Sonia, are you kidding me? The day when we arrived, I felt like a heavy stone rolled from my shoulders. My Jewishness is not an issue anymore. I am like everyone else, not a stranger within enemy territory. It's a fabulous feeling to feel freedom and not be ashamed to be different. You could not win in Minsk. Among Goym, I was always Jewish. Here, sometimes among Jews, I feel Russian, but it is temporary, I hope. I could never live in Minsk today. It would choke me."

"Amazing. You are lucky that your parents had Polish citizenship."

"Sonia, you have no idea how lucky I feel. I could never express my feelings there the way I can here in Israel. The freedom I feel in my heart and in my bones is just waiting to be exposed."

"It shows in your painting."

"I am glad you say it. I want to be a professional painter."

"In Israel, you throw an apple and hit an artist, so much art, creativity. It is in the air."

"I totally agree with you, Sonia. This is why I love and adore this tiny gem of a country with its numerous artistic communities. Eventually I would like to live in Safed or in Ein Hod. Safed is not only artistic, it's a very spiritual place."

"Olga, for me, the most spiritual place is Jerusalem. When I graduate, I will look for a position there."

But there were other young newcomers who were more like Rina, disappointed very quickly with what they found in Israel. Sonia felt particularly badly for Joseph, a young engineer from Czechoslovakia who, after being disenchanted with Marxist-Leninist ideology, had chosen to embrace Zionism.

Joseph was madly in love with his fiancée Blanca, who left Prague with him, bought tickets to Vienna, and then to Israel. Blanca, who sat next to him through five years of studies, who did the best drawings in the Faculty of Mechanical Engineering, who was supposed to become his wife in the new country of Israel, met a fifty-two-year-old, wealthy, Italian businessman in Vienna and disappeared with him before Joseph could say "wow!"

Joseph arrived sad and then became poisoned by the fact that ordinary people push and shove each other and are rude. He expected a

Jewish country to be civilized, with its suffering people being particularly nice to each other.

Joseph suffered from broken heart. It completely coloured his impression and total perception of everything that happened to him in the last two years.

"I cannot believe I could not find a better job," Joseph complained. "I came here to do something important and to contribute. What did I get? Night shifts, no respect, and no appreciation. They chase you and boss you around like a little puppy."

"Many people work in much worse conditions than you, willing to do anything to build the country. They are real Zionists," Sonia argued.

"Leave me alone with so-called Zionists! Where are they? Please show them to me! Maybe it is my director who lives in a bungalow with ten rooms, drives an American Cadillac, and takes a vacation every year in Switzerland. Is he a real Zionist?

How can you tolerate constant noise on the streets, in the restaurants, and the aggressive pushing on the busses? You are lucky if it does not bother you."

"It does not. When I look at the Israeli crowd, I see smart, confident people who know exactly what they want. I feel inferior to them."

Sonia woke up each morning expecting that something good was going to happen on that particular day. And it usually did. Her happiness was in her hands and in her head. She soon learned that her feelings were completely dependent on her thinking.

Sonia had been to a synagogue once in her life in Vilnius. She remembered being curious, remembered passing by a pre-war building to find a neglected room with a few old men making loud and unpleasant sounds. If anything, Sonia found it a bit repulsive.

Now there were so many thoughts in her confused mind that she had a need to talk more to some higher power. If it existed or not almost did not matter.

Reciting *Modeh Ani* every morning suddenly was not enough. Sonia dressed up on a Saturday morning, putting on a skirt instead of her regular jeans, and went to the nearest shul. It was like being on another planet. Men were busy praying with big shawls over their heads. Sonia could not make any sense of the prayers and couldn't recognize the words although she understood spoken Hebrew fairly well by this point. Nevertheless, she stayed until the end and joined others for *Kiddush* after services.

"How did you like our services?"

"I don't know how to pray. I didn't understand the prayers."

"I don't understand much either, but I come often."

"Why?"

"Being here and listening to Hazan *davening* has miraculous healing power for me. Prayer is not just reading *Sidur* or *Machzor*. While praying, I feel my history and the passionate yearnings of my people for two thousand years, our tragedies."

"Without understanding what they are saying?"

"Yes. I don't read much of the text. I mostly listen, listen to the cries of my people."

"Very powerful. You must be very spiritual and lucky to believe in God. Me? I don't really believe there is a God that makes things happen in this world."

"Start praying and start learning. Belief will come. Did you notice that we always pray, 'Us, Give Us, Lord?' We never say just 'I.' Jewish prayer is not about the personal encounter of a lonely man with his lonely God. It is more of a collective prayer when you have to include the needs of all our people."

"It makes sense. I personally cannot comprehend how our people could have faith so deeply rooted in their everyday life, and how they never lost hope for two thousand years being far away from their land and scattered all over the globe."

"That is the reason we are here now after two thousand years. It's our ability to have faith in our God, to follow our Torah, and to pray. We were conquered, destroyed, deprived, and viciously prosecuted, but we never gave up hope."

"Maybe this is a magic secret of our survival."

The next week Sonia went again to the same *shul*, hoping to meet this intelligent woman she spoke to. After having such a nice conversation, she didn't even know her name. The woman was not there. Sonia stayed for a *Kiddush*, this time mingling with the crowd. She was surprised to see so many young people and was sincerely envious of their deep belief in God and their commitment to the old traditions. Sonia could not relate to the rules, could not yet believe that the Torah was God's spoken words on Mount Sinai, and that there really was a Moses who took his people out of Egypt after ten horrible plagues.

15

(Voice of Israel)

Sonia wanted to be the best she could be, the best G-d meant and intended her to be.

Ariel was becoming her mentor. She goes to a lot of classes taught by his Rabbi. Sonia still isn't religious, but somehow, after each of the Rabbi's lectures, Sonia feels like a better human being who is closer to Truth, to inner peace, and to simple wisdom.

She doesn't understand the words of the prayers. With a soothing melody, she finds her own words that can somehow convey her feelings to the Highest Power.

My daughter talks to me, whom she doesn't remember. But she feels that I am always somewhere around her.

For her G-d is too far. She isn't observant enough to pray to him directly. Sonia likes to pray in the synagogue. She doesn't understand the words of the Torah. She listens to the Hazan, looks up to the Habima, and then talks to me, longing for my approval and my encouragement. There is so much passion in her words.

I watch her serene, radiant, and trusting face. I protect her. She thanks me constantly. It is hard for me to keep distant from her.

I hear her loving prayer:

"Papochka, you may think that I am crazy, but you must hear me. It doesn't matter that I cannot see you, but I feel you. The world is miraculous place. I don't understand how G-d handles His affairs. There is a lot of mystery. I don't understand how heavy planes can fly or how I can hear someone's voice on the other end of a planet. It doesn't matter that I don't see you. Papochka, you must see me and you must hear me. I know that you will guide me. Please, please!"

Her lips tremble. Sonechka gets very emotional.

I cannot keep away as I did for years. She didn't talk to me before. Now she does, she pleads. She expects me to be there for her. My dear Sonechka, it is okay to pray. Up above, He hears you too, but I will stand by.

I touch her shoulders. They are tense. I stroke her hair. She relaxes.

Why so much fascination with storybook romance?

She knows how much Raisa was in love with me. My Sonechka wants the same all-consuming love. She doesn't want just a rainbow. Sonia wants fireworks and sparks. In that sense, she inherited my intense temperament. I was happy most of the time. I was happy with what I had while Raisa was unhappy with what was missing.

Now I see my Sonechka preparing for an upcoming exhibition. Her back is curved in an uncomfortable position, her forehead perspires, her eyebrows stretch. She loves to paint; she loves art. She speaks with colours. She feels through colours. She has a lot of dreams.

Childish innocence radiates through her juicy naturmorts of cherries and peaches. She loves Cézanne. Sonia adores Matisse and his colours of the Mediterranean Sea. My daughter also loves van Gogh. She examines each of his paintings over and over, mesmerized by his thick brush strokes, the energy and passion that scream from his canvases, and his peaceful, poetic apple blossoms in his last months at Arles.

She is also inspired by Israeli art. There is so much of it in this little place; so much creativity, energy, and passion. I watch her carefully. Her small place is full of charm. She picks up an old art book and sits down in her enormous grandfather chair she picked up at the antique auction. It is a funny story. I saw her there.

A few times a year, antique dealers and artisans who work from home have the chance to bring China, jewelry, and pictures to an exhibit for people in their neighbourhood. Small stuff. One elderly lady watched Sonia admiring her custom jewelry. She got up from her chair to help Sonia choose some of it.

"Which piece would you like to try? They are fun."

"Wow!" Sonia's eyes focused on the green, velvet armchair on which the lady had been sitting. "I would like that chair."

"The chair is not for sale," the lady answered, categorically.

"Maybe by the end of the show you will change your mind. Today is the first day. I will pass by again."

This is how she got the chair.

Initially Sonia had hoped to change the fabric. Meanwhile she got used to it and got to like it. The huge armchair swallowed her, giving her a lot of comfort. Many nights my Sonechka fell asleep in it with a book on her lap and her glasses on the carpet.

Sonia sits flipping through a magnificent book of pictures from Gardner's gallery in Boston. Her face has a glow of pleasure and understanding. I know she will paint tonight. The show is next month. She is far from ready now, but she will be ready for the exhibit. Sonia performs well under pressure. It is a pleasant pressure. She wants to show her work. Red, turquoise, purple, and numerous other strong colours fight for space on her canvases. There is a magical energy to her paintings. They beg one to look at them. I am bewitched. How can one be taught to paint? Your heart is open. You seem to be naked, vulnerable, lying, sitting, and standing across your brilliant compositions, full of dreams, fantasies, and longings. Paint darling, paint.

My Sonechka is full of excitement; she loves Israel, is happy to be in this magical land, and to finally be Jewish. She never experienced antisemitism and never felt like a second-class citizen. She knew nothing about her original family or about our life before she was born. Why, then, did she want to be Jewish? She wanted to belong. Having been born Jewish, Sonia did not think there was a choice. She decided to be what she was born to be. That was it. It was as simple as that. The Truth and only the Truth.

She loves to write poems and paint. She is good at her work and loves her job.

It is already past midnight. The world around you is sleeping You are excited. I don't want to disturb you. You may sense my presence. My presence may contaminate your innocence. I am leaving for now.

It had been a long time since they spoke last, so Sonia was startled to find Raisa sitting in her room in the Technion dormitory talking to her roommate, Rina.

"Surprised?" Raisa looked straight at her.

There was sadness in her big eyes.

"I understand you haven't missed me, but I missed you."

Sonia kept quiet, not knowing what to say.

"I see you have a nice suntan. Going a lot to the beach? With whom?"

"With friends."

"Thank God you have many friends." Raisa spoke unusually slowly, stretching out her words. "I am glad that you are happy. You are a big girl. You don't need a mother anymore. It is good to be so independent."

Sonia sat down on one of a few chairs in the room. She felt tense and uneasy.

"Sonechka, you rejected me like an old rag, but I understand you today. I am not angry with you. I know you are angry with me. I know you hate me."

"I don't," Sonia interrupted, almost whispering. "I don't. Not at all."

"I felt thrown out and forgotten. You were right. You have decided that I did not understand you, that strangers are smarter, more patient, not so nervous like me. You found a way that worked better for you. I am glad." Raisa had a smile on her face, but her chin trembled and her face was covered with red spots.

Sonia leaned closer and took her hand.

"I am sorry, really sorry that I hurt you so much. It is amazing you came today. I am painting a lot and this week I am having exhibit with some other people. They choose five of mine I always liked art. Do you want to come see them?"

"I am proud of you, Sonechka. Sure, I come if you want me to."

"Thank you. Ima, since you are here and you would know can I ask you a delicate question?"

"Sure, if I can answer."

"Is Esther dating Professor Steg?"

"They are living together. Fania is not very happy about it."

"Ima, I am shocked. Do you want to know something? I am very, very jealous. Professor Steg is the most remarkable, brilliant person I have met in my life."

"I thought you will like him. I planned to make a *shiduch* for you since he arrived in Israel."

"Imale, many times I cried that it was one of my biggest mistakes to refuse your suggestion. My silly, stupid stubbornness. Maybe he would have liked me after all."

"Sonechka, don't think about it. It is water under the bridge. You will meet the right person who will love and appreciate you."

Raisa and Sonia met again the following week at Marcaz Carmel. From the top of Marcaz of Mount Carmel, life looked splendid. They sat at a cozy, attractive table. Someone stopped to say hello. She was a young, attractive woman.

"Iris, please join us. This is my daughter, Sonia."

"I didn't know you had such a grown-up, beautiful daughter. She looks like you. I would gladly join you but I have a dentist appointment across the street."

When the woman left, Sonia asked, "Who was that person?"

"One of my new friends. A year ago, I joined a book club."

"She did not know I exist?"

"The way you rejected me, how could I tell people that I have a daughter who never visits me, who actually ignores me?"

"You are right. I'm sorry about it."

"It was too humiliating. I was ashamed to admit the truth." Sonia extended her hand and gently touched Raisa's fingers.

"I love you, Sonechka," Raisa said, suddenly.

"I love you too. I also need you."

"Any more coffee? Another croissant?" asked their young, olive-skinned waitress in a tiny, leather miniskirt and silver, platform shoes. Sonia wished to say yes, but something choked inside her throat.

July 17 was Raisa's birthday. Sonia planned to invite her to a Chinese restaurant she saw not far from Technion. Maybe after dinner they would see the play starring Haim Topol. The Habima Theatre from Tel Aviv was coming to Haifa.

There was nobody in the restaurant. Sonia showed up before Raisa.

"Sorry, I am late." Raisa wore a very elegant suit Sonia hadn't seen yet.

"Did you dress up for me?" Sonia asked.

"Definitely. I even had my hair done this afternoon to look young and pretty tonight."

"Ima, you always look young and pretty."

"Sonechka, I arrived in Israel many years ago, exactly at this time of the year. In the hot summer. I have never been to a restaurant in Israel. When I was young, we used to go to a restaurant twice a week with your father."

"I was in a restaurant only once. In Moscow during the Youth Festival in 1957. But not in Vilnius."

The waiter was very attentive, explained every dish, gave interesting choices, and suggested their specialty, Peking duck. Raisa and Sonia ordered half of the duck with stir-fried noodles and vegetables.

When the Peking duck was ready, it was carted out on a large platter and put in front of them on a table with a sparkling, white tablecloth. After skillfully removing the crispy skin, the waiter, who spoke in excellent Hebrew, sliced the brown, juicy breast into thin slivers. Sonia and Raisa watched, fascinated by his skill.

"Now you take the small pieces and dip them into this delicious sauce." He took two pieces to demonstrate. Then he placed the two pieces on the edge of hot, wheat-based pancakes.

"Some guests want to spread the sauce on the pancake, but it is a much cleaner process if you dip the duck into the sauce and place it on the edge of the pancake. This is how we do it in Beijing."

The waiter placed some chopped pickles, white scallions, and cucumber batons next to the duck.

"Now all you have to do is wrap carefully. One takes the bottom over the top to create a sealed package and to prevent juices from leaking."

Sonia was first to bite her paper-thin wrap.

"Ima, yummy, really yummy. Now it is your turn to try. Do you want me to make you one?" The friendly, sweet waiter stayed for a few minutes to make sure they got it.

"What is your name?" Sonia asked him before he left their table.

"My name is Li."

"Li, you are very nice. Thank you very much. Ima, this is so much fun. Do you agree?"

"Sonia, today, you made me very happy. I hope that Izia is looking at us at this moment, smiling from high above."

"I know he is. He is looking at you ... at us."

They talked for a long time. Raisa wanted Sonia to know about life in Vilna before the war, a life that had vanished as if it did not exit.

"Let me tell you a joke. An Israeli joke," Raisa said with a smile. " There is a very well-known Israeli journalist named Ephraim Kishon. He goes out with his grandchildren in a baby carriage and meets two friends on the main street. They stop to admire what good-looking grandchildren he has. Ephraim Kishon looks at them seriously and whispers, "This is nothing. Wait till you see the pictures."

Sonia laughed until tears came to her eyes. Was it really so funny? She was not so sure. But she was sure that she wanted to see Raisa happy.

After surprisingly long time it was such a coincidence to see Ariel at Roni's birthday party. Ariel did not touch the food. Obviously, it was not his level of kashrut. Sonia walked over.

"Ariel, you disappeared. How long has it been since we saw each other last?"

"Since you moved to Jerusalem. You never got in touch with any of your classmates. I didn't disappear. You seem to be too busy. I met your classmates. Guys asked me about you, they talked about you a lot."

"What did they say?"

"Good things. They admired you changing professions after so many years of studying."

"I had to. I never wanted to be an engineer."

"Still, so much energy put, so much time. Strong determination. Like a true *sabra*."

"That is the biggest compliment I've ever heard."

"Not a compliment, just a fact."

"Ariel, thank you so much for these kind words. What are you up to these days?"

"At the present, I am working with Professor Stern in his research lab."

"So you too moved to Jerusalem. I had no idea. Do you like it?"

"Very much so. It is very challenging but very exciting. And you? What are you up to?"

"It is all very fresh and new to me but I like my job and people at work. It is not stressful. Besides, I paint. I actually take classes twice a week. You may be surprised, but I am becoming more interested in our tradition, in our religion. I know very little, not like you. Occasionally I go to *shul*."

"I am not surprised. It always struck me that you had a spiritual side you may explore eventually."

"What made you think so?"

"Your questions, my gut feeling."

"I still have difficulty with the existence of God."

"We all do."

"You don't question the existence of God. For you, it is clear. You have strong faith. More than that, you have a commitment."

"I have learned from very smart Rabbis. Once you start learning, your belief will grow exponentially. Like they say, 'Yard by yard is hard, but inch by inch is cinch.'" Once you start learning, our divine Torah will open its secrets to you."

"It is hard to find the right teacher. An inspiring teacher. There are many lectures, but most of them are tedious and boring."

"Come with me on Thursday night to Rabbi Ben Gadi's class. He is amazing."

"What does he talk about?"

"Everything. He is *Chabadnik*; he teaches *Tanya*. Jewish mysticism."

"I know nothing about these topics."

"You don't have to. He is extremely knowledgeable, a brilliant scholar."

"How old is he?"

"Maybe forty, wise as one-twenty, has ten children. People go to him for advice. He is very patient, very helpful."

"My biggest difficulty is believing that the Torah was written by God."

"Who wrote it, according to you?"

"Very wise sages put it together."

"There are many people who think like you. The majority of Israelis probably think that men wrote "The Book."

"And you, what do you think?"

"I know that *Hashem* gave us the Torah through Moses. Every single word in it is the word of God. Once you believe that *Hashem* gave us the Torah on Mount Sinai, everything flows smoothly. If you don't, nothing makes sense."

By now they were sitting outside on the roof of a 120-year-old Arab house. They faced the city spreading out in front of them. Sonia knew that the next time she saw Ariel would be at his Rabbi's class.

"We Jewish people are the only ones who experienced God. God appeared to us in front of all the nation; three million people witnessed *Hashem* talking to them. Nobody else on the entire planet can claim this type of experience."

Sonia listened to Ariel quietly, afraid to interrupt. She had nothing to add. For her, all Jewish history and the Jewish Bible seemed to be beautiful legends written by wise people. She wished to believe in a personal God who could reward and punish his creations—human beings.

"Why didn't Jesus come from the cross in front of thousands of people?" Ariel continued. "We Jews argue about everything, small or big. But one thing nobody argues about is our experience at Mount Sinai. This is very, very powerful. It cannot be made up."

Sonia said nothing. Silence warmly embraced them.

"You don't seem to be convinced."

"I understand what you are saying, but it is still not proof that our Torah is the word of God."

"It was given to us more than three thousand years ago. It is full of prophecies. Real prophecies. All of them did happen."

"What makes a prophecy real?"

"That is a topic for another discussion. I don't want to bore you with it today."

"Ariel, believe me. I want to know. Convince me how prophecy proves God gave us the Torah."

"Sonia, these prophecies could not be given by a mortal human being. How could any man announce what is going to happen a thousand years down the line? It is impossible for a man to predict. Remember, the most irrational, the most unpredictable events took place over these past 3,000 years. We were warned by *Hashem* in advance. We were told they would happen. They did."

"Ariel, with your knowledge, with your passion, with your enthusiasm, you could make even me a religious person."

"Maybe I should." Ariel smiled. "It might help to think of yourself as one of God's beloved creations, and to love yourself is to honour God in a very direct way. As long as you remember gratitude, simple humility, include others as creations of God, and stay tuned to what feels the most appropriate in terms of giving and receiving in each situation, you are on the right track. You can always give yourself the suggestion before falling asleep that you would like some insight into a particular question."

"When I need a solution, I talk to *Hashem* to help me take care of it? Do you believe that *Hashem* meant us to meet? That he sent you to teach me, to make me a real Jewish girl?"

"It would be a big *mitzvah*."

After the birthday party was over, Ariel walked Sonia home.

"How did you become friends with Roni? He is completely secular."

"Roni is a terrific and sensitive soul. We were in the army together."

Before falling asleep, Sonia couldn't help but think about Ariel, his gentle mannerisms, his green eyes, and their long, meaningful conversation.

The following Thursday she went to Rabbi Ben Gadi's lecture. Ariel was already in the room. Sonia sat next to him.

"I'm happy you came. I didn't expect you."

"Why not? I told you I was curious to learn more."

Sonia was as much interested in seeing Ariel as she was learning from Rabbi Ben Gadi. There were about twenty people in the Rabbi's study. Rabbi Ben Gadi had a calm voice. Occasionally he got very enthusiastic while walking in front of his audience.

"The only thing we have to fear is God. Everything in our life has a purpose. Everything is in *Hashem*'s hands. Life is like a surfboard on the waves. Wherever the wave takes you, is where you are supposed to be. Are there any questions at this point?"

"How do you feel about all the horrible and unjust things that are happening in the world if everything that happens is God's will?" Sonia dared to ask.

"It is the way it is. There is no explanation. We don't question God. God knows. It is divine providence."

"Why do I have such a difficulty with the concept of *Ulam Habah*?" Sonia asked Rabbi Ben Gadi after the class.

"When a person dies, because he or she is Jewish, they die on *Kiddush Hashem*. Their souls go directly to Heaven, to a beautiful place."

"All these people who died in the Holocaust are now next to *Hashem*? My poor father? Six million people?"

Sonia had a problem with it.

"Why do you have a problem with *Ulam Habah*? I believe that *Hashem* runs the world and decides where our souls should go. We are not just a body. Our body is a vessel to hold our soul. Our souls exist independent of our bodies. There definitely is another reality that we cannot understand, another universe. Many universes. We all have a mission in this world to fulfill. If we don't, we will come again. There are angels watching over us. Good angels and bad ones. Some people have the chance to meet their angels. I did. I clearly heard a voice talking to me, telling me what to do. I am glad I can talk to you about it. Some people, in hearing me talk about angels, would suggest locking me up. We may think that we are in control of our lives. We are not. *Hashem* is."

"Do you believe in *Mashiach* coming?" Sonia asked Ariel.

"One hundred percent."

"Why would you want *Mashiach* to come?"

"Don't you?"

"I don't relate to *Mashiach* coming. What would you like to happen when Mashiach comes?"

"I would like to meet our forefathers, David Hamelech, Rabbi Akiva. I find the character of Rabi Akiva very moving: his noble spirit, the way he thought, the way he served God. The most I would like to know is how *Hashem* wants me to serve him better. There is physical reality and there is spiritual reality. I accept them both."

Sonia had caught herself lately going places she would meet Ariel as if by chance.

One night when she couldn't sleep, she got up and went to sit on the balcony. She took a pen and wrote while thinking about her life and about Ariel.

> Along the journey of our life
> So little warning.
> We drive along
> Follow the signs.
> When we miss and try to get back
> They seldom show again.
> I wish someone to touch my hair,
> My cheeks, my hand.
> Gently, my heart.
> I close my eyes to dream.
> Outside, small leaves smile shyly
> Hiding in the bushes
> Wind whispers and they tremble
> Begging for warmth.
> Buds open like a dusty green
> They claim their space
> They take their time
> Gently giving pleasure
> Teasing with their fresh beauty
> Promising to be different from last time.
> Each bush, each flower claimed to be a poet.

Sonia decided to keep a kosher house. She bought two new sets of dishes. One was avocado-green with little, pink roses and trimmed with gold. There were twenty-four plates with cute matching salad bowls with a butterfly design in the middle. This was Sonia's dairy set. The other set of dishes were cobalt-blue with white decorated with intricate Chinese dragons. She used them for *fleishig* dishes.

Setting the table in an attractive way was fifty percent of her dinner experience. Sonia was not lazy about shopping, cooking, and preparing for her guests. It gave her a lot of pleasure. She had no cookbooks and loved to invent her own recipes. Her friends adored her dinners. Mama would be very proud of her. Irina most probably would not believe that Sonia was capable of entertaining in such an elegant fashion.

Sonia had also furnished her apartment in a very traditional, comfortable style.

On this particular Friday night, Sonia invited Ima, her young, American neighbour Bracha with her academic husband Aaron, and Jossi, a young musician she met recently at her art class.

Sonia did not cook on Shabbat. Everything was prepared in advance. She had a hot plate to keep her chicken soup warm.

Jossi was very helpful in the kitchen.

Sonia set her table very nicely with four dishes: first the gold charger, then the plate for the main course, then a smaller plate with a soup bowl on top of it.

Before long, the conversation turned to Jewish religion.

"We live in an open world. There is a core of Jewish heritage; Jewish culture that we inherited from generation to generation for more than two thousand years. There is so much knowledge outside of the Torah that enriches our life," said Aaron who started the topic because he felt that Jossi was too religious for his liking. "I have a problem with Jews who claim that what is outside of the Torah is invalid. I agree that everything in the Torah has precious value, but things outside the Torah should not be ignored or be considered nonsense."

"In my book, Jewish people survived because of Jews with strong feelings for our heritage and our culture, not necessarily a strict adherence to the Halacha," said Raisa, pleased to participate in the discussion. "The strictly Orthodox want you to believe that we survived because of them, their rigidity. Maybe they are actually right."

"They may be right. Do you believe in God?" asked Bracha, who did not want to create heated disagreements.

"They are not right. Do I believe in God? God as what? As a superior force? Yes, but…" Aaron was not giving up.

"I think that one of many reasons that we Jews survived as a people is because Goym didn't want us to assimilate, to be part of their world. Whatever God's plan is for us, we had, and still have today, so much trouble, so much hate directed toward us for no other reason than being born Jewish. If they had let us assimilate, I don't believe there would be Jewish people as a nation," Raisa said, really enjoying the conversation.

"We would be smaller in numbers, but those who are committed and are ready to sacrifice for Hashem would still be around, along with the Torah, to remind us that we were at Har Sinai, that Hashem talked to us, gave us guidance. But like Adam and Eve, we were deaf," said Jossi, who had been pretty quiet until now.

"The Torah was given to us. I am not certain we understand the message. Every word in the Torah is interpreted by different Rabbis, and each one has disciples who claim theirs is the right and the only way. So, we argue and fight and don't hear each other. We are very difficult people, unfortunately." Sonia was pleased to share her thoughts.

We paid such a heavy price for being so difficult, for not listening to Hashem's commandments, so much punishment.…" Jossi was not pleased that Aaron and Bracha could not see his point.

"I am very upset about not being counted for minyan. In which way I am inferior to the men in our congregation?" asked Bracha.

"Bracha, it has nothing to do with inferiority or intelligence. I have no problem with traditional restrictions," Sonia said, trying to convince her friend. "The way I see an Orthodox synagogue is actually as a men's club. We women have clubs of our own. Jewish women, in particular, have a superior position in the home. Women run Jewish households. Nothing ever happens without a wife's permission. A Jewish woman makes all the decisions as far as kid's education, finances, what to buy, whom to invite. You name it. And in a strictly Orthodox home, women don't even go to shul on the Sabbath. I never understood the bitter rage that feminists unleash on traditional Judaism. I don't have any desire to count for a minyan. Who needs extra responsibility? We have more than enough. It has nothing to do with respect, with equality, with intelligence. There are so many clever and intelligent Jewish women, and men are ready to consult with them and listen to their wisdom."

As her main course, Sonia served turkey with mangoes. Everyone loved it. After the main course, they continued talking about religion, eventually switching to politics. It was after eleven thirty when Jossi got up from the table to leave.

"I am going early to the synagogue tomorrow."

Once Jossi left, Aaron and Bracha got up from the table to leave.

"Thank you so much. It was a lovely evening. It had a real Sabbath atmosphere. Sonia, I am impressed by how much you know."

"Aaron, I know very little. I just go to some classes every Thursday afternoon from four to six o'clock. Bracha, you can join me."

"Maybe."

"Sonechka, I have no words for how proud I am of you. You cook like a real Jewish balabusta. Now you have to teach me." Raisa hugged her, keeping her close for a few seconds.

"Imale, don't go yet. I will walk you home."

On Saturday morning, Sonia woke up at six thirty as usual. She wanted to go to the shul where Ariel prayed.

A new, young, *Hazan* read the text very fast. Sometimes Sonia was able to follow his prayers, but she mostly lost the place on the page.

"How was your dinner last night?" Ariel asked her after the services.

"Actually, better than I expected. We had a lengthy discussion about God and the Torah. My neighbour Bracha was a bit confused. She is very American, secular. She wants to learn, but she has difficulty with religion, with *Halacha*."

"Too bad. Judaism, if you practice it right, is actually a way of life. It is something that you are aware of from the moment you get up in the morning. Christians are Christians on Sunday only. The first thing a religious Jew does is thank *Hashem* for giving them back their *neshoma*. It is so beautiful."

"The Modeh Ani is the only prayer I know and like to say in Hebrew. Otherwise, I don't pray, cannot really pray. My Hebrew is not good enough," said Sonia.

"*Hashem* understands all languages. What really counts are the feelings in your heart. Words are there to help you start. From the beginning when God gave us the Torah, He gave us the choice to take it or not take it. This week, Parsha Moshe told us that we have a choice.

Choice is very important. We can only feel right if we choose it. Feelings cannot be forced. Without the feelings, observance doesn't have the same value. The Jewish religion is not a passive religion. It is doing things like observing commandments and doing mitzvahs, but it has to feel right. Our purpose as Jews is to bring light to the nations and to be an example. We are different from all other nations. We were given the Torah by G-d! I remember in my family, when we were little and fighting, my father would come and gently say, "Kindale, remember Kol Yaakov, no fights. We deal with soft voices. We learn the Torah with our voice. We argue by discussing, and we solve everything by talking. Revenge is not our value. Justice, yes, but never revenge. We have to learn through struggle, we always struggle, but we pray and never give up hope."

All three mothers, Sara, Rivka, and Rachel, had difficulty conceiving. They prayed and prayed. Hashem listened to them. Their story teaches us the power of prayer! We also learn from them to have hope and to not give up when nothing works. Every one of us here is a messenger of Divine providence to teach other, to improve this world, to bring more goodness to it. Everything that happens is the will of G-d. Nothing ever happens without the Divine plan."

"Ariel, how can I believe in it when the world seems crazy with so much going on at this very moment? How can you believe that everything is the will of G-d?"

"I have no choice. What is the alternative? That everything happens at random and there is no design, no reason for it? This would be much worse. It would make our life meaningless. There must be a reason that we are put on this planet."

Talking about Torah, Jewish values was Ariel's passion. As always, listening to Ariel was music to Sonia's starving soul. She just wanted to be in the same space as he, to hear his voice, to catch some wisdom. She wanted more knowledge about her culture and her rich heritage that she hardly knew about.

Sonia would be a birthday girl in two days. There was nothing planned. Nobody even knew except Raisa.

Her doorbell rang very early at six o'clock. Sonia grabbed her housecoat and ran to open it.

"Oh my God, a big bouquet of white lilies! From whom?" Who had guessed that lilies were her favourite flowers?

"There is a note," said the dark-eyed Israeli *sabra* who worked in the flower shop on the corner of Aza Street.

Dear Sonia,
    Happy birthday.
    Take a deep breath and smell the flowers.
    Warmest wishes for your beautiful spiritual journey.

                                      Your friend, Ariel

The short note and the sweet fragrance melted her itching heart.

That afternoon, Sonia called Ariel to thank him for the beautiful lilies and to invite him for dinner. She bought every delicious thing from Glad Kosher Bakery and served them on her pretty new plates.

"Are you in a hurry?" Sonia asked when Ariel got up to leave.

"Sonia, don't tempt me to stay longer. It is not about you. It is about me. I've worked very hard to do what is right, not what I feel like." Ariel gently took her hand and touched her fingers with his soft, full lips.

Sonia blushed. While saying goodbye at the door, Sonia gives him a gentle hug for a split second.

It was already midnight. She was still looking at her hand and touching her fingers, unable to believe that Ariel had actually kissed them. She sat on the balcony with a song in her heart, talking to *Hashem* and Ariel at the same time.

    Sing me a song
    About sky so blue
    About grass so green
    About birds so free
    Sing me a song about love forever.
    Sing me a song that never ends
    Sing me a song about life so big
    Sing me a song about sky so high
    About life so free
    Sing me a song about love forever
    Sing me a song about dreams and joy.
    Did you really kiss my hand?

> Was it really, really you?
> Was it really, really me?
> You touched my soul,
> You hold my heart.
> Sing me a song…

Sonia peeked at the clock on her night table a few times: one o'clock, two o'clock, three thirty… By four o'clock, she closed her tired eyes, expecting an interesting dream.

Sonia woke up at eleven o'clock in the morning. The very first thing she wished to do after saying *Modeh Ani* was visit Raisa's small apartment.

Raisa had moved to Jerusalem soon after Sonia had gotten her new position.

Raisa's flat was on the first floor with an entrance from the garden. The door was open. Sonia watched Raisa sweeping the floor in the kitchen for a few seconds.

"Imale, I don't know how to say it." She moved forward.

"Sonechka, I know." Raisa hugged her, holding her tight for a while. "Is it Ariel?"

"What makes you say that?" Sonia said, shocked.

They sat down at the kitchen table to have a lunch. Raisa served herring, kefir, hummus, and Israeli salad.

"I know how you feel about Ariel. He loves you. It is impossible not to love you. Just have patience. For now, Ariel has a lot of influence on you. He knows it, and he cherishes it."

"What are you talking about?"

"Sonechka, just the way you think, the way you have grown spiritually in the last year, the way you forgave me."

"Please, don't say a word about it. I still feel guilty about the way I treated you, the way I had a *chutzpah* to judge you. I am ashamed."

"Don't be. You are very young and very innocent. You don't know life. Try my borsch. Do you want sour cream with it? I've started cooking again. I did not cook for years."

"How is it that you have such yummy food in the house? It is not like you."

"I knew you would come." Raisa smiled.

"You didn't."

Raisa looked tired. But, as usual, everything was spotless. Her silk, fuchsia housecoat had seen brighter days. Raisa's slippers, too, looked wilted, but there was still something elegant and charming in her posture. Ima looked straight at Sonia. It was heartwarming to admit that they had the same colour and same shape of eyes.

Sonia tried to envision her Ima as a little girl in Vilnius with no worries, being spoiled and loved by her parents and grandparents. She imagined innocent and stunning Raisa at seventeen meeting Israel, who was twenty-four at the time, and feeling about him the way that Sonia felt about Ariel.

"Ima, please tell me more about how you met my father. Did you love him so very, very much from the very beginning?"

"Did I love him very much?" Raisa's eyes moistened. "I didn't think I could live without him."

"How often do you think about him?"

"Sonechka, I think about him every single day. I talk to him every morning and every night. I believe I will meet him. I have to meet him. Not only my Izia. I will meet my parents, my sisters, my brother, and all my family. I have to."

"Ima, you talk like Ariel. I never expected to hear it from you."

"Why? How could I breathe or wake up in the morning if I didn't believe…?"

"If you do believe in *Ulam Habah*, how come you never go to synagogue?"

"You are right. I don't know why."

"Ima, I feel like I've made so many mistakes in my life."

"Everybody makes mistakes. Don't look back. At twenty, our brain and our thoughts are different than at thirty or forty."

"One is not allowed to be so utterly stupid."

"You were never stupid. You just perceived things differently. Me too. When you arrived, I did not let you be yourself. I tried to change you. I paid the price."

"We both paid the price. I did not have the compassion or depth to understand your pain, your grief."

"How could you at twenty?"

That night Sonia tossed in bed until four o'clock in the morning. She thought about her Mama in Vilnius. She felt guilty for not writing enough to her, guilty for leaving her and not thinking at the time that they most probably would never meet again.

Sonia still had nightmares about going back to Vilnius to visit Mama and Irina and not being able to leave. A few times a week for the first few years, Sonia had very vivid dreams about it. In her dreams, Sonia would board a train. Then the train would stop.

In other dreams, she would leave their apartment and there would be strangers with guns pointing at her, not letting her move. She screamed and cried, but nobody paid attention, she was completely ignored when she tried to talk to someone. Most often, she woke up sweating, not sure where she really was.

And then she called Mama.

Irina answered.

"How is Mama? Can I speak to her?"

"Mama, mamochka," Sonia tried to scream, but there was silence. "Do you hear me? Can you hear me? Do you remember me?" Not a sound. Nothing.

Sonia felt utterly devastated by Mama's anger. Mama is so upset, she does not want even to speak to her, to say Hello. One word. Prickly sharp pain pierced her chest and stayed there. Sonia crouched into fetal position trying to hide her face from the world, from herself.

Sonia could not sleep. How would she function tomorrow? She finally dozed off at five thirty and slept until seven thirty. The bright, warm, Jerusalem sun welcomed her in the morning.

She prayed her beautiful prayer *Modeh Ani*, thanking *Hashem* for giving her back her soul, for giving her eyesight, the ability to hear, and nice clothes to wear. She thanked him for giving her energy, a zest for life, and for bringing her to Israel. Each morning Sonia felt calmer and better after this prayer.

Sonia cried many times after this telephone call. Mama did not want to speak to her. She did not forgive her for leaving. She had lost Mama's love. Sonia felt sorry for herself; she cried for mistakes she had made in her life, and cried for losing a precious, irreplaceable place in Mama's big heart. If Sonia did not exist anymore for her loving Mama.

Would anybody ever care again if she existed or not?

I knew, I didn't want to know, but I knew when you were gone, completely gone. Mama, mamochka, it wasn't when you died; it was after that telephone call when I said, "Mama, Mama," again and again. There was complete silence on your end. I cried so hard. I cried feeling sorry for myself, cried for all the mistakes I had made, cried for losing you. I could not have dreamed that you had Alzheimer's. I did not realize that you didn't recognize my voice. All I felt was that there was no more place for me in your big, warm heart. I thought that I did not exist for you anymore. My heart froze inside my chest. Mama, mamochka can you hear me now? I need you more than ever. You always took care of everything. I still believe you are taking care of me when I stumble, when I am confused…

Sonia excelled in her new position in Jerusalem. Jerusalem was magic.

Sonia adored her boss, Moshe Stern. He patiently and consistently taught her everything he knew.

"My dear young lady, you have chosen the right profession. Maybe the profession chose you because you have a very original, creative mind." He was very encouraging.

Sonia's office was bright with a spectacular view. She was asked to participate in a new project at Ramat Eshkol. Sonia put all her energy and her heart into it.

She was keen to embrace different and new direction. She focused on modern designs that fit into this spirited, unique, and young country. Her country. She did not care about salary. Sonia would do it for free. Some evenings, she stayed in the office until ten o'clock.

The first project Sonia designed was a modern office building. She placed all of the offices along the edge of the building with huge glass windows from floor to ceiling. All the corridors were connected toward a central core inside. With Moshe Stern's help, encouragement, and astonishing people skills, Sonia hoped her unconventional design would be accepted.

On many levels, Jerusalem was soothing for her soul. But Sonia did suffer from the heat. Hamsin was torture. She hung many wet towels and sheets in her small apartment to cool the air.

Ariel moved to Jerusalem the year he graduated from Technion, two years before her. He, too, suffered from the heat. They both walked to work.

Once or twice, Sonia had spotted him jogging to work in the morning in his running shoes.

The heat hung in the air as heavy as invisible smoke. It was hard to breathe. Ariel's T-shirt clung to sweaty body. Walking to work and back home was nearly his only exercise. The sun was high, the air hot. The trees lured one into the shade under heavy curly braids spreading like wild mushrooms from one solid trunk.

Ariel spotted Sonia sitting under a willow tree. The sweat on her forehead formed tiny bubbles that shone through the branches of the tree. Her eyes were closed, her head tilted slightly to the left. The right strap of her sundress had slid from her shoulder. Sonia appeared frozen, her fingernails gripping, almost biting into her left foot.

Ariel tiptoed away, embarrassed to catch her in such private, vulnerable position. His heart squeezed painfully. Ariel realized how much he cared about this young woman. She stirred his emotions, but he could not allow himself to get involved with her.

"Ariel?" he heard Sonia call him.

He came to sit next to her. They sat quietly for a few minutes.

"Ariel, how come you are so calm? You never interrupt, even if the other person doesn't make sense. Did you inherit it from your mother or from your father?" Sonia asked, breaking the silence.

"I don't know. There is a need to be at peace with myself by empowering another person to listen to their inner voice, to their intuition."

"Your wisdom must come from studying the Torah!"

"Maybe. The Torah has the Truth. Every person longs for Truth."

"Obviously."

"It is not obvious. Sometimes it is not best to tell the Truth. It is better to say nothing."

"Why?" Sonia touched his hand.

"If you tell me what you think of me, I cannot hear you. Maybe all I want is you to be there to listen to my feelings and to show me empathy." Ariel moved on the grass to sit closer.

"I am not sure I get it."

"Sonia, your mind is somewhere else."

"You are right."

How could she tell him that her mind was on his lips and his green eyes? She felt his shoulders occasionally touching hers. A stream of electricity rushed through her blood, all the way up to her heart and to her burning cheeks. She could hear her heart pounding.

The sky above was light blue. Fluffy and inviting clouds were floating like gigantic pillows. Mature greenery offered respite from the debilitating heat. The tops of leaves shone a deep-avocado green, but the bottoms shimmered with a silvery glow. Not a single leaf stirred. Time stopped. It was hard to get up and go to the office.

"Ima, do you remember your dreams? Do you have any?" Sonia eagerly asked Raisa on her next visit.

"I do. For years I had nightmares. My family, war, everything. Every night."

"Still?"

"Not lately."

"Ima, I mean happy dreams, like a desire to do something interesting, to have an adventure, to meet someone, to fall in love."

"Not that. I was in love. If I could have a secret wish, I would want to go to Italy."

"Why Italy?"

"We were planning to go there with your father."

"Wow!"

For Raisa's birthday, Sonia arranged a two-week trip to Italy. They would go through Amalfi, drive for a week, and then visit Venice.

In Positano, Sonia bought Raisa beautiful, Italian shoes with sparkling stones.

"These shoes are much too fancy for me. They are for young people." Raisa objected.

"Ima, you are young. These shoes are very fashionable today."

"Sonechka, you have exquisite taste. Like your father."

Raisa wore those shoes every day for the rest of their trip.

Raisa had the rare ability to keep the same dress for many years and each time she wore the dress, it looked like new.

Raisa knew to how live extremely modestly yet appear rich. Her elegance shone through in everything she did. While in Venice, Sonia took her shopping.

"Don't spoil me. These gorgeous outfits are not for me." Raisa protested.

"It is very much for you. I want you to look young and sexy."

"Oh, Sonechka, my God! Sexy is not a word in my vocabulary. Nobody has found me sexy for many, many years."

"They will."

Sonia took Raisa for a walk away from the busy tourist areas. They found a wonderful, little pizza place by one of the charming canals. The canal was filled with little ducks and water lilies. Grasshoppers whispered their gentle songs. Modest boats cuddled next to the shore. Two canoes glided in front of them, synchronizing their paddles. What would it feel like to be a water lily or a duck with purple wings and green neck?

"Excuse me, do you know what time it is?" A handsome, elegantly dressed gentleman appeared in front of their table. He looked at Raisa. He was no more than fifty.

"Sorry, we don't have a watch. We are happy. Happy people don't need a watch." Sonia smiled at him. "You can join us if you want."

"No, not now." Raisa didn't want company.

Feeling unwelcome, he left.

"Why not? I would like you to meet a nice gentleman."

"I don't want any distractions. You are kind and loving to me. I want to cherish our time."

"Aren't you pleased someone found you so attractive?"

"So attractive? He was lonely."

"Ima, he was a pleasant, handsome man. He was not interested in me. He was interested in you. How do you feel about it?"

"I am not used to this type of attention," Raisa claimed, but there was a sparkle in her eyes.

Sonia couldn't wait to share her experiences with Ariel once she returned.

"The highlight of my trip was seeing Ima smile, to see the same expression on her face as in the precious pictures with my father before the war."

"Ima, come with me to *shul* this Sabbath."

"Sonechka, I don't remember when I was last in shul. G-d doesn't hear my voice."

"He will. I promise. You don't even have to pray. Just come and meet people."

On Friday Sonia arrived to pick up Raisa to walk to her little *shtible*. Raisa had put on her best dress, a nice, silk scarf, and a bit of makeup.

"I see you are pleased," Raisa said in a soft voice as if asking for approval.

"You look beautiful. You should always look like that."

"I tried for you. I want you to be proud of me."

"Ima, thank you. I am very proud of you." Sonia hugged her, surprised by how small Raisa felt.

Everyone in her little *shul* knew Sonia and they knew a lot about Raisa from Sonia.

"Your Sonia is such a nice, interesting person. We are so privileged that she joined our *shul*. Everyone loves her and her young spirit. You can be very proud of her."

"I am." Raisa was beaming with delight.

"You look like sisters. My parents are also from Vilna. Maybe you know the family? Family Korinsky," said a woman who was holding Raisa's hands as if in admiration.

"Which Korinsky? Hasia Korinsky?"

"Yes, my mother's name was Hasia! You knew my mother?" the woman grabbed Raisa into her arms.

"Hasia? We went to the same Yiddish school in Vilna. She was my classmate." Raisa was not used to displays of affection or attention from strangers.

"Ima, they are my friends. They are like family. I come here every Sabbath. I also come for classes. It is okay. Completely okay."

It was the Rabbi's 90th birthday. There was generous *Kiddish* after Sabbath services and good speeches.

"I think I am going to give the same speech today that I gave at my Bar Mitzvah," the Rabbi said when asked to say something. He was funny, articulate, animated, and happy.

Sonia felt comfortable being with this committed and intelligent crowd.

Almost everyone had left. Sonia and Ariel sat at the table discussing *Parshat Hashavua* called *Shmini*, miracles, and the mystery of the number eight.

"Sonia, you have changed."

"How?"

"You have grown spiritually."

"What makes you think so?"

"The way you talk, the way you act."

"Ariel, I am still full of doubts, full of questions."

"This is a good sign. Me too. I am also full of questions."

"I have been waiting for a long time but have been reluctant to ask."

"Ask!"

"Ariel, I have a problem believing in *Ulam Habah*. I understand that one cannot be an Orthodox Jew and not believe in the next world, but...."

"But? Do you believe that you exist? You know that you exist. You understand, but there is so much that you don't know and don't understand. Do you understand how a baby is born?"

"Ariel, the birth of a child is the biggest miracle for me. Bigger than *Mashiach*."

"Why?"

"Because it is from nothing. From a little invisible seed, something grows inside a woman's body into a big, grown-up man like you. From nothing."

"So why is it harder to believe that after we die some part of us goes somewhere else into another reality, a reality that we don't understand with our limited five senses?"

Sonia goes to her little *shtible* almost every Sabbath. It is a Chabad House. They don't have a *minyan* often, but she likes the people, she likes the Rabbi, and she feels very welcomed. There are very few really observant people; most come to feel Jewish, to experience Sabbath, to feel different from other days. Occasionally Ariel comes to her shul.

"If one doesn't follow *Halacha*, if one doesn't observe rituals, what makes them Jewish?" Sonia asked him one afternoon.

"Technically, once you are born Jewish, you have a privilege to be Jewish, as do your children, no matter what your level of observance."

"I understand, but in my everyday life, what makes me Jewish if I don't observe holidays?"

"Being Jewish is much more than religious observance. Most Jews are not religious. It is a very strong identity if you want it. You can throw it away if you don't want it and decide not to be Jewish. But I don't think one has such a choice. Even if one doesn't want to be Jewish, one always stays Jewish to the outside world."

"I don't know what to say. I wish I believed twenty-five percent of the way you do, but I don't know how."

"You do. You are learning. Once you learn about our laws and our traditions, you will develop belief. *Na'aseh V'nishma*. This is what our religion is all about. We learn in order to improve what was given, to grow into people we can become without being stuck in the first draft no matter how successful."

"Ariel, did I ever tell you that my Mama died from Alzheimer's?"

"You did not."

"For long time, I thought Mama stopped loving me and that she did not want to talk to me." At this point, Sonia could not continue. "I don't know why I am telling you this now."

"Because it is on your mind. You suffered because you did not know the truth."

"What is painful is that I seldom called. I was not there. Irina was there. Irina ended up being the good daughter. She tells me she misses Mama now. Can you understand it? She misses taking care of her, changing her diapers, feeding her. I don't know if I could have done it. I am so riddled with guilt."

"Guilt is such a Jewish emotion. We thrive on it."

"It is easy for you. You believe that *Hashem* rules the world and everything that happens is His will. Very little seem to bother you."

"If I worry too much, that means I don't have trust in *Hashem*."

"Does it always work for you?"

"Not always. I too get upset but I try hard to remind myself that I have to trust Him."

"When I am stressed, I don't know what to do."

"Pray, talk to *Hashem*, ask for his guidance."

"I tried. It doesn't work for me."

"Sonia, another good strategy is to have *pushka*. Put some change inside it every day. Small *mitzvah*. It will bring you luck and you will feel better."

"How much?"

"It does not matter how much. Whatever you feel like. It does not have to be the same every day. One day more, the next day less."

"Thank you. I will start tomorrow."

"Do you have *pushka* at home?"

"Believe it or not, I do. A very, very nice one."

My life is finally taking shape. I feel my father here with me. He will help with my every move, he will breathe a divine spirit, he will breathe magic into my place… Mamochka, forgive me for leaving you, for not appreciating you enough. Forgive me. I need you now, more than ever before. Mamochka, I am becoming more religious, more and more as I learn. I am afraid I am in love. Bless me. Guide me.

Ariel left for Boston. Sonia bought him a small camera as a present. She believed he would write. Sometimes. He may even miss her. They had spent a lot of time together lately. Ariel was her best friend. She could tell him exactly what was on her mind. Ariel understood. She wanted to be his best friend, but it was not up to her. She hoped he trusted her the way she trusted him.

The main difference between them was that Sonia needed Ariel, needed his guidance. Ariel was completely independent. When Sonia had a problem, she wanted to talk to Ariel, to hear his opinion and to get his advice. When Ariel had a problem, he talked to *Hashem*. *Hashem* was his partner.

She dreamed about him often. He was not her lover in life, but he was in her dreams. That part she would be embarrassed to share with him. Did Ariel know that Sonia loved him? Sonia hoped he didn't, but on the other hand, he must have guessed. Could he ever love her as a woman? Was he attracted to her? Ariel never even hinted that Sonia was attractive. When would he write to her from the States? Would he miss her? Probably, not really.

The first thing Sonia did every morning was run to pick up her mail. She could not help it. Ten days after Ariel left, there was a letter from Boston. She kissed the envelope before opening it.

> *Dear Sonia,*
> *I write this letter, my sweetheart, to tell you that you are the one I will always love, the one who is everything to me. I love you. I love you more than I have*

ever loved another. I love you to the very core. I love your Mona Lisa smile, I love your walk, I love your soul, I love the way you think. I love the way you look at me when we talk. I love everything about you. I love your interest in Judaism. I embrace the rare opportunity to become true soulmates. We can meet and defeat any and all challenges. Forever yours, Ariel

As you can see, I could never say it, but Hashem *guided me to write it to you. Now you know.*

Only after reading his letter three times, and still not believing Ariel could write these loving words he had never said to her, Sonia prayed *Modeh Ani*, grateful to *Hashem* for answering her prayers. Then she put money into the *pushka*.

Two months later, at six o'clock, her bell rang. Ariel stood in her doorway.

"Why didn't you let me know? I would have come to the airport."

He stood there, tall and gorgeous, smiling with open arms. Her prince! Sonia could hear the beating of her jumping heart. There was a magic in the room. Was she dreaming?

Glossary for Yiddish Words

1. DACHA—Russian country house for summer vacations.
2. GOYM—all non-Jewish nations came to be called goym.
3. HALACHA—is the way Jew is directed to behave encompassing civil, criminal and religious Law.
4. LIKI—Leningrad Institute for Cinematography.
5. MADRICHA—female instructor in Hebrew.
6. NATIAT JADAIM—washing your hands the first thing in the morning according to Jewish tradition.
7. NESHOMA—Jewish notion of the soul.
8. PROTECZIA—favouritism, nepotism, doing someone a favour like getting a good position not on merit but by just knowing them personally.
9. SABRA—people born in Israel are given this name. It is a name of a local cactus plant which is prickly on outside and sweet inside.
10. SHIKSA—disparaging term applied to a non-Jewish girl or woman.
11. SHUL—Jewish house of praying, another word for synagogue.

12　AFIKOMAN—a hidden piece of matzah put aside to be eaten at the end of the meal during a Seder.

13　BALABUSTA—mistress of the house in Hebrew but used more as a compliment for an accomplished housewife.

14　BASHERT—soulmate, the one person whom an individual is divinely destined to marry.

15　BATUSHKA—Russian Orthodox priest.

16　BORSCH—traditional Russian soup.

17　CHALA—special Jewish bread for Friday night.

18　CHALIAPIN—famous Russian opera star.

19　CHERNOVITZ—town in Bokovina that is now in the Ukraine. It had a large Jewish population between the two World wars.

20　CHOLENT—traditional Sabbath food cooked over night.

21　CHUTZPAH—brazen nerve, personal confidence or courage that allows someone to do or to say things that may seem shocking to others.

22　DADIA—Russian for Mister.

23　DAVEN or DAVENING—to pray or praying.

24　FLEISHIG—Yiddish for "meaty", refers to any food made with meat or foul products to keep strict separation between meat and diary products according to Jewish Law of kashrut.

25　FOUTEIL—comfortable arm chair.

26　HABIMA—name of famous Yiddish theatre that started in Moscow and moved to Israel.

27　HAPUNES—abductors, Lithuanians and Poles, willing to do the dirty work for Nazis grabbing Jews on the street and arresting them.

28 HASHEM—instead of saying God.

29 HATIKVAH—Israeli National Anthem.

30 ISRAEL, IZA, IZENKA—the same name in more endearing way.

31 JUDENDRAT—administrative body of Jewish self-government in a ghetto.

32 KASHRUT—is the body of Jewish Law dealing with what foods we can eat and cannot eat and how those foods must be prepared and eaten.

33 KIBBUTZ —communal settlement in Israel where workers live together and share everything.

34 KIDUSH—blessing recited over wine followed by a festive meal on the Sabbath and special occasions.

35 KINDALECH—Yiddish for little children.

36 KUGEL—Ashkenazi Jewish dish. Baked pudding made from egg noodles or potato.

37 MACHZOR —is a prayer book used by Jews on Holy Days and Yom Kippur.

38 MAIDALE—young girl in Yiddish.

39 MALINA—secret hiding places for Jews to avoid deportation by Nazis during second World War.

40 MASHIACH—Hebrew Messiah.

41 MATUSHKA—wife of Russian priest.

42 MINYAN —a quorum of ten men over the age of 13 required for traditional Jewish public worship.

43 MISNAGDIM—followers of Vilna GAON opposing HASSIDIM, real Hebrew word for opposition.

44 MITZVA—- good deed done from religious duty.

45 MODEH ANI—morning prayer of thanking God.

46 MUJIK—Russian peasant prior to 1917.

47 NACHAS—understood to be pride and joy in Yiddish.

48 NASEH V'NISHMA—Jews accepted Torah with statement "We will do, and we will hear!"

49 NES—miracle in Hebrew.

50 PELLMENI—It forms the heart of Russian cuisine, type of dumpling consisting of a different filling that is wrapped in thin uneven dough.

51 PILSUTZKY—Polish leader from 1922 to 1940.

52 PIROZKY—Russian baked buns stuffed with a variety of feelings.

53 PURIM—Jewish festival to commemorate the defeat of plot to massacre the Jews in the book of Esther.

54 PUSHKA—box for charity to collect.

55 SHERUT—Israeli taxi system.

56 SHIDUCH—Jewish tradition of choosing marriage partner with the help of matchmaker.

57 SHLACHMONES—gifts delivered on PURIM by Jewish people to their friends and relatives.

58 SHMATTES—old, cheap, tattered clothes more like rags.

59 SHTETL—small town with large Jewish population which existed in Central and Eastern Europe before the Holocaust.

60 SHTIBLE—Yiddish word for a little house of prayer like shul, very small synagogue.

61 SIMCHA—joyous occasion to celebrate.

62 SONIA, SONKA, SONECHKA—the same name in more endearing form.

63 TALLIT—fringed garment traditionally worn under one's clothing by Jewish males.

64 TANYA—is an early work of Hasidic philosophy by Rabbi Shneur Zalman of Liadi.

65 TROKAI—ancient village with an old, thirteenth-century castle outside of Vilnius.

66 TSIMES—sweet stew made from carrots, raisins, and dried fruit.

67 ULAM HABAA—literally "next world" in Hebrew.

68 VILNA GAON—the foremost leader of mitnagdim movement of the past few centuries.

69 VILNIUS, VILNO, WILNA—the name of the capital of Lithuania used by Lithuanians, Polish people, and Russians at different times.

www.ingramcontent.com/pod-product-compliance
Lightning Source LLC
Chambersburg PA
CBHW021441070526
44577CB00002B/241